TROPHIES

Intervention
TEACHER'S GUIDE
Grade 2

Harcourt

Orlando   Boston   Dallas   Chicago   San Diego

Visit *The Learning Site!*
www.harcourtschool.com

Copyright © by Harcourt, Inc.

All rights reserved. No part of this publication may be reproduced or transmitted in any form or by any means, electronic or mechanical, including photocopy, recording, or any information storage and retrieval system, without permission in writing from the publisher.

Requests for permission to make copies of any part of the work should be addressed to School Permissions and Copyrights, Harcourt, Inc., 6277 Sea Harbor Drive, Orlando, Florida 32887-6777. Fax: 407-345-2418.

HARCOURT and the Harcourt Logo are trademarks of Harcourt, Inc., registered in the United States of America and/or other jurisdictions.

Printed in the United States of America

ISBN 0-15-325344-4

7 8 9 10 048 10 09 08 07 06 05 04

Table of Contents

Lesson 1 • "The Mixed-Up Chameleon" 8
and "Mac's Wish Comes True"

Lesson 2 • "Get Up and Go!" 18
and "Company Is Coming!"

Lesson 3 • "Henry and Mudge Under the Yellow Moon" 28
and "A Walk in the Woods"

Lesson 4 • "Days With Frog and Toad" 38
and "One Fine Night"

Lesson 5 • "Wilson Sat Alone" 48
and "Just You and Me"

Lesson 6 • "The Enormous Turnip" 58
and "A Turnip's Tale"

Lesson 7 • "Helping Out" 68
and "Tools That Help"

Lesson 8 • "Mr. Putter and Tabby Fly the Plane" 78
and "The Promise"

Lesson 9 • "Hedgehog Bakes a Cake" 88
and "Too Many Cupcakes"

Lesson 10 • "Lemonade for Sale" 98
and "A Lemonade Surprise"

Lesson 11 • "Johnny Appleseed" 108
and "Anna's Apple Doll"

Lesson 12 • "From Seed to Plant" 118
and "A Day in the Life of a Seed"

Lesson 13 • "The Secret Life of Trees" 128
and "The Old Tree"

Lesson 14 • "Watermelon Day" 138
and "Mr. Carver's Carrots"

Lesson 15 • "Pumpkin Fiesta" 148
and "Miss Owl's Secret"

Table of Contents • Intervention Teacher's Guide

Lesson 16 • "The Day Jimmy's Boa Ate the Wash"..................158
and "The Not-So-Boring Night"

Lesson 17 • "How I Spent My Summer Vacation"..................168
and "The Matador and Me"

Lesson 18 • "Dear Mr. Blueberry"..................178
and "Mr. Whiskers"

Lesson 19 • "Cool Ali"..................188
and "Sounds All Around"

Lesson 20 • "The Emperor's Egg"..................198
and "Little Blue Penguins"

Lesson 21 • "The Pine Park Mystery"..................208
and "A Secret Place"

Lesson 22 • "Good-bye, Curtis"..................218
and "Hello from Here"

Lesson 23: "Max Found Two Sticks"..................228
and "The Music Maker"

Lesson 24 • "Anthony Reynoso: Born to Rope"..................238
and "Rodeo!"

Lesson 25 • "Chinatown"..................248
and "Happy New Year!"

Lesson 26 • "Abuela"..................258
and "If I Could Fly"

Lesson 27 • "Beginner's World Atlas"..................268
and "Map Games"

Lesson 28 • "Dinosaurs Travel"..................278
and "When You Visit Relatives"

Lesson 29 • "Montigue on the High Seas"..................288
and "Zelda Moves to the Desert"

Lesson 30 • "Ruth Law Thrills a Nation"..................298
and "An Amazing Feat"

What are Intervention Strategies?

Intervention strategies are designed to facilitate learning for those students who may experience some difficulty no matter how well we have planned our curriculum. These strategies offer support and guidance to the student who is struggling. The strategies themselves are no mystery. They are based on the same time-honored techniques that effective teachers have used for years—teaching students on their instructional reading level; modeling previewing and predicting; and giving direct instruction in strategic-reading, vocabulary, phonics, fluency, and writing.

Intervention works best in conjunction with a strong core program. For an intervention program to be effective, instruction should focus on specific needs of students, as determined by systematic monitoring of progress.

Components of the Intervention Program

The goal of the *Trophies* Intervention Program is to provide the scaffolding, extra support, and extra reading practice that below-level readers need to succeed in the mainstream reading program. The program includes the following components:

- ***Skill Cards*** to preteach and reteach the Focus Skill for each lesson
- ***Intervention Practice Book*** with the following practice pages for each lesson:

    Fluency Page with word lists and phrase-cued sentences that parallel the reading level of the *Intervention Reader* selection

    Phonics Practice Page that reinforces prerequisite phonics/decoding skills and can be used as a teacher-directed or independent activity

    Comprehension Practice Page that gives students an opportunity to respond to the *Intervention Reader* selection and show that they have understood it

    Focus Skill Review Page that provides an additional opportunity to practice and apply the focus skill for that lesson

- ***Intervention Reader*** to provide reading material at students' instructional reading level
- ***Vocabulary Game Boards*** and related materials to provide additional practice and application of vocabulary skills
- ***Intervention Assessment Book*** opportunities to monitor progress and ensure success

Introduction • Intervention Teacher's Guide

Using the *Intervention Teacher's Guides* with *Trophies*

The *Intervention Teacher's Guide* gives support for below-level readers in key instructional strands of *Trophies*, plus prerequisite phonics skills and oral-reading fluency. Each *Intervention Teacher's Guide* lesson includes the following resources:

- The **Phonics/Decoding Lesson** reviews prerequisite phonics and word analysis skills. Each skill is systematically applied in the corresponding *Intervention Reader* selection.

- **Preteach/Reteach Vocabulary** activities to teach key vocabulary that appears in both the *Intervention Reader* selection and the corresponding *Trophies Pupil Edition* selection.

- **Fluency Builders** reinforce important vocabulary while providing reading practice to promote oral reading fluency. You may also wish to use the *Oral Reading Fluency Assessment* periodically to measure student progress.

- **Preteach/Reteach Focus Skill** activities reinforce the objective of *Trophies* Focus Skills, ensuring that below-level readers get the in-depth instruction they need to reach grade skill-level standards.

- **Preview and Summarize** provide support for comprehension of each main selection in *Trophies Pupil Editions*.

- **Directed Reading Lesson** for the *Intervention Reader* selection that reinforces basic comprehension skills, using questions and teacher modeling.

- **Writing Support** for writing lessons in *Trophies* provides interactive writing experiences for the key aspects of the corresponding writing forms and skills.

- **Weekly Review** provides additional support as students review phonics, vocabulary, and focus skills and prepare for testing.

- **Self-Selected Reading** suggests titles that students can read independently with success and also offers specific suggestions for encouraging student expression and participation through conferencing.

The *Intervention Teacher's Guide* lessons clearly identify the most appropriate times during the *Trophies* lesson plan to provide supplemental instruction. Look for the BEFORE or AFTER tag that appears next to each of the key instructional strands, along with page numbers from the core pogram. For example:

BEFORE
Reading
pages 314–330

This tag alerts you that *before* children read the literature selection that appears in *Trophies* on pages 314–330, intervention strategies may be useful. Appropriate preteaching activities are provided. Reteaching activities are indicated by the AFTER tag.

Depending on your individual classroom and school schedules, you can tailor the "before" and "after" instruction to suit your needs. The following pages show two options for pacing the instruction in this guide.

Suggested Lesson Planners

Option 1:

DAY 1

BEFORE Building Background and Vocabulary

Review Phonics
- Identify the sound
- Associate letters to sound
- Word blending
- Apply the skill

Introduce Vocabulary
- Preteach lesson vocabulary

AFTER Building Background and Vocabulary

Apply Vocabulary Strategies
- Use decoding strategies
- Reteach lesson vocabulary

Fluency Builder
- Use *Intervention Practice Book*

DAY 2

BEFORE Reading the *Trophies* Selection

Focus Skill
- Preteach the skill
- Use Skill Card Side A

Prepare to Read the *Trophies* selection
- Preview the selection
- Set purpose

AFTER Reading the *Trophies* Selection

Reread and Summarize

Fluency Builder
- Use *Intervention Practice Book*

Option 2:

DAY 1

AFTER Weekly Assessments

Self-Selected Reading
- Choosing books
- Conduct student-teacher conferences

Fluency Performance
- Use passage from *Intervention Reader* selection

BEFORE Building Background and Vocabulary

Review Phonics
- Identify the sound
- Associate letters to sound
- Word blending
- Apply the skill

Introduce Vocabulary
- Preteach lesson vocabulary

DAY 2

AFTER Building Background and Vocabulary

Apply Vocabulary Strategies
- Use decoding strategies
- Reteach lesson vocabulary

Fluency Builder
- Use *Intervention Practice Book*

BEFORE Reading the *Trophies* Selection

Focus Skill
- Preteach the skill
- Use Skill Card Side A

Prepare to Read the *Trophies* selection
- Preview the selection
- Set purpose

DAY 3

BEFORE — **Making Connections**

Directed Reading of *Intervention Reader* selection
- Read the selection
- Summarize the selection
- Answer *Think About It* Questions

AFTER — **Skill Review**

Focus Skill
- Reteach the skill
- Use Skill Card Side B

Fluency Builder
- Use *Intervention Practice Book*

DAY 4

BEFORE — **Writing Lesson**

Writing Support
- Build on prior knowledge
- Construct the text
- Revisit the text
- On Your Own

AFTER — **Spelling Lesson**

Connect Spelling and Phonics
- Reteach phonics
- Build and read longer words

Fluency Builder
- Use passage from *Intervention Reader* selection

DAY 5

BEFORE — **Weekly Assessments**

Review Vocabulary
- Vocabulary activity

Review Focus Skill
- Use *Intervention Practice Book*

Review Test Prep
- Use the core *Pupil Edition*

AFTER — **Weekly Assessments**

Self-Selected Reading
- Choosing books
- Conduct student-teacher conferences

Fluency Performance
- Use passage from *Intervention Reader* selection

DAY 3

AFTER — **Reading the *Trophies* Selection**

Reread and Summarize

Fluency Builder
- Use *Intervention Practice Book*

BEFORE — **Making Connections**

Directed Reading of *Intervention Reader* selection
- Read the selection
- Summarize the selection
- Answer *Think About It* Questions

DAY 4

AFTER — **Skill Review**

Focus Skill
- Reteach the skill
- Use Skill Card Side B

Fluency Builder
- Use *Intervention Practice Book*

BEFORE — **Writing Lesson**

Writing Support
- Build on prior knowledge
- Construct the text
- Revisit the text
- On Your Own

DAY 5

AFTER — **Spelling Lesson**

Connect Spelling and Phonics
- Reteach phonics
- Build and read longer words

Fluency Builder
- Use passage from *Intervention Reader* selection

BEFORE — **Weekly Assessments**

Review Vocabulary
- Vocabulary activity

Review Focus Skill
- Use *Intervention Practice Book*

Review Test Prep
- Use the core *Pupil Edition*

Suggested Lesson Planners

Fluency

"So that students will understand why rereading is done, we have involved them in a discussion of how athletes develop skill at their sports. This discussion brings out the fact that athletes spend considerable time practicing basic skills until they develop speed and smoothness at their activity. Repeated readings uses this same type of practice."

S. Jay Samuels
The Reading Teacher, February 1997
(originally published January 1979)

In the years since S. Jay Samuels pioneered the technique of repeated reading to improve fluency, continuing research has confirmed and expanded upon his observations. Ideally, oral reading mirrors the pacing, smoothness, and rhythms of normal speech. Fluency in reading can be defined as a combination of these key elements.

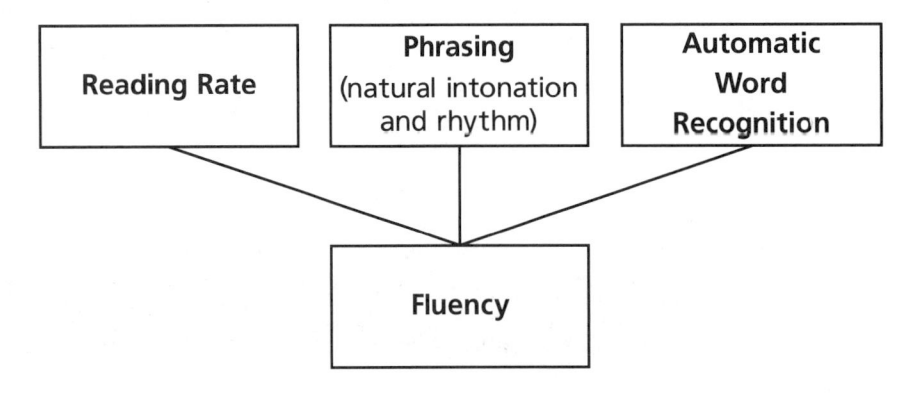

```
    Reading Rate      Phrasing              Automatic
                   (natural intonation       Word
                     and rhythm)          Recognition
                           │
                        Fluency
```

How Do Students Become More Fluent Readers?

Research and the experiences of classroom teachers make it clear that certain practices can and do lead to significant improvements in reading fluency. Techniques that have been shown to be successful include

- Teacher modeling
- Repeated reading of short passages
- Daily monitoring of progress

A program that incorporates these three elements will help struggling readers gain fluency and improve their comprehension.

Using Fluency Builders in the *Intervention Teacher's Guide*

The plan for each lesson in the *Intervention Teacher's Guide* includes daily fluency practice that incorporates the elements of teacher modeling, repeated reading, and self-monitoring.

The fluency portion of the lesson is designed to be completed in five or ten minutes, although you may adjust the time according to students' needs and as your schedule allows.

About the *Intervention Practice Book* Fluency Page

The *Intervention Practice Book* Fluency page is designed to correlate with the phonics elements taught in the *Intervention Teacher's Guide*, as well as with key vocabulary from the *Trophies* and *Intervention Reader* selections. A total of twenty words that fall into these three categories are listed at the top of the Fluency Page for each lesson.

On the bottom half of the page, you will find a set of numbered sentences that incorporate the words from the lists. Slashes are used to divide each sentence into phrases. To help students improve natural phrasing, model reading each phrase smoothly, as a unit, and encourage students to follow the same procedure in their repeated-reading practice.

This chart gives an overview of the fluency portion of the Intervention Program.

Day	Materials	Explanation
1	*Intervention Practice Book* Fluency Page	Teacher models reading aloud word lists. Students then practice reading aloud the word lists with partners.
2	*Intervention Practice Book* Fluency Page	Teacher models reading aloud the phrased fluency sentences. Students then practice repeated rereadings of the sentences with partners.
3	*Intervention Practice Book* Fluency Page	Students read the fluency sentences on tape, assess their own progress, and then reread the sentences on tape to improve pacing and tone.
4	*Intervention Reader* selection	Students read aloud a selected short passage from the *Intervention Reader* selection three times, monitoring their progress after each reading.
5	*Intervention Reader* selection	Students read the same passage aloud to the teacher. Both teacher and student assess the student's progress.

Fluency

Phonemic Awareness

Rhyming Activities

Rhyme-a-Day

Start each day by teaching students a short rhyme. Periodically throughout the day, repeat the rhyme with them. Say the rhyme together, have them say it alone, pause and leave out words for them to insert, or ask volunteers to say each line. Students will develop a repertoire of favorite rhymes that can serve as a storehouse for creating their own rhymes.

Rhyme Sort

Place on a tabletop pictures of items that rhyme. Have students sort the pictures into groups, according to names that rhyme. You may also want to try an "open sort" by having students create categories of their own to sort the picture cards

Rhyme Pairs

To assess students' ability to recognize pairs of words that rhyme, say a list of twenty or more pairs of words. Half of the word pairs should rhyme. Students tell which word pairs rhyme and which do not. Have students indicate *yes* with a card marked *Y* or another symbol.

If working with **one child** (or small group), have students use one of the Game Boards. From each correct response, the player can move a marker ahead one space. Provide word pairs until the player has completed the game.

What Word Rhymes?

Use theme-related words from across the curriculum to focus on words that rhyme. For example, if you are studying animals, ask: *What rhymes with snake? bear? fox? deer? ant? frog? goat? hen? fish? whale?* If a special holiday is approaching, ask: *What rhymes with flag, year, or heart?* Use these word groups for sound-matching, sound-blending, or sound-segmenting activities.

Sound-Matching Activities

Odd Word Out

Form a group of four students. Say a different word for each group member to repeat. The student with the word that does not begin (or end) like the other words must step out of the group. For example, say *basket, bundle, cost, bargain*. The student whose word is *cost* steps from the group. The odd-word-out player then chooses three students to form a new group and the procedure continues.

Head or Toes, Finger or Nose?

Teach students the following rhyme. Be sure to say the sound, not the letter, at the beginning of each line. Recite the rhyme together several times while touching the body parts.

/h/ is for *head*.
/t/ is for *toes*.
/f/ is for *finger*.
/n/ is for *nose*.

Phonemic Awareness Activities • Intervention Teacher's Guide

Explain that you will say a list of words. Students are to touch the head when you say a word that begins with /h/, the toes for the words that begin with /t/, a finger for words that begin with /f/, and the nose for words that begin with /n/. Say words such as *fan, ten, horn, hat, feet, nut, ham, nest, toy, fish, note, tub, nail, time, fox,* and *house.*

Souvenir Sound-Off

Have students imagine that a friend has traveled to a special place and has brought them a gift. Recite the following verse, and ask a volunteer to complete it. The names of the traveler, the place, and the gift must begin with the same letter and sound.

- My friend [person]
  My friend Hannah
- who went to [place]
  who went to Hawaii
- brought me back a [gift].
  brought me back a hula skirt.

After repeating this activity a few times, ask **partners** to recite the missing words. As an alternative, you can focus on words with initial blends and digraphs. Students can focus on social studies and phonics skills by using a world map or globe to find names of places.

Match My Word

Have students match beginning or ending sounds in words. Seat students in pairs, sitting back-to-back. One student in each pair will say a word. His or her partner will repeat the word and say another word that begins with the same sound. Repeat the activity, reversing the roles of partners and focusing on ending sounds.

Sound Isolation Activities

What's Your Name N-N-N-Name?

Invite students to say their names by repeating the initial phoneme in the name, such as *M-M-M-M-Michael* or by drawing out and exaggerating the initial sound, such as *Sssss-erena*. Have students say the names of others, such as friends or family members.

Singling Out the Sounds

Form groups of three students. Students can decide who will name the beginning, the middle, and the ending sounds in one-syllable picture names. Given a set of pictures, the group identifies a picture name, and then each group member isolates and says the sound he or she is responsible for. Group members can check one another.

Chain Reaction

Have students form a circle. The student who begins will say a word such as *bus*. The next child must isolate the ending sound in the word, /s/, and say a word that begins with that sound, such as *sun*. If the word is correct, the two students link arms, and the procedure continues with the next child isolating the final sound in *sun* and giving a word that begins with /n/. You will want all students to be able to link arms and complete the chain, so provide help when needed.

Phonemic Awareness Activities

Sound-Addition, Deletion, or Substitution Activities

Add-a-Sound

Explain that the beginning sound is missing in each of the words you will say. Students must add the missing sound and say the new word. Some examples follow.

Add:

/b/ to *at* (bat)	/f/ to *ox* (fox)	/k/ to *art* (cart)
/f/ to *ace* (face)	/p/ to *age* (page)	/h/ to *air* (hair)
/w/ to *all* (wall)	/j/ to *am* (jam)	/r/ to *an* (ran)
/b/ to *and* (band)	/d/ to *ark* (dark)	/f/ to *arm* (farm)
/d/ to *ash* (dash)	/s/ to *it* (sit)	/s/ to *oak* (soak)
/h/ to *eel* (heel)	/b/ to *end* (bend)	/m/ to *ice* (mice)
/n/ to *ear* (near)	/f/ to *east* (feast)	/b/ to *each* (beach)
/f/-/l/ to *at* (flat)	/sk/ to *ate* (skate)	/t/-/r/ to *eat* (treat)
/g/ /r/ to *ill* (grill)	/sh/ to *out* (shout)	/p/-/l/ to *ant* (plant)

Remove-a-Sound

Reinforce rhyme while focusing on the deletion of initial sounds in words to form new words. Ask students to say:

- *hat* without the /h/ (at)
- *fin* without the /f/ (in)
- *tall* without the /t/ (all)
- *box* without the /b/ (ox)
- *will* without /w/ (ill)
- *peach* without the /p/ (each)
- *nice* without the /n/ (ice)
- *meat* without the /m/ (eat)
- *band* without the /b/ (and)

Continue with other words in the same manner.

Mixed-Up Tongue Twisters

Think of a simple tongue twister such as *ten tired toads*. Say the tongue twister for students, but replace the initial letter in each word with another letter, such a *p*, to create nonsense words: *pen pired poads*. Explain to students that you need their help to make sense of the tongue twister by having them replace /p/ with /t/ and say the new tongue twister. Use the same procedure for other tongue twisters.

- copper coffee cups
- nine new nails
- two ton tomatoes
- long lean legs

Then ask partners to do this activity together.

The Name Game

Occasionally when a new sound is introduced, students might enjoy substituting the first sound of their names for the name of a classmate. Students will have to stop and think when they call one another by name, including the teacher. For example, Paul would call Ms. Vega, Ms. Pega; Carmen becomes Parmen; Jason becomes Pason; and Kiyo becomes Piyo. Just make certain beforehand that all names will be agreeable.

Take Away

New words can be formed by deleting an initial phoneme from a word. Have students say the new word that is formed.

flake without the /f/ (lake)

swing without the /s/ (wing)

shrink without the /sh/ (rink)

spread without the /s/-/p/ (read)

fright without the /f/ (right)

score without the /s/ (core)

bride without the /b/ (ride)

spoke without the /s/ (poke)

bring without the /b/ (ring)

swell without the /s/ (well)

shred without the /sh/ (red)

gloom without the /g/ (loom)

snout without the /s/-/n/ (out)

slip without the /s/ (lip)

block without the /b/ (lock)

snail without the /s/ (nail)

Sound-Blending Activities

I'm Thinking of a Word

Play a guessing game with students. Tell students that you will give them clues to a word. Have them listen closely to blend the sounds to say the word.

- I'm thinking of something that has words— /b/-/o͝o/-/k/. (book)
- I'm thinking of something that comes in bunches— /g/-/r/-/ā/-/p/-/s/. (grapes)
- I'm thinking of something that shines in the night sky— /s/-/t/-/är/-/s/. (stars)
- I'm thinking of something that moves very slowly— /s/-/n/-/ā/-/l/. (snail)

What's in the Box?

Place various objects in a box or bag. Play a game with students by saying **In this box is a /c/-/r/-/ā/-/o/-/n/. What do you think is in the box?** (crayon) Continue with the other objects in the box, segmenting the phonemes for students to blend and say the word.

Sound-Segmenting Activities

Sound Game

Have **partners** play a word-guessing game, using a variety of pictures that represent different beginning sounds. One student says the name on the card, separating the beginning sound, as in **p-late**. The partner blends the sounds and guesses the word. After students are proficient with beginning sounds, you could have them segment all the sounds in a word when they give their clues, as in **d-o-g**.

Count the Sounds

Tell students that you are going to say a word. Have them listen and count the number of sounds they hear in that word. For example, say the word *task*. Have children repeat the word and tell how many sounds they hear. Students should reply *four*.

tone (3)	four (3)
great (4)	peak (3)
pinch (4)	sunny (4)
stick (4)	clouds (5)
flake (4)	feel (3)
rain (3)	paint (4)

Phonemic Awareness Activities

Vocabulary Games

Vocabulary Game Boards

To give students additional vocabulary practice, use the Vocabulary Game Boards and copying masters provided in the Intervention Kit. Two different games can be played on each game board. Directions for each game are printed on the back of the board on which the game is played. There are a total of five game boards, which students can use to play ten different games. For best results, use the games to review vocabulary at the end of each theme, so that there are more words to play with.

Copying Masters

The copying masters that accompany the game boards provide some other materials that students will need to play the games. These include:

- spinners
- game pieces
- game cards

Illustrated directions on the copying masters show students how to create the game materials. They may need scissors, crayons or colored markers, and glue. Pencils and paper clips are used to construct spinners. When game markers are called for, provide students with buttons, counters, or some other small item.

Additional Materials

When the directions for a game call for **word cards**, use the vocabulary word cards from *Trophies*. In addition, some games require the use of a vocabulary list, definition cards that students can create, a dictionary, and commonly available items such as a paper bag.

Use the following charts to plan for and organize the vocabulary games.

Game Board 1: Hopscotch

Games	Skills Practiced	Players	Additional Materials
Wordscotch	definitions	2	Wordscotch Copying Master *Trophies* word cards dictionary game markers
Syllable Hop-Along	number of syllables	2	Syllable Hop-Along Copying Master *Trophies* word cards dictionary game markers

Game Board 2: Tic-Tac-Toe

Games	Skills Practiced	Players	Additional Materials
Tic-Tac-Know	creating sentences	2	word cards with meaning on back (to be made by students) game markers
Riddle Me	definitions and number of syllables	4	word cards with meaning on back (to be made by students) paper bag vocabulary list game markers

Game Board 3: Do You Remember?

Games	Skills Practiced	Players	Additional Materials
Match a Pair	definitions	2	word cards with meaning on back (to be made by students) *Trophies* word cards
Syllable Match	number of syllables	2	*Trophies* word cards dictionary

Game Board 4: Safari

Games	Skills Practiced	Players	Additional Materials
Safari Spin	number of syllables	2	Safari Spin Copying Master *Trophies* word cards dictionary
Safari Wordwatch	definitions	2–4	Safari Wordwatch Copying Masters vocabulary list dictionary

Game Board 5: Word Castle

Games	Skills Practiced	Players	Additional Materials
Castle Construction	definitions	2	Castle Construction Copying Master *Trophies* word cards dictionary
Knight's Syllable Spin	number of syllables	2	Knight's Syllable Spin Copying Masters *Trophies* word cards dictionary

Vocabulary Games

Vocabulary Activities

The six activities on the following pages provide additional opportunities for vocabulary practice and application. Two activities are offered for individual students, two for pairs of students, and two for small groups of three or four students. All require a minimum of preparation and call for materials that are readily available in the classroom.

Word Book

INDIVIDUAL ACTIVITY

MATERIALS
- paper
- markers
- stapler
- simple binding materials

As students progress through a theme, encourage them to identify new vocabulary that they find interesting or that they think will be useful to them. Have students create a page for each of the special words they choose. Encourage them to check the spelling of the word and to include the definition and other information they might find helpful, such as how the word is divided into syllables, how it is pronounced, whether it has a prefix or a suffix, synonyms and antonyms, and how the word may be related to other words they know. Students can also draw pictures and include captions and labels.

Upon completion of the theme, have students make a cover for the book. Staple the pages together or help students use simple materials to bind them. Encourage them to share their word books with classmates and to use them as a resource for their writing.

Vocabulary Activities • Intervention Teacher's Guide

Draw a Smile

PARTNER ACTIVITY

MATERIALS
- list of vocabulary words from a complete theme
- two sheets of paper and markers or chalk and chalkboard
- dictionary

Pairs of students can play this game on paper or on the board. Players should be designated Player 1 and Player 2. Player 1 begins by choosing a vocabulary word from the list for Player 2 to define. If Player 2 defines the word correctly, he or she gets to draw one part of a smiling face. If Player 2 cannot define the word correctly, he or she cannot draw on that turn. Players take turns choosing words for each other to define and adding parts to their drawings each time they define a word correctly. Encourage students to use a dictionary to check definitions as necessary.

A completed drawing has five parts, to be drawn in this order: (1) head, (2) one eye, (3) the other eye, (4) nose, (5) smile. The first player to draw a complete smiling face wins the game.

1. face
2. one eye
3. other eye
4. nose
5. smile

Vocabulary Activities

Make a Word Garden

SMALL GROUP ACTIVITY

MATERIALS
- bulletin board
- colored construction paper
- markers
- scissors
- masking tape
- pencil
- paper

Students can create a word garden by drawing and cutting out large flowers from construction paper. Encourage them to use their imaginations to create flowers in a variety of shapes and colors. Have students use markers to write a vocabulary word on each flower and then arrange the flowers to make a garden on the bulletin board.

Then have students create a key on a separate sheet of paper by making a small drawing of each of the large flowers and writing the definition of the word that appears on the matching large flower. Students should display the key on the bulletin board with their garden.

What's the Score?

INDIVIDUAL ACTIVITY

MATERIALS
- list of vocabulary words from a theme or several lessons within a theme
- pencil and paper
- dictionary

Make a list of six to eight vocabulary words that may have given students some difficulty. Have students copy the words from the list and write a definition for each word from memory. Then have them use a dictionary to check their definitions. Tell them to keep score by writing down the number of words they defined correctly.

Then have students copy the words from the list in reverse order, beginning at the bottom. Have them again write a definition for each word from memory, check the definitions in a dictionary, and count the words they defined correctly. Tell students to compare this score to their first score to see how much they improved.

Finger Puppets

SMALL GROUP ACTIVITY

MATERIALS
- finger puppet pattern
- construction paper
- markers
- scissors
- tape
- list of vocabulary words from a theme

Give students a simple pattern that they can trace to make finger puppets. Have students use construction paper and markers to create puppets that represent favorite characters from a particular theme. Have students work together to make up simple dramatizations using the finger puppets. Challenge students to use as many words as possible from the vocabulary list. They can keep track of the words they use by checking them off the list.

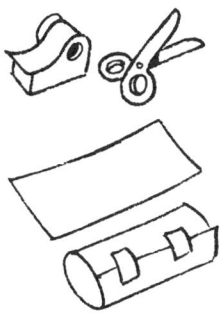

Guess My Word

PARTNER ACTIVITY

MATERIALS
- list of vocabulary words from a theme
- scrap paper
- pencils

Display the list of vocabulary words where both players can see it. Students take turns choosing a word from the list for each other to guess. The student who is guessing may ask questions about the meaning of the word, how it is spelled, the number of syllables, or any other information they think may help them, as long as the questions can be answered with *yes* or *no*. Encourage students to jot down information that they find out about the word that can help narrow down the list. You may want to give examples of questions that players might ask and explain how they can use the information they obtain.

QUESTION: Does the word begin with a consonant?

INFORMATION: If the answer is *yes*, you can look at the words that begin with consonants and ask more questions to figure out which of those is the correct word. If the answer is *no*, you can rule out the words that begin with consonants and focus on those that begin with vowels.

QUESTION: Does the word have an *-ed* ending?

INFORMATION: If the answer is *no*, you can rule out all words with *-ed* endings. If the answer is yes, focus on the words with *-ed* endings. Ask more questions to figure out which of those words is the correct one.

Vocabulary Activities 7

LESSON 1

BEFORE
Building Background and Vocabulary

Use with

"The Mixed-Up Chameleon"

Review Phonics: Short Vowel /a/a

Identify the sound. Read aloud the following sentence: *The cat sat on Dan's lap*. Ask children to repeat the sentence three times, identifying the words that have the /a/ sound. (*cat, sat, Dan's, lap*)

Associate letters to sound. Write on the board the sentence *The cat sat on Dan's lap*, and have a volunteer underline the words that contain the letter *a*. Tell children that in these words, the letter *a* stands for the /a/ sound.

Word blending. Model how to blend and read the word *cab*. Slide your hand under the word as you elongate the sounds /kkaabb/. Then say the word naturally—*cab*. Follow a similar procedure for the words *tap, ran,* and *sad*.

Apply the skill. *Consonant Substitution* Write the following words on the board, and have children read each one aloud. Make the changes necessary to form the words in parentheses. Have volunteers read aloud each new word.

ran (man)   **sad** (mad)   **pat** (bat)
fan (pan)   **pad** (had)   **sat** (cat)

INTERVENTION PRACTICE BOOK
page 4

Introduce Vocabulary

PRETEACH lesson vocabulary. Tell children that they are going to learn seven new words that they will see again when they read a story called "The Mixed-Up Chameleon." Teach each Vocabulary Word by using the process shown in the box.

Use the following suggestions or similar ideas to give the meaning or context.

> Write the word.
> Say the word.
> Track the word and have children repeat it.
> Give the meaning or context.

dull — Relate to surfaces in the classroom that are not shiny.

exciting — Point out the *-ing* ending. Related words: You can *excite* someone by having fun; the person will get *excited*.

handsome — Point out the two word parts *hand* and *some*. Relate to *beautiful* or *nice-looking*.

hardly — Point out the *-ly* ending. Relate to a very small amount.

sideways — Point out the two small words *side* and *ways*. Demonstrate by looking from side to side.

sparkling — Point out the *-ing* ending. Relate to glitter or another bright object in the classroom.

spotted — This is a multiple-meaning word. Children may be more familiar with another meaning. Relate to *saw*.

For vocabulary activities, see Vocabulary Games on pages 2–3.

> **Vocabulary Words**
> **dull** not bright or clear
> **exciting** lively and interesting
> **handsome** good-looking
> **hardly** barely, only just
> **sideways** from side to side
> **sparkling** shiny, bright
> **spotted** saw

AFTER
Building Background and Vocabulary

Apply Vocabulary Strategies

Use spelling patterns. Write the word *hardly* on chart paper and underline the letters *ar*. Tell children that they can sometimes figure out how to pronounce new words by looking for letter patterns that they know.

MODEL The letter combination *ar* is a spelling pattern I have seen before in words. When I blend the letter patterns that I know all together with the initial consonant *h* and the ending *ly*, I read *hardly*. Guide children in using a similar procedure to decode the word *sparkling*.

RETEACH lesson vocabulary. Have children listen to each of the following sentences. Tell them to hold up the word card that completes each riddle. Reread the sentence aloud with the correct answer. Then discuss how children made their choices.

1. I saw things with my eyes. (*spotted*)
2. I am the opposite of dull. (*sparkling*)
3. I am lots of fun. (*exciting*)
4. I am not sparkling or shiny. (*dull*)
5. This is when I look from side to side. (*sideways*)
6. I am not a lot. (*hardly*)
7. I am very good-looking. (*handsome*)

FLUENCY BUILDER Using *Intervention Practice Book* page 3, read each word in the first column aloud and have children repeat it. Then have children work in pairs to read the words in the first column aloud to each other. Follow the same procedure with each of the remaining columns. After partners have practiced reading aloud the words in each column separately, have them practice the entire list. (Save *Intervention Practice Book* page 3 for use on pages 11 and 13.)

INTERVENTION PRACTICE BOOK
page 3

The Mixed-Up Chameleon/Mac's Wish Comes True

BEFORE
Reading "The Mixed-Up Chameleon"
pages 16–45

USE SKILL CARD 1A

Focus Skill: Main Idea

PRETEACH the skill. Point out to children that the main idea of a story is the most important idea. Explain that often the first sentence states the main idea, but sometimes they have to read the whole piece to figure out which idea is the most important. Discuss why it helps readers to know which idea in a story is the most important one.

Have children look at **side A of Skill Card 1: Main Idea**. Read the definition of main idea. Next read the paragraph and then have children reread it with you.

Now call attention to the chart and have volunteers take turns reading the sentences aloud. Ask:

- **How can you tell that you have chosen the right main idea?** (*Possible response: All the clues tell about the main idea.*)

- **Why is it important to have a main idea?** (*Possible response: so readers can understand what the story or paragraph is about*)

Prepare to Read: "The Mixed-Up Chameleon"

Preview. Tell children that they are going to read a selection titled "The Mixed-Up Chameleon." Explain that this is a fantasy selection. Tell children that "The Mixed-Up Chameleon" tells about a make-believe chameleon. Then preview the selection.

JUST FOR YOU
pages 16–45

- **Pages 16–17:** I see the title, "The Mixed-Up Chameleon," and the name of the author on page 17. I see a picture of a chameleon on pages 16–17 and I think that this must be the mixed-up chameleon.

- **Pages 18–19:** On these pages, I see pictures of the chameleon. He looks different in each picture. I think the selection must tell about how the chameleon changes.

- **Pages 20–21:** I see a picture of the chameleon about to eat a fly. I think the selection must tell about what the chameleon eats and what his life is like.

- **Pages 22–23:** There are a lot of different animals on these pages. They look very different from the chameleon. Maybe the chameleon thinks they look different, too.

Set Purpose. Model setting a purpose for reading "The Mixed-Up Chameleon."

MODEL From what I have seen in my preview, I think I will probably find out what happens to make the chameleon change the way he looks and get mixed up. I will read to find out if he is still a chameleon at the end of the story.

Lesson 1 • Intervention Teacher's Guide

AFTER

Reading "The Mixed-Up Chameleon"
pages 16–45

Reread and Summarize

Have children reread and summarize "The Mixed-Up Chameleon" in sections, as described below.

> Pages 19—23
>
> **Let's reread pages 19–23 to recall what the chameleon is like and how he lived until something happened.**
>
> Summary: The chameleon was small and green and could change colors. He did not have an exciting life until one day he saw many animals in a zoo.
>
> Pages 24–41
>
> **Let's reread pages 24–41 to recall how the chameleon got mixed up.**
>
> Summary: The chameleon wanted to be like all the animals in the zoo. Every time he wished to change, he did, until he was a little bit like all the animals. Then he did not look like a small, green chameleon anymore.
>
> Pages 42–43
>
> **Let's reread pages 42–43 to remember why the chameleon could not catch the fly.**
>
> Summary: The chameleon was a little bit like all the animals and people instead of like himself, so he did not know how to catch a fly anymore.
>
> Pages 44–45
>
> **Let's reread pages 44–45 to recall what happened to the mixed-up chameleon.**
>
> Summary: He wished that he could be like himself, and his wish came true. Then he was able to catch the fly.

FLUENCY BUILDER Use *Intervention Practice Book* p. 3, which you used for the previous Fluency Builder activity. Call attention to the sentences on the bottom half of the page. The slashes break the sentences into phrases to allow you to work on natural phrasing. Tell children that their goal is to read each phrase or sentence smoothly. Model appropriate pace, expression, and phrasing as you read each sentence, and have children read it after you. Then have children practice by reading the sentences aloud three times to a partner.

INTERVENTION PRACTICE BOOK
page 3

The Mixed-Up Chameleon/Mac's Wish Comes True

BEFORE
Making Connections
pages 50–51

Directed Reading: "Mac's Wish Comes True," pp. 6–12

Ask a volunteer to read aloud the title. Help children to see that the character Mac is a turtle. Read pages 6–7 while children listen to find out what Mac is feeling.

SOUNDS OF SUNSHINE
pp. 6–13

Ask: **How does Mac feel about his life?** (*Possible response: He is bored with his friends and is not happy about the way he looks.*) **INTERPRET STORY EVENTS**

Ask: **What is the main idea of these pages?** (*Possible response: Mac is not satisfied with his life.*) **MAIN IDEA**

Model using the Decoding/Phonics strategy by writing the word *hungry* on the board. Slide your hand slowly underneath the letters elongating each sound.

MODEL When I read this page, some of the words on it are new to me. I look for vowel sounds or consonant sounds that I know to help me figure out these new words. I also use blending to put the different sounds together. I look at the letters in the word *hungry* and think about the sounds the letters stand for. I say the word slowly to myself—(hhuunnggrrēē). Then I say the word again quickly—*hungry*.
USE DECODING/PHONICS

Pages 8–9
Have children read pages 8–9 to find out what happens when Mac's wishes come true. Ask: **How does Mac change each time his wish comes true?** (*Possible response: He looks different and can do different things.*) **IMPORTANT DETAILS**

Pages 10–11
Discuss the strategies children use to help them figure out how to pronounce unfamiliar words. Have a volunteer read aloud page 11. Ask: **How did you know what the word *handsome* should sound like?** (*Possible response: I looked at the letters and thought about the sounds the letters stand for.*)

Page 12
Have children read page 12 to find out what Mac learned at the end of the story. Ask: **What lesson did Mac learn after his last wish came true?** (*Possible response: Being himself and having his pals was not so bad after all.*) **DRAW CONCLUSIONS**

Lesson 1 • Intervention Teacher's Guide

INTERVENTION PRACTICE BOOK *page 5*

Summarize the selection. Ask children to think about why people sometimes wish to be like someone else.

Answers to *Think About It* Questions

1. Mac does not look like a turtle anymore. **CAUSE AND EFFECT**
2. He and his pals are not so bad. **NOTE DETAILS**
3. Accept reasonable responses. **EXPRESS OPINIONS**

AFTER
Skill Review *page 5 II*

USE SKILL CARD 1B

(Focus Skill) Main Idea

RETEACH the skill. Have children look at **side B of Skill Card 1: Main Idea**. Read the skill reminder with them, and have a volunteer read the paragraph aloud.

Read aloud the set of directions. Explain that children will work with partners to create their own charts. Remind them to think about the difference between a clue and the main idea.

After children have completed their main-idea charts, have them display and explain their work. Point out that the selection "Mac's Wish Comes True" has a main idea and clues that tell about the main idea. Ask volunteers to name the main idea and some clues from the selection.

Review the Phonics Skill from "The Mixed-Up Chameleon"

RETEACH phonograms *-id* and *-ide*. Read aloud the following sentence: *The kid hid behind the slide.* Have children listen for phonograms *-id* and *-ide*. Then read this list aloud and have children raise their hands when they hear phonograms *-id* and *-ide*: *big, hid, glide, fish, had, slide, bid, hide.*

FLUENCY BUILDER *Use Intervention Practice Book* page 3. Explain that children will practice the sentences on the bottom half of the page by reading them aloud on tape. Assign new partners. Have children take turns reading the sentences aloud to each other and then reading them on tape.

INTERVENTION PRACTICE BOOK *page 3*

The Mixed-Up Chameleon/Mac's Wish Comes True

BEFORE
Drafting a Journal Entry
page 53C

Developing Ideas and Topics: Journal Entry

Build on prior knowledge. Tell children that they are going to discuss things they might write in a journal. Explain that they can use their journals to brainstorm ideas for writing longer pieces. Guide children to see that a person writes a journal for him- or herself, but parts of it may be shared with others. Explain that to develop ideas they might make a web or list of ideas and circle the idea they like best. Display and read aloud the following list:

> Journal Topic: Dogs
> Idea 1: my dog Snoopy
> Idea 2: games dogs like to play
> Idea 3: kinds of dogs

Construct the text. "Share the pen" with children. Guide them in writing a short journal entry based on the topic *games dogs like to play*. For example, model:

> My dog, Snoopy, is a puppy and likes to play games like other young dogs. Snoopy likes to play fetch. Snoopy can shake hands.

Revisit the text. Go back and read the journal entry. Ask: **If I did not have a topic, what would I write about?** (*Possible response: I might feel stuck or would not know how to get started.*)

- Guide children to combine ideas and use connecting words, such as *and*, to make the ideas flow more smoothly. For example: *Snoopy likes to play fetch and can shake hands.*

- Ask: **What pronoun can we use to replace the word *Snoopy* in the second sentence?** (*he*) Make the appropriate change.

- Have volunteers suggest other things Snoopy might do and add a sentence to the writing.

- Have children read the completed journal entry aloud and then copy it on their papers.

On Your Own

Have children brainstorm a list of journal topics. Ask them to choose one and write a list of ideas for it. Then have children write a three-sentence journal entry about their topic.

Lesson 1 • Intervention Teacher's Guide

AFTER

Spelling Lesson
page 47H

Connect Spelling and Phonics

RETEACH short vowel /a/a. Tell children to number their papers 1–8. Dictate the following words, and have children write them. After each word is written, write it on the board so children can proofread their work. They should draw a line through a misspelled word and write the correct spelling below it.

| 1. Mac* | 2. sat* | 3. pals* | 4. can* |
| 5. at* | 6. bad* | 7. that* | 8. ran* |

* Word appears in "Mac's Wish Comes True."

Dictate the following sentence and have children write it: *Pam looked at the fat cat.*

Build and Read Longer Words

Remind children that they have learned how to decode words with short vowel /a/. Explain that now they will use what they have learned to help them read some longer words.

Write the word *handsome* on the board. Tell children that they can sometimes figure out how to pronounce long words by looking for syllables. Cover *some* and have a volunteer read *hand*. Then cover *hand* and have a volunteer read *some*. Point out that *hand* has the sound /a/. Have children blend the word parts to read the longer word *handsome*. Follow a similar procedure with these words: *knapsack*, *happen*, *ladder*, and *matter*. Encourage children to read other long words like these. Suggest that they use a dictionary to look up words they are not sure about.

INTERVENTION ASSESSMENT BOOK

FLUENCY BUILDER Have children choose a passage from "Mac's Wish Comes True" to read aloud to a partner. You may have children choose a passage that they found particularly interesting, or have them choose one of the following options:

- Read pages 6–8. (From *Mac sat. . . through. . . an animal ran up.* Total: 87 words.)
- Read pages 9–11. (From *What is that. . .through . . . That was not so bad!* Total: 82 words.)

SCALE
1 Not so good
2 Pretty good
3 Good
4 Great!

Children should read the selected passage aloud to their partners three times. Have the child rate each reading on a scale from 1 to 4.

The Mixed-Up Chameleon/Mac's Wish Comes True

BEFORE Weekly Assessments

Review Vocabulary

To revisit Vocabulary Words prior to the weekly assessment, use these sentence frames. Have volunteers take turns reading aloud the sentence stems and choices. Students identify the correct choice and explain why that choice makes sense in the sentence.

1. If something is **dull**, it is probably not
   a. shiny.
   b. cold.
2. I **spotted** my favorite dog, and so I
   a. could not find it.
   b. went to pet it.
3. If you see a **sparkling** rock, it might be
   a. a jewel.
   b. mud.
4. The **handsome** prince was
   a. scary.
   b. nice to look at.
5. If something is turned **sideways**, it is
   a. upside down.
   b. turned on its side.
6. An **exciting** party is
   a. a lot of fun.
   b. very boring.
7. If something is **hardly** there, it is
   a. difficult to see it.
   b. not very soft.

Correct responses: 1a, 2b, 3a, 4b, 5b, 6a, 7a

Focus Skill ★ Review Main Idea

To review Main Idea before the weekly assessment, distribute *Intervention Practice Book* page 6. Have volunteers read aloud the first direction line and the paragraph. Guide children to think about the most important thing that they read.

Review Test Prep

Ask children to turn to page 53 of the *Pupil Edition*. Call attention to the tips for answering the test questions. Tell children that paying attention to these tips can help them answer not only the test questions but also other test questions like these.

JUST FOR YOU page 53

Have children follow along as you read each test question and the tip that goes with it. Discuss how each sentence in question 1 relates to the other sentences in the paragraph.

Lesson 1 • Intervention Teacher's Guide

AFTER
Weekly Assessments

Self-Selected Reading

Have children select their own books to read independently. They might choose books from the classroom library shelf, or you may wish to offer a group of appropriate books from which children can choose.

- *Looking for Animals* (See page 530 of the *Teacher's Edition* for lesson plan.)
- *Frogs* by Laura Driscoll. Grosset & Dunlap, 1998.
- *Who is the Beast?* By Keith Baker. Harcourt, 1990.

After children have chosen their books, give each child a copy of "My Reading Log," which can be found on page R35 in the back of the *Teacher's Edition*. Have children fill in the information at the top of the form. Then have them use the log to keep track of their reading and to record their responses to the literature.

Conduct student-teacher conferences. Arrange time for each child to conference with you individually about his or her self-selected reading. Have children bring their Reading Logs to share with you at the conference. Children might also like to choose a favorite passage to read aloud to you. Ask questions about the book designed to stimulate discussion. For example, you might ask what information the child learned from a nonfiction text or how the animals in the story compare to a turtle.

FLUENCY PERFORMANCE Have children read aloud to you the passage from "Mac's Wish Comes True" that they selected and practiced with their partners. Keep track of the number of words the child reads correctly. Ask the child to rate his or her own performance on the 1–4 scale. If children are not happy with their oral reading, give them an opportunity to continue practicing and then to reread the passage to you.

See *Oral Reading Fluency Assessment* for monitoring progress.

The Mixed-Up Chameleon/Mac's Wish Comes True

LESSON 2

BEFORE Building Background and Vocabulary

Use with

"Get Up and Go!"

Review Phonics: Blends with *s, r, l*

Identify the sound. Read aloud the following sentence: *Stan can skip and snap*. Ask children to repeat the sentence three times, identifying the words that have the /s/ sound combined with another consonant sound. (*Stan, skip, snap*)

Associate letters to sounds. Write the sentence *Stan can skip and snap* on the board, and underline the consonant blends in *Stan, skip,* and *snap*. Tell children that when they see two consonants together in a word, they should try blending the sounds of the two letters.

Word blending. Model how to blend and read the word *Stan,* having children repeat each step after you. Slide your hand under the word as you elongate the sounds /ssttaann/. Then say the word naturally—*Stan*. Follow a similar procedure for the words *skip* and *snap*. Then write these words on the board: *stop, trip, drag, clip,* and *flag*. Have volunteers take turns blending the sounds in each word and reading them aloud.

Apply the skill. *Consonant Substitution* On the board, write the first word in each pair of the following words, one at a time, and have children read each aloud. Make the changes necessary to form the words in parentheses. Have volunteers read aloud each new word.

| **pin** (spin) | **skip** (slip) | **prop** (drop) | **band** (brand) | **sill** (still) |
| **top** (stop) | **grip** (trip) | **grab** (crab) | **dip** (drip) | **sand** (grand) |

INTERVENTION PRACTICE BOOK page 8

Introduce Vocabulary

PRETEACH lesson vocabulary. Tell children that they will learn five new words that will help them when they read a story called "Get Up and Go!" Teach every vocabulary word using the following process.

Use the following suggestions or similar ideas to give the meaning or context.

> Write the word.
> Say the word.
> Track the word and have children repeat it.
> Give the meaning or context.

always   Point out the small word *ways*. Talk about things that always happen, such as the sun rising and setting.

homework   Point out the two small words *home* and *work*. Demonstrate with a volunteer's homework assignment.

minutes   Point out the minutes on an analog clock.

18   Lesson 2 • Intervention Teacher's Guide

snuggle	Demonstrate by making two stuffed animals hug and cuddle.
treat	Point out the small word *eat*. Explain that sometimes a treat can be eaten.

For vocabulary activities, see Vocabulary Games on pages 2–7.

Vocabulary Words
always all the time
homework schoolwork that is done at home
minutes units of time; sixty minutes make one hour
snuggle hug and cuddle
treat a special gift

AFTER
Building Background and Vocabulary

Apply Vocabulary Strategies

Use familiar patterns. Write the word *snuggle* on chart paper and underline the letters *ug*. Tell children that they can sometimes figure out a new word by looking for letter patterns that they know.

MODEL The letter pattern *ug* is familiar to me because I have seen it in words like *hug*. I have seen the ending *le* in words like *paddle*. I have seen the letter pattern *sn* in words like *snore*. When I blend all the letter patterns together, I can figure out how to read *snuggle*.

RETEACH lesson vocabulary. Guide children in using a similar procedure to decode the other Vocabulary Words.

Vocabulary activity. Have children write each vocabulary word on a word card and then listen to each of the following groups of words. Tell them to hold up the word card that matches each group. Reread the group aloud with the correct answer. Then discuss how children made their choices.

1. eat, special, gift (*treat*)
2. schoolbook, paper, bedroom (*homework*)
3. clock, watch, time (*minutes*)
4. never, forever, sometimes (*always*)
5. cozy, comfortable, touch (*snuggle*)

FLUENCY BUILDER Using *Intervention Practice Book* page 7, read each word in the first column aloud and have children repeat it. Then have partners read the words in the first column aloud to each other. Tell children to follow the same procedure with each of the remaining columns. After partners have practiced reading aloud the words in each column, have them practice the entire list. (Save *Intervention Practice Book* page 7 to use on pages 21 and 23.)

INTERVENTION PRACTICE BOOK
page 7

Get Up and Go!/Company Is Coming!

BEFORE
Reading "Get Up and Go!"
pages 56–76

USE SKILL CARD 2A

Focus Skill: Author's Purpose

PRETEACH the skill. Point out to children that the author's purpose is the reason why the author wrote the story. Explain that there are many purposes, or reasons, why authors write stories. Give examples of author's purposes, such as *to entertain*, and *to tell facts*. Discuss why it helps an author to have a purpose before she or he begins to write.

Have children look at **side A of Skill Card 2: Author's Purpose**. Read the definition of author's purpose. Next read the story, and then have children reread it with you. Then have volunteers take turns reading the information in the chart aloud. Ask:

- **How would the story be different if the author's purpose was to teach readers about real ladybugs?** (*Possible responses: The story would not be made-up; there would not be a silly bug in the story.*)

- **How do the clues help you understand the author's purpose?** (*Possible response: They show us what kind of story it is and help us know the author's reason for writing it.*)

Prepare to Read: "Get Up and Go!"

Preview. Tell children that they are going to read an informational story called "Get Up and Go!" Explain that this is a rhyming story about how much time it takes a girl to get ready for school. Then preview the selection.

JUST FOR YOU pages 56–76

- **Pages 56–57:** I see the title, "Get Up and Go!," and the name of the author and the illustrator. I see a picture of a little girl sleeping with her teddy bear. I think that the story must be about this little girl and what happens when she gets up out of bed.

- **Pages 58–59:** I see a dog with the girl. The words tell me that someone is talking to the girl. I think that it is the dog. He's trying to get the girl to wake up so she'll get ready and not be late for whatever she is going to do.

- **Pages 60–61:** The words tell me that the dog is keeping track of how much time the girl takes to do things so she will not be late. The pictures of lines show me how many minutes the girl takes to do things.

Set purpose. Model setting a purpose for reading "Get Up and Go!"

MODEL From my preview, I think I will probably find out how much time it takes the girl to get ready. I will read to find out how to add minutes and to see if the girl will be late or on time.

Lesson 2 • Intervention Teacher's Guide

AFTER
Reading "Get Up and Go!"
pages 56–76

Reread and Summarize

Have children reread and summarize "Get Up and Go!" in sections, as described below.

Pages 58–65

Let's reread pages 58–65 to recall who is keeping track of the time and why.

Summary: The dog is keeping track of how much time the girl takes to do things so she won't be late for school.

Pages 66–69

Let's reread pages 66–69 to recall the things the girl did and how much time it took her.

Summary: She took 6 minutes to brush her teeth and hair and 7 minutes to get dressed. It took her 13 minutes. So far, it has taken the girl 31 minutes to get ready.

Pages 70–73

Let's reread pages 70–73 to recall more things the girl did and how much time it took her.

Summary: She took 4 minutes to pack and 1 minute to hug her dog. These things took her 5 minutes to do.

Pages 74–76

Let's reread pages 74–76 to recall everything the girl did and how long it took her to get ready for school.

Summary: She took 5 minutes to snuggle, 3 minutes to wash, 8 minutes to eat, 2 minutes to give her dog a treat, 6 minutes to brush her teeth and hair, 7 minutes to dress, 4 minutes to pack, and 1 minute to hug her dog. All together, it took her 36 minutes to get ready for school.

FLUENCY BUILDER Use *Intervention Practice Book* page 7. Call attention to the sentences on the bottom half of the page. The slashes break the sentences into phrases to allow you to work on natural phrasing. Tell children that their goal is to read each phrase or sentence smoothly. Model appropriate pace, expression, and phrasing as you read each sentence, and have children read it after you. Then have children practice by reading the sentences aloud three times to a partner.

INTERVENTION PRACTICE BOOK
page 7

BEFORE
Making Connections
pages 78–79

Directed Reading: "Company Is Coming!" pp. 14–20

Ask a volunteer to read aloud the title. Help children to see that the family's house is messy. Read pages 14–15 while children listen to find out what the family is doing. Ask: **What is the problem?** (*Possible response: Company is coming and the family is not ready.*) **INTERPRET STORY EVENTS**

SOUNDS OF SUNSHINE
pp. 14–20

Ask: **What is the author's purpose?** (*Possible response: To entertain; to teach about telling time.*) **AUTHOR'S PURPOSE**

Pages 16–17 Have children read pages 16–17 to find out who else isn't ready and what they are doing. Ask: **What are the family members doing?** (*Possible response: Cass is snuggling with Alf and Stan is reading.*) **IMPORTANT DETAILS**

Pages 18–19 Read aloud pages 18–19 to children. Then reread aloud page 18. Model using the Reread Aloud strategy to figure out how Dad is feeling.

> **MODEL** I'm not sure what the sentence *Dad is in a flap* means. I know Dad is in a hurry to clean up, but I'm not sure exactly what the sentence means. I will reread the page aloud to figure out the meaning. Oh, I understand now. The sentence means that Dad is upset and that he is really moving fast to try to get the house ready for company.
> **REREAD ALOUD**

Have children reread page 19 and predict where Dad is. (*Possible responses: He is resting . . . he is looking out the window to see if the company is there.*) **MAKE PREDICTIONS**

Page 20 Have children read page 20 to find out what happened to Dad at the end of the story. Ask: **Was the whole family ready in time to greet their company?** (*Possible response: Everyone was ready except Dad.*) **DRAW CONCLUSIONS**

INTERVENTION PRACTICE BOOK
page 9

Summarize the selection. Ask children to think about why people want their houses to be neat when company comes to visit. Then have them complete *Intervention Practice Book* page 9.

Lesson 2 • Intervention Teacher's Guide

Answers to *Think About It* Questions

1. The house is messy and no one wants to help him clean it. **NOTE DETAILS**
2. Yes, because Dad cares about the house and other people. **EXPRESS PERSONAL OPINIONS**
3. Dad tried so hard to get everything ready that he tires himself out. When the doorbell rings, Dad will not be awake to greet the company. **DRAW CONCLUSIONS**

AFTER
Skill Review
pages 81C–81D

USE SKILL CARD 2B

(Focus Skill) Author's Purpose

RETEACH the skill. Have children look at **side B of Skill Card 2: Author's Purpose**. Read the skill reminder with them, and have a volunteer read the paragraph aloud.

Read aloud the directions. Explain that children will work with partners to create their own charts. Remind them to think about the difference between the author's purpose and the clues to the purpose.

After children have completed their author's purpose charts, have them display and explain their work. Point out that the author of the selection "Company Is Coming!" had a purpose in writing it. Ask volunteers to tell what they think the author's purpose is and some clues to that purpose that are found in the selection.

Review Phonics Skill from "Get Up and Go!"

RETEACH phonograms *-ame, -ake*. Read the following sentence aloud and have children repeat it three times: *Let's bake a cake and then play the same game.* Ask volunteers to write the words on the board that have the phonograms *-ame* and *-ake*.

FLUENCY BUILDER Use *Intervention Practice Book* page 7.
Explain that children will practice the sentences on the bottom half of the page by reading them aloud on tape. Assign new partners. Have children take turns reading the sentences aloud to each other and then reading them on tape. Have children listen to the tape and tell how they think their reading has improved. Then have them record the sentences one more time.

INTERVENTION PRACTICE BOOK
page 7

BEFORE
Drafting Detail Sentences
page 81G

Writer's Craft: Adding Details

Build on prior knowledge. Tell children that they are going to talk and write about adding details so their writing can be clearer and more interesting to readers. Guide children to see that details give readers more information and help answer questions that they may have about what they read. Display and read aloud the following information:

> rode bicycle
> went to park
> saw a man
> saw flowers
> had a picnic lunch

Construct the text. "Share the pen" with children. Guide them in writing sentences based on the information. For example:

> I rode my bicycle to the park. I saw a man and some flowers. Then I had a picnic lunch.

Revisit the text. Go back and read the sentences. Ask: **How can you make the sentences more interesting?** (*add details to give readers more information*)

- Guide children to add details to make the sentences more interesting. For example: *I rode my new bicycle to the park near my house. I saw an old man and some purple flowers.*

- Ask: **What details can we use to describe the lunch?** (*delicious; homemade*) Make appropriate changes.

- Have children read the completed detail sentences aloud and then copy them onto their papers.

On Your Own

Have children write detail sentences describing what they see in the classroom. Encourage them to include words that tell about size, shape, and color.

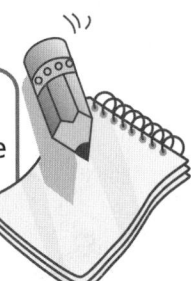

24 Lesson 2 • Intervention Teacher's Guide

AFTER

Spelling
page 81A

Connect Spelling and Phonics

RETEACH blends with *s, r, l*. Tell children to number their papers 1–8. Dictate the following words, and have children write them. After children write each word, write it on the board so that they can proofread their work. They should draw a line through a misspelled word and write the correct spelling beside it.

| 1. Brad* | 2. snuggle* | 3. Fran* | 4. treat* |
| 5. flap* | 6. claps* | 7. Stan* | 8. black* |

* Word appears in "Company Is Coming!"

Dictate the following sentence and have children write it: *Brad skids to a stop.*

Build and Read Longer Words

Remind children that they have learned how to decode words with consonant blends containing *s, r,* and *l*. Explain that now they will use what they have learned to help them read some longer words.

Write the word *clapping* on the board. Tell children that they can sometimes figure out long words by looking for syllables. Cover *ping* and have a volunteer read *clap*. Point out that *clap* has a consonant blend with *l*. Then cover *clap* and have a volunteer read *ping*. Have children blend the word parts to read the longer word *clapping*. Follow a similar procedure with these words: *skipping, swimming,* and *snapping*. Encourage children to build other long words like these. Suggest that they use a dictionary to look up words they are not sure about.

INTERVENTION ASSESSMENT BOOK

FLUENCY BUILDER Have children choose a passage from "Company Is Coming!" to read aloud to a partner. You may have children choose passages that they found particularly interesting, or have them choose one of the following options:

- Read pages 14–15. (Total: 78 words.)
- Read pages 16–17. (Total: 83 words.)

Children should read the selected passage aloud to their partners three times. Have children rate each of their own readings on a scale from 1 to 4.

SCALE
1 Not so good
2 Pretty good
3 Good
4 Great!

Get Up and Go!/Company Is Coming!

BEFORE Weekly Assessments

Review Vocabulary

To review the Vocabulary Words prior to the weekly assessment, use these sentences. Have volunteers take turns reading aloud the sentence stems and choices. Children identify the correct choice and explain why that choice makes sense.

1. If you **always** do something, you do it
    a. once in a while.
    b. all the time.
2. You probably do your **homework**
    a. at home.
    b. while you are taking a test.
3. If something lasts for six **minutes**, it lasts less than
    a. six hours.
    b. six seconds.
4. When you **snuggle** with a pet, it feels
    a. nice.
    b. horrible.
5. If someone gives you a **treat**, you should
    a. give it back.
    b. thank the person.

Correct responses: 1.b, 2.a, 3.a, 4.a, 5.b

You may want to display the Vocabulary Words and definitions from page 19, and have children copy them to use when they study for the vocabulary test.

Focus Skill — Review Author's Purpose

To review Author's Purpose before the weekly assessment, distribute *Intervention Practice Book* page 10. Have volunteers read aloud the first direction line and the paragraph. Guide children to think about the reason the author wanted to write the paragraph.

INTERVENTION PRACTICE BOOK
page 10

Review Test Prep

Ask children to turn to page 81 of the *Pupil Edition*. Call attention to the Tips for answering the test questions. Tell children that paying attention to these tips can help them answer not only the questions on this page but also other test questions like them.

JUST FOR YOU
page 81

Have children follow along as you read each test question and the tip that goes with it. Discuss how to find clues that help readers understand an author's purpose. Remind children to check their answers when they finish taking the test.

INTERVENTION ASSESSMENT BOOK

Lesson 2 • Intervention Teacher's Guide

AFTER Self-Selected Reading
Weekly Assessments

Have children select their own books to read independently. They might choose books from the classroom library, or you may wish to offer appropriate books from which children can choose, such as these:

- *What Time Is It?* by Judy Mayer. INDEPENDENT READER
- *There's an Alligator Under My Bed* by Mercer Mayer. E.P. Dutton, 1987.
- *The Day I Had to Play with My Sister* by Crosby Bonsall. HarperCollins, 1988.

After children have chosen their books, give them a copy of My Reading Log, which can be found on page 35R in the back of the *Teacher's Edition*. Have children fill in the information at the top of the form. Then have them use the log to keep track of their reading and to record their responses to the literature.

Conduct student-teacher conferences. Arrange time for each child to conference with you individually about his or her self-selected reading. Have children bring their Reading Logs to share with you at the conference. Children might also like to choose a favorite passage to read aloud to you. Ask questions about the book designed to stimulate discussion. For example, ask what information the children learned, why they chose the book, and whether the book was what they expected.

FLUENCY PERFORMANCE Have children read aloud to you the passage from "Company Is Coming!" that they practiced. Observe children's pronunciation, intonation, phrasing, and the amount of words, in general, that they read correctly. Have children use the 1–4 scale to rate their performance. Give them a second chance to read if they are not satisfied with their performance. See *Oral Reading Fluency Assessment* for monitoring progress.

LESSON 3

Use with

"Henry and Mudge Under the Yellow Moon"

BEFORE
Building Background and Vocabulary

Review Phonics: Short Vowel: /i/*i*

Identify the sound. Ask children to repeat the following sentence aloud three times: *Did Tim win that pin and that hat?* Have children identify the words that have the /i/ sound. (*Did, Tim, win, pin*)

Associate letters to sound. Write *Did Tim win that pin and that hat?* on the board. Ask a volunteer to underline the words that contain the letter *i*. Tell children that in these words, the *i* stands for the /i/ sound. Have children read the underlined words with you.

Word blending. Model how to blend and read the word *fin*. Slide your hand under the word as you elongate the sounds /ffiinn/. Then say the word naturally—*fin*. Follow a similar procedure for the words *tin* and *Kim*.

Apply the skill. *Vowel Substitution* On the board, write the first word in each pair of the following words, one at a time, and have children read each aloud. Make the changes necessary to form the words in parentheses. Have volunteers read aloud each new word.

INTERVENTION PRACTICE BOOK
page 12

tan (tin)   **tap** (tip)   **pan** (pin)   **bat** (bit)   **sat** (sit)

Guide children to see that when a vowel is in between two consonants, the word usually has a short vowel sound.

Introduce Vocabulary

PRETEACH **lesson vocabulary.** Tell children that they are going to learn five new words that they will see again when they read a story called "Henry and Mudge Under the Yellow Moon." Teach the vocabulary words using the following process.

Use the following suggestions or similar ideas to give the meaning or context.

chipmunks	Show photographs of chipmunks and have children tell where the animal lives.
picked	Point out the *-ed* ending. Demonstrate by picking up a classroom object.
sniffing	Point out the *-ing* ending. Demonstrate by sniffing a flower or something aromatic.
south	Draw a compass rose on the board. Relate to directions.

> Write the word.
> Say the word.
> Track the word and have children repeat it.
> Give the meaning or context.

woods   Relate to trees and to stories that are set in the woods.

For vocabulary activities, see Vocabulary Games on pages 2–7.

AFTER
Building Background and Vocabulary

Apply Vocabulary Strategies

Use familiar word parts. Write the word *picked* on chart paper and underline the letters *ed*. Tell children that they can sometimes figure out the meaning of the word by looking for endings that they know.

> **MODEL** The ending *ed* is familiar to me because I have seen it in words like *talked* and *looked*. I know that this ending tells me that something happened in the past. I can read the word *pick* and blend it with the ending *ed* to figure out how to read *picked*.

Guide children in using a similar procedure to decode the words *sniffing*, *woods*, and *chipmunks*.

RETEACH lesson vocabulary. Have children listen to each of the following descriptions. Tell them to hold up the word card that is the opposite of each description. Reread the descriptions aloud with the correct answer. Then discuss how children made their choices.

1. the direction on the compass points north (*south*)
2. holding your breath (*sniffing*)
3. a desert with no trees (*woods*)
4. huge creatures that live in the sky (*chipmunks*)
5. throwing something away (*picking*)

Vocabulary Words
chipmunks small, striped members of the squirrel family that live underground
picked gathered with the hands or fingers
sniffing smelling by taking short breaths through the nose
south in the direction opposite of north; one of the four directions on the compass
woods forest

FLUENCY BUILDER Using *Intervention Practice Book* p. 11, read each word in the first column aloud and have children repeat it. Then have children work in pairs to read the words in the first column aloud to each other. Follow the same procedure with each of the remaining columns. After partners have practiced reading aloud the words in each column, have them practice the entire list.

INTERVENTION PRACTICE BOOK
page 11

Henry and Mudge Under the Yellow Moon/A Walk in the Woods

BEFORE

Reading "Henry and Mudge Under the Yellow Moon"
pages 84–93

USE SKILL CARD 3A

(Focus Skill) Narrative Elements (Setting)

PRETEACH the skill. Point out to children that every story has a setting. Explain that the setting of a story is the time and place in which it happens. Give examples of story settings, such as the woods or the city. Discuss how readers can tell what the setting of a story is by looking for words that describe a place.

Have children look at **side A of Skill Card 3: Narrative Elements (Setting)**. Read the definition of *setting*. Next, read the story and then have children reread it with you.

Now call attention to the chart and have volunteers take turns reading the information in the boxes aloud. Ask:

- **What would happen to the setting if the author told about a special ocean called Fish Park?** (*Possible response: The setting of the story would probably be a special ocean called Fish Park.*)

- **How do the clues help you understand the setting?** (*Possible response: They tell details about when and where.*)

Prepare to Read: "Henry and Mudge Under the Yellow Moon."

Preview. Tell children that they are going to read a selection entitled "Henry and Mudge Under the Yellow Moon." Explain that this is a realistic fiction story about a boy and his dog taking a walk in the woods. Then preview the selection.

JUST FOR YOU
pages 84–93

- **Pages 84–85:** I see the title, "Henry and Mudge Under the Yellow Moon," and the name of the author and the illustrator. I see a picture of a little boy and his dog with leaves blowing around them. I think that the story must take place outdoors during the fall season.

- **Pages 86–87:** On these pages, I see a picture of a boy and his dog. I think the boy and the dog in the picture must be Henry and Mudge.

- **Pages 88–89:** The photos show what Henry and Mudge like to do in the fall in the woods. I see Henry looking at the colors of the leaves, and Mudge is eating some of the leaves.

- **Pages 90–91:** I see Henry and his dog Mudge eating apples.

- **Pages 92–93:** In these photos, Henry and Mudge look happy together on a windy fall day.

Lesson 3 • Intervention Teacher's Guide

Set Purpose. Model setting a purpose for reading "Henry and Mudge Under the Yellow Moon."

> **MODEL** From what I have seen in my preview, I think I will probably find out what happens on Henry and Mudge's walk. I will read to find out if they do the same things or different things in the woods.

AFTER

Reading "Henry and Mudge Under the Yellow Moon" *pages 84–93*

Reread and Summarize

Have children reread and summarize "Henry and Mudge Under the Yellow Moon" in sections, as described below.

Pages 86–87

Let's reread pages 86–87 to recall the setting of the story and who is there.

Summary: The setting of the story is the woods in the fall. Henry and his dog Mudge are there.

Pages 88–89

Let's reread pages 88–89 to recall what Henry and Mudge did with the fall leaves.

Summary: Henry enjoyed looking at the colors of the leaves. Mudge liked to sniff the ground and eat a few leaves.

Pages 90–92

Let's reread pages 90–92 to recall how Henry and Mudge were different.

Summary: Henry was a boy, and Mudge was a dog. Henry counted birds, and Mudge watched for chipmunks. Henry picked apples, and Mudge licked apples. Henry put on a coat, and Mudge grew one. Henry's ears turned red, and Mudge's turned inside out.

Page 93

Let's reread page 93 to recall how Henry and Mudge were the same.

Summary: They both liked being together in the fall.

FLUENCY BUILDER Be sure children have copies of *Intervention Practice Book* p. 11. Call attention to the sentences on the bottom half of the page. Model appropriate pace, expression and phrasing as you read each sentence and have children read it after you. Then have children practice by reading the sentences aloud three times to a partner.

INTERVENTION PRACTICE BOOK

page 11

BEFORE
Making Connections
pages 96–97

Directed Reading: "A Walk in the Woods," pp. 22–27

Have a volunteer read the title aloud. Then ask children to describe the setting. Ask: **What is the setting of the story?** (Possible response: the woods in fall)
(Focus Skill) **NARRATIVE ELEMENTS (SETTING)**

SOUNDS OF SUNSHINE
pp. 22–27

Ask: **What does the girl like about walking in the woods?** (Possible response: walking in the fall leaves.) **NOTE DETAILS**

Ask: **What does the dog like?** (Possible response: sniffing the leaves) **NOTE DETAILS**

Pages 24–25

Have children read pages 24–25 to compare Kim's and Tip's experiences in the woods. Ask: **How are Kim's experience and Tip's experience in the woods alike? How are they different?** (Possible response: Kim and Tip both love the woods in fall; Kim picks apples and Tip looks for chipmunks.) **COMPARE AND CONTRAST**

Page 25

Ask children to predict whether Kim and Tip will follow the chipmunk. Have them read page 25 to find out. Ask: **Will Kim and Tip follow the chipmunk?** (Possible response: yes) **MAKE PREDICTIONS** Ask: **How do you know?** (Possible response: because Kim asks, "Can you find his tree?") **DRAW CONCLUSIONS**

Page 26

Have children describe what has happened in the illustration on page 26. Then have them read the page to find out what the chipmunk will do. Ask: **Does the chipmunk come down from the tree?** (Possible response: no) **NOTE DETAILS**

Ask: **Why doesn't the chipmunk come down?** (Possible response: It is probably afraid of Tip.) **CAUSE AND EFFECT**

Page 27

Read aloud page 27 to children. Model using the Self-Correct strategy so children can help themselves when they notice that a word they read does not make sense with the other words in the sentence. Then say,

> **MODEL** As I read page 27, I read the word *sniffing* as *snoring*. I know that this does not make sense, so I read the word again, slowly, to correct my mistake and figure out what the sentence means.
> (Focus Strategy) **SELF-CORRECT**

Lesson 3 • Intervention Teacher's Guide

INTERVENTION PRACTICE BOOK
page 13

AFTER
Skill Review
pages 99C

USE SKILL CARD 3B

Summarize the selection. Ask children to work in small groups and summarize the story by acting it out. They might use crumpled balls of paper for apples. One child can play Kim talking to Tip, and another can describe the walk in the woods.

Answers to *Think About It* Questions

1. Kim and Tip loved to take walks in the woods. They watched a chipmunk in its tree. **SUMMARY**
2. It may be afraid. **INTERPRETATION**
3. Accept reasonable responses. **TASK**

(Focus Skill) Narrative Elements: Setting

RETEACH the skill. Have children look at **side B of Skill Card 3: Narrative Elements (Setting).** Read the skill reminder with them, and have a volunteer read the paragraph aloud.

Read aloud the set of directions. Explain that children will work with partners to complete their own charts. Remind them to think about the difference between clues that tell when and clues that tell where.

After children have completed their setting charts, have them display and explain their work. Point out that the selection "A Walk in the Woods" has a setting and clues that tell when and where. Ask volunteers to name the setting and some clues that tell about when and where.

(Focus Skill) Review Phonics Skill from "Henry and Mudge Under the Yellow Moon"

RETEACH inflections *-ed*. Write the base words below on the board. Print the *-ed* ending on a slip of paper. Ask volunteers to pick a base word, and use it in a sentence. Then add the *-ed* ending after the base word and use it in a different sentence.

| play | sniff | watch |
| walk | pick | look |

FLUENCY BUILDER Be sure that children have copies of *Intervention Practice Book* page 11. Explain that today children will practice the sentences on the bottom of the page by reading them aloud on tape. Assign new partners. Have children take turns reading the sentences aloud to each other and then reading them on tape.

INTERVENTION PRACTICE BOOK
page 11

Henry and Mudge Under the Yellow Moon/A Walk in the Woods

BEFORE
Drafting a Paragraph
page 97A

Writing Process: Paragraph

Build on prior knowledge. Tell children that they are going to talk and write about paragraphs. Lead children to see that paragraphs are made up of sentences that are put in order to tell about the same topic. Display and read aloud the following sentences:

> Harry is white with a black spot on his ear.
> Harry loves to play.
> I have a dog named Shep.
> Harry is the best pet in the world.
> Today, I got a new kitten named Harry.

Construct the text. "Share the pen" with children. Guide them in organizing the sentences into a paragraph. Help them see that not all the sentences can be used. For example:

- Today, I got a new kitten named Harry. Harry is white with a black spot on his ear. Harry loves to play. Harry is the best pet in the world.

Revisit the text. Go back and read the sentences. Ask: **What word can we use in some of the sentences to replace the word** *Harry*? (*he*) Make the appropriate change.

- Guide children to think of another sentence that they could add to the paragraph after the sentence *He loves to play*. For example: His favorite game is chasing a stuffed mouse.

- Ask: **Why can't we use the sentence that tells about Shep?** (*It is not about the same topic as the rest of the sentences.*)

- Have children read the completed paragraph aloud and then copy it on their papers.

On Your Own

Have children write a paragraph that begins with the sentence *I have a dog named Shep*. Have them write three or more sentences that tell what Shep likes to do.

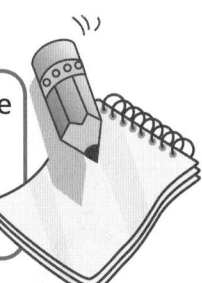

AFTER
Spelling Lesson
page 95H

Connect Spelling and Phonics

RETEACH short vowel /i/ *i*. Tell children to number their papers 1–8. Dictate the following words, and have children write them. After children write each word, write it on the board so they can proofread their work. They should draw a line through a misspelled word and write the correct spelling below it.

1. pin	2. lip	3. sit*	4. sip
5. tin	6. did*	7. bit*	8. fit

*Word appears in "A Walk in the Woods."

Dictate the following sentence and have children write it: *Kip sits on the tip of the big bin.*

Build and Read Longer Words

Remind children that they have learned how to decode words with short vowel /i/. Explain that now they will use what they have learned to help them read some longer words.

Write the word *sitting* on the board. Tell children that they can sometimes figure out long words by looking for syllables. Cover *sit* and have a volunteer read *ting*. Then cover *ting* and have a volunteer read *sit*. Point out that *sit* has the short sound of /i/i/. Have children blend the word parts to read the longer word *sitting*. Follow a similar procedure with these words: *tipping, winning,* and *ripping*. Encourage children to build other long words like these. Suggest that they use a dictionary to look up words they are not sure about.

INTERVENTION ASSESSMENT BOOK

FLUENCY BUILDER Have children choose a passage from "A Walk in the Woods" to read aloud to a partner. Tell children they may select an interesting passage, or have them choose one of the following options:

- Read pages 22–24. (From *Kim and Tip loved*. . . through. . . *looking for chipmunks*. Total: 48 words.)
- Read pages 25–26. (From "*Look over*". . . through . . . *come down*. Total: 60 words.)

SCALE
1 Not so good
2 Pretty good
3 Good
4 Great!

Children should read the selected passage aloud to their partners three times. Have children rate each of their own readings on a scale from 1 to 4.

BEFORE Weekly Assessments

Review Vocabulary

To revisit Vocabulary Words prior to the weekly assessment, use these sentence frames. Have volunteers take turns reading aloud the sentence stems and choices. Children identify the correct choice and explain why that choice makes sense in the sentence.

1. If you **picked** something up, you probably
   a. did it already.
   b. are about to do it.
2. You probably see **chipmunks**
   a. swimming in the ocean.
   b. hurrying up trees in the woods.
3. If a dog is **sniffing** something, she is
   a. sleeping.
   b. smelling it.
4. When you travel **south**, you are moving away from
   a. the sun.
   b. the north.
5. When you walk in the **woods**, you see a lot of
   a. cars.
   b. trees.

Correct responses: 1. a, **2.** b, **3.** b, **4.** b, **5.** b

You may want to display the Vocabulary Words and definitions on page 29 and have children copy them to use when they study for the vocabulary test.

Focus Skill: Narrative Elements (Setting)

To review Narrative Elements (Setting) before the weekly assessment, distribute *Intervention Practice Book* p. 13. Have volunteers read aloud the first direction line and the paragraph. Guide children to think about the setting of the paragraph.

Review Test Prep

Ask children to turn to page 99 of the *Pupil Edition*. Call attention to the Tips for answering the test questions. Tell children that paying attention to these tips can help them answer not only the test questions on this page but also other test questions like these.

Have children follow along as you read each test question and the tip that goes with it. Remind children to think about the reasons for their answers.

INTERVENTION PRACTICE BOOK
page 13

INTERVENTION ASSESSMENT BOOK

JUST FOR YOU
page 99

Lesson 3 • Intervention Teacher's Guide

AFTER
Weekly Assessments

Self-Selected Reading

Have children select their own books to read independently. They might choose books from the classroom library shelf, or you may wish to offer a group of appropriate books from which children can choose.

- *Chipmunks Do What Chipmunks Do* by Julie Verne. See page 99S of the *Teacher's Edition* for an Independent Reading Plan.
- *Who Will Be My Friends?* by Syd Hoff. HarperCollins, 1988.
- *Frog and Toad Together* by Arnold Lobel. HarperCollins, 1972.

After children have chosen their books, give each child a copy of "My Reading Log," which can be found on page R35 in the back of the *Teacher's Edition*. Have children fill in the information at the top of the form. Then have them use the log to keep track of their reading and to record their responses to the literature.

Conduct student-teacher conferences. Arrange time for each child to meet with you individually to discuss his or her self-selected reading. Have children bring their Reading Logs to share with you at the conference. Children might also like to choose a favorite passage to read aloud to you. Ask questions designed to stimulate discussion of the book. For example, you might ask what information the child learned about things that friends do together, or what people do when they go to the woods.

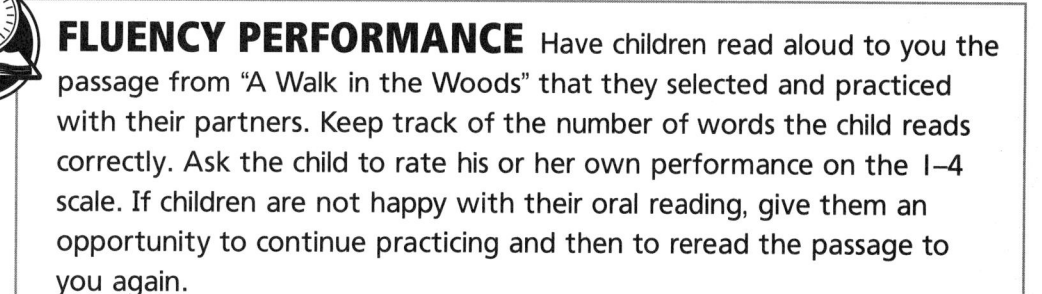

FLUENCY PERFORMANCE Have children read aloud to you the passage from "A Walk in the Woods" that they selected and practiced with their partners. Keep track of the number of words the child reads correctly. Ask the child to rate his or her own performance on the 1–4 scale. If children are not happy with their oral reading, give them an opportunity to continue practicing and then to reread the passage to you again.

See *Oral Reading Fluency Assessment* for monitoring progress.

LESSON 4

BEFORE Building Background and Vocabulary

Use with

"Days With Frog and Toad"

Introduce Vowel Variant: /ôl/*all*

Identify the sound. Ask children to repeat the following sentence aloud several times: *All the balls hit the wall*. Have children identify the words that have the /ôl/ sound. (*all, balls, wall*)

Associate letters to sound. On the board, write: *All the balls hit the wall*. Ask a volunteer to underline the letters *all* in each word. Tell children that in these words, the letters *all* stand for the /ôl/ sound.

Word blending. Write the words *call, wall, tall,* and *fall* on the board and underline the *all* in each. Model how to blend and read the word *call*. Slide your hand under the letters as you slowly elongate the sounds /kkôôll/. Then read the word naturally—*call*. Follow a similar procedure for *wall, tall,* and *fall*.

Apply the skill. *Consonant Substitution* On the board, write the word *call* and model replacing the *c* in *call* with *b* to form *ball*. Continue replacing the initial consonant as shown below to form new words that have the /ôl/ sound. Have children take turns reading each new word aloud.

INTERVENTION PRACTICE BOOK page 16

call   ball   fall   hall   mall   wall   tall

Introduce Vocabulary

PRETEACH lesson vocabulary. Tell children that they are going to learn six new words that they will see again when they read a story called "Days With Frog and Toad."

Teach each Vocabulary Word using the following process.

Use the following suggestions or similar ideas to give the meaning or context.

alone	Relate by grouping children singularly and in small groups.
cheer	Relate by role-playing the act of cheering up a sad person.
fine	Relate to other words: *good, nice, beautiful*.
meadow	Relate by showing pictures of meadows, describing a large area of grass and flowers.
reason	Relate to cause and effect. Demonstrate a simple cause and effect in the classroom.

> Write the word.
> Say the word.
> Track the word and have children repeat it.
> Give the meaning or context.

spoiled   Relate by showing a whole, clean piece of paper and a dirty, torn piece of paper.

For vocabulary activities, see Vocabulary Games on Intervention Teacher's Guide pages 2–7.

> **Vocabulary Words**
> **alone** not with anyone
> **cheer** make glad
> **fine** very good
> **meadow** grassy land
> **reason** cause
> **spoiled** ruined

AFTER
Building Background and Vocabulary

Apply Vocabulary Strategies

Use familiar patterns. Write the word *cheer* on chart paper and underline the letters *ch*. Tell children that they can sometimes figure out a new word by looking for letter patterns that they know.

> **MODEL** The letter combination *ch* is familiar to me because I have seen it in words like *chair*. I have seen the letter combination *ee* in *feet*. When I blend the letter patterns that I know all together with the ending consonant *r*, I read *cheer*.

Guide children in using a similar strategy to decode the words *spoiled* (page 113) and *meadow* (page 106).

RETEACH lesson vocabulary. Have children listen to each of the following groups of words. Tell them to hold up the word card that matches each group. Reread the group aloud with the correct answer. Then discuss how children made their choices.

1. bad ruined dirty (*spoiled*)
2. one only single (*alone*)
3. grass outdoors flowers (*meadow*)
4. happy glad funny (*cheer*)
5. good nice well done (*fine*)

FLUENCY BUILDER Using *Intervention Practice Book* page 15, read aloud each word in the first column and have children repeat it. Then have children work in pairs to read the words in the first column aloud to each other. Follow the same procedure with each of the remaining columns. After partners have practiced reading aloud the words in each separate column, have them read aloud the entire list. (Save *Intervention Practice Book* page 15 to use on pages 41 and 43.)

INTERVENTION PRACTICE BOOK
page 15

Days With Frog and Toad/One Fine Night

BEFORE

Reading
"Days With
Frog and Toad"
pages 102–116

USE SKILL CARD 4A

(Focus Skill) Compare and Contrast

PRETEACH the skill. Point out to children that they can compare things that happen with what they already know. For example, they can compare new people they meet to people they already know, or contrast new places with familiar ones. Discuss how readers can compare and contrast characters in stories.

Have children look at **side A of Skill Card 4: Compare and Contrast.** Read the definition of compare and contrast. Next, read the stories and have children read them with you.

Now call attention to the diagram and have volunteers take turns reading the information aloud. Ask:

- **Why is it helpful to compare and contrast characters?** (*Possible response: to understand what you read*)

Prepare to Read: "Days With Frog and Toad"

Preview. Tell children that they are going to read a selection titled "Days With Frog and Toad." Explain that this is a story. Tell children that "Days With Frog and Toad" tells about a make-believe pair of friends. Then preview the selection.

JUST FOR YOU
pages 102–116

- **Pages 102–103:** I see the title, "Days With Frog and Toad," and the name of the author, on pages 102–103. I see a picture of a frog and a toad and I think that they must be the two friends in the story.

- **Pages 104–105:** On page 104, I read about a note that Frog left for his friend Toad. On page 105, I see a picture of Toad reading the note that Frog left. I think the selection must be about why Frog wants to be alone.

- **Pages 106–107:** On page 106, I read about all the places that Toad looks for Frog. On page 107, there is a picture of Frog sitting alone on an island. I read that Toad thinks Frog is sad. I think the selection must tell how Frog feels about being alone.

- **Pages 108–116:** On these pages, I see the things that Toad does to make Frog happy. I see the friends together on page 116.

Set Purpose. Remind children to think about how the characters are alike and different as they read the story.

> **MODEL** From what I have seen in my preview, I think I will probably find out why Frog wants to be alone, and whether Frog and Toad will have a picnic. I will read to find out if Frog is happier being alone or being with Toad.

AFTER

Reading "Days With Frog and Toad"
pages 102–116

Reread and Summarize

Have children reread and summarize "Days With Frog and Toad" in sections, as described below.

Pages 102–106

Let's reread pages 102–106 to recall what happens when Frog writes Toad a note.

Summary: Frog writes Toad a note saying that he wants to be alone. Toad does not understand why Frog wants to be alone and goes looking for him.

Pages 107–109

Let's reread pages 107–109 to recall where Frog is and what Toad does when he finds Frog.

Summary: Frog is sitting alone on an island. Toad goes home to pack a picnic lunch and then hurries back to Frog.

Pages 110–112

Let's reread pages 110–112 to recall what Toad does after Frog does not see him or hear him call.

Summary: Toad climbs on a turtle's back and rides out to the island where Frog is sitting. Toad apologizes to Frog and then falls in the river.

Pages 113–116

Let's reread pages 113–116 to remember what happened to Frog and Toad.

Summary: Frog pulled Toad onto the island. The sandwiches were wet, and the iced tea was gone. Frog told Toad how happy he was to be alive and have Toad for a friend. They ate their picnic lunch and sat together.

FLUENCY BUILDER Be sure children have copies of *Intervention Practice Book* page 15, which you used for yesterday's Fluency Builder activity. Call attention to the sentences on the bottom half of the page. The slashes break the sentences into phrases to allow you to work on natural phrasing. Tell children that their goal is to read each phrase or sentence smoothly. Model appropriate pace, expression, and phrasing as you read each sentence and have children read it after you. Then have children practice by reading the sentences aloud three times to a partner.

INTERVENTION PRACTICE BOOK
page 15

BEFORE

Making Connections
pages 120–121

Directed Reading: "One Fine Night," pp. 30–36

Sounds of Sunshine pp. 30–37

Ask a volunteer to read aloud the title. Help children to see that Hal is an owl who is sitting at home alone. Read pages 30–31 while children listen to find out how Hal is feeling. Ask: **How does Hal feel about being alone?** (*Possible response: He feels sad.*) **NOTE DETAILS**

Ask: **How are Hal and Rip alike? How are they different?** (*Possible response: Hal and Rip are both animals and are at home; Hal is sad, Rip is napping.*) **COMPARE AND CONTRAST**

Pages 32–33

Have children read pages 32–33 to find out what Hal will do next. Ask: **What does Hal do next? What does he do after that?** (*Possible response: He calls Mack; he calls Gil.*) **SEQUENCE OF EVENTS**

Pages 34–35

Read aloud pages 34–35 to children. Model using the Create Mental Images strategy in order for children to picture how Hal is feeling and what he is doing.

> **MODEL** In these pages, the other characters talk about Hal. I cannot see what Hal is doing. The other characters say that Hal is sad and does not like to be alone. In my mind, I create a picture of what I think Hal looks like and what he might be doing all alone. I remember how I have felt when I was sad or alone, and I use this to help me create a mental image of Hal. This helps me to better understand what is happening in the story. **CREATE MENTAL IMAGES**

Pages 36–37

Have children look at the picture on page 36 and read page 37 to find out what happened to Hal in the end of the story. Ask: **Why is being alone fine for some?** (*Possible response: Not all people like to be alone.*) **DRAW CONCLUSIONS**

Lesson 4 • Intervention Teacher's Guide

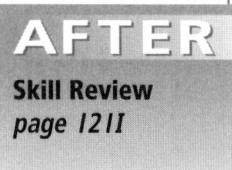

Summarize the Selection. Ask children to think about why people might feel sad being home all alone. Then have them complete *Intervention Practice Book* page 17.

Answers to *Think About It* Questions

1. They didn't want Hal to be sad and lonely. **SUMMARY**
2. Hal liked playing with friends more than playing alone. **INTERPRETATION**
3. Accept reasonable responses. **TASK**

(Focus Skill) Compare and Contrast

RETEACH the skill. Have children look at **side B of Skill Card 4: Compare and Contrast**. Read the skill reminder with them, and have a volunteer read the stories aloud.

Read aloud the set of directions. Explain that children will work with partners to create their own diagrams. Remind them to look for all the ways in which the characters are alike and different.

After children have completed their compare and contrast diagrams, have them display and explain their work. Point out that the selection "One Fine Night" has characters that are alike and different from each other. Ask volunteers to name some of the ways these characters are alike and different.

Review Phonics Skill from Days with Frog and Toad

RETEACH Inflections: -ed (*y* to *i*) On the board write the word *try* and model changing the *y* to *i* and adding *-ed* by erasing the *y* and writing *i* and then writing *-ed* as you tell children that words that end with a consonant and *y* change *y* to *i* before *-ed* is added. Read the word *tried* with children. Remind children that the ending is added to show that the action happened in the past. Have children take turns, at the board, and follow the same procedure with these words.

dry (dried)   **fry** (fried)   **pry** (pried)   **multiply** (multiplied)

FLUENCY BUILDER Be sure that children have copies of *Intervention Practice Book* page 15. Explain that today children will practice the sentences on the bottom half of the page by reading them aloud on tape. Assign new partners. Have children take turns reading the sentences aloud to each other and then reading them on tape.

BEFORE

Drafting a Friendly Letter
page 121A

Writing Process: Friendly Letter

Build on prior knowledge. Tell children that they are going to talk and write about information they might share in a friendly letter. Explain that a friendly letter is a message that may be written from someone to a friend or relative. Guide children to see that friendly letters may tell about all sorts of things.

> Yours truly, Toad
>
> We can eat sandwiches by the lake.
>
> I want to invite you to a picnic.
>
> Dear Frog,
>
> I hope you will come.

Construct the text. "Share the pen" with children. Help them organize the list above into a friendly letter. For example:

> Dear Frog,
>
> I want to invite you to a picnic. We can eat sandwiches by the lake. I hope you will come.
>
> Yours truly,
>
> Toad

Revisit the text. Go back and read the letter together. Ask: **Is there any important information that Toad forgot?** (*day and time of picnic*) Make the appropriate changes.

- Guide children to see the different parts of the friendly letter. Ask: **How do I know who this letter is for?** (*It is for Frog, because it says, "Dear Frog,".*)

- Ask: **How do I know who wrote this letter?** (*Toad wrote the letter, because it says, "Yours truly, Toad."*)

- Have children read the completed friendly letter aloud and then copy it on their papers.

On Your Own

Have children write a list of topics for friendly letters they would like to write. Encourage them to write who each letter is for.

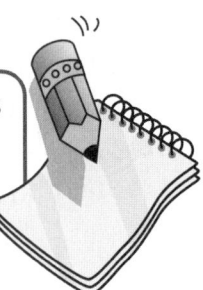

44 Lesson 4 • Intervention Teacher's Guide

AFTER
Spelling Lesson
page 117H

Connect Spelling and Phonics

RETEACH Vowel Variant: /ôl/*all*. Tell children to number their papers 1–7. Write *tall* on the board and tell children that all the words you will say will rhyme with *tall* and will have the same spelling pattern for the /ôl/ sound. Dictate the following words, and have children write them. After each word is written, write it on the board so children can proofread their work. They should draw a line through a misspelled word and write the correct spelling below it.

| 1. ball | 2. fall | 3. hall | 4. all* |
| 5. call* | 6. wall | 7. mall | |

* Word appears in "One Fine Night."

Dictate the following sentence and have children write it: *That bat will fall*.

Build and Read Longer Words

Remind children that they have learned how to decode words with the /ôl/ sound. Explain that now they will use what they have learned to help them read some longer words.

Write the following words on the board: *calling, malls, falling, halls*. Remind children that they should look for words they know in longer words. Point to *calling* and read it aloud. Ask children which part of the word says *call* and which part says *ing*. Ask children what *call* and *ing* together say. Have children blend the word parts to form the longer word *calling*. Repeat this procedure with each word on the board.

INTERVENTION ASSESSMENT BOOK

FLUENCY BUILDER Have children choose a passage from "One Fine Night" to read aloud to a partner. You may have children choose passages that they found particularly interesting, or have them choose one of the following options:

- Read pages 30–32. (From *Hal sat . . .* through . . . *I'm not digging.*") Total: 78 words.
- Read pages 33–34. (From *Hal sat . . .* through . . . *to be alone.*") Total: 85 words.

Children should read the selected passage aloud to their partners three times. Have children rate each of their own readings on a scale from 1 to 4.

SCALE
1 Not good
2 Pretty good
3 Good
4 Great

Days With Frog and Toad/One Fine Night

BEFORE Weekly Assessments

Review Vocabulary

To revisit vocabulary words prior to the weekly assessment, use these sentence frames. Have volunteers take turns reading aloud the sentence stems and choices. Then have children identify the correct choice and explain why that choice makes sense in the sentence.

1. If something is **spoiled**, it is probably
    a. good
    b. rotten
2. You can go to a **meadow** and
    a. have a picnic
    b. sail a boat
3. If you have a **reason**, you have a
    a. cause
    b. problem
4. If you did **fine** on your test, you did
    a. very well
    b. badly
5. When your friend wants to **cheer** you up, it might be because
    a. you are happy
    b. you are sad
6. If your friend is **alone**, she is
    a. with friends
    b. by herself

Correct responses: 1b, 2a, 3a, 4a, 5b, 6b

You may want to display the vocabulary words and definitions on page 39 and have children copy them to use when they study for the vocabulary test.

★ Focus Skill Review Compare and Contrast

To review compare and contrast before the weekly assessment, distribute *Intervention Practice Book* p. 18. Have volunteers read aloud the first direction line and the sentences. Guide children to think about the ways in which characters are alike and different.

INTERVENTION PRACTICE BOOK
page 18

Review Test Prep

Ask children to turn to page 123 of the *Pupil Edition*. Call attention to the tips for answering the test questions. Tell children that paying attention to these tips can help them answer not only the test questions on this page but also other test questions.

JUST FOR YOU
page 123

INTERVENTION ASSESSMENT BOOK

Have children follow along as you read each test question and the tip that goes with it. Discuss how it is important to reread each question to make sure you understand what is being asked.

Lesson 4 • Intervention Teacher's Guide

AFTER
Weekly Assessments

Self-Selected Reading

Have children select their own books to read independently. They might choose books from the classroom library shelf, or you may wish to offer a group of appropriate books from which children can choose.

- *Alone Time, Together Time* by Jesse Levine. See page 123M of the *Teacher's Edition* for an Independent Reading Plan.
- *Frog and Toad Together* by Arnold Lobel. HarperCollins, 1972.
- *Kit and Kat* by Tomie dePaola. Grosset & Dunlap, 1986.

After children have chosen their books, give each child a copy of "My Reading Log," which can be found on page R35 in the back of the *Teacher's Edition*. Have children fill in the information at the top of the form. Then have them use the log to keep track of their reading and to record their responses to the literature.

Conduct Student-Teacher Conferences. Arrange time for each child to conference with you individually about his or her self-selected reading. Have children bring their Reading Logs to share with you at the conference. Children might also like to choose a favorite passage to read aloud to you. Ask questions about the book designed to stimulate discussion. For example, you might ask what children like to do when they are alone and how their activities might differ if they are with friends.

FLUENCY PERFORMANCE Have children read aloud to you the passage from "One Fine Night" that they selected and practiced with their partners. Keep track of the number of words the child reads correctly. Ask the child to rate his or her own performance on the 1–4 scale. If children are not happy with their oral reading, give them an opportunity to continue practicing and then to read the passage to you again.

See *Oral Reading Fluency Assessment* for monitoring progress.

Days With Frog and Toad/One Fine Night

LESSON 5

BEFORE Building Background and Vocabulary

Use with

"Wilson Sat Alone"

Review Phonics: Short Vowel /o/o

Identify the sound. Ask children to repeat the following sentence aloud several times: *This pot has a hot top.* Have children identify the words that have the /o/ sound. (*pot, hot, top*) Ask children to raise their hands each time they hear a word with the /o/ sound. Then repeat with these words: *top, tip, tap, cap, pop, job, hot, hit.* (*top; pop, job; hot*)

Associate letter to sound. On the board, write: *This pot has a hot top.* Ask a volunteer to underline the words with the /o/ sound. Tell children that in these words, the letter *o* stands for the /o/ sound.

Word blending. Model how to blend and read the word *pot*. Write the word *pot* on the board, and slide your hand under the letters as you slowly elongate the sounds /ppoott/. Then read the word naturally—*pot*. Follow a similar procedure for *hot* and *top*.

Apply the skill. *Vowel Substitution* Write the following words on the board, one at a time, and have children read them aloud. Then change the vowel in each word to form the word in parentheses. Have children take turns reading each new word aloud.

| **pat** (pot) | **cab** (cob) | **hat** (hot) |
| **tap** (top) | **hip** (hop) | **map** (mop) |

INTERVENTION PRACTICE BOOK page 20

Introduce Vocabulary

PRETEACH lesson vocabulary. Tell children that they are going to learn five new words that they will see again when they read a story called "Wilson Sat Alone."

Teach each Vocabulary Word shown in the box below using the following process.

Use the following suggestions or similar ideas to give the meaning or context.

amazing	Relate by role-playing facial expressions and gestures that people show when seeing something amazing.
clustered	Relate by grouping classroom objects.
gathered	Relate by gathering classroom objects into a bag.
raced	Point out the *-ed* ending. Relate by having pairs of children race to the board and back to their seats.

> Write the word.
> Say the word.
> Track the word and have children repeat it.
> Give the meaning or context.

wandered   Point out the *-ed* ending. Relate by role-playing someone wandering through the classroom without a plan.

For vocabulary activities, see Vocabulary Games on pages 2–7.

> **Vocabulary Words**
> **amazing** surprising
> **clustered** formed a group
> **gathered** came together
> **raced** ran quickly
> **wandered** went from place to place without a plan

AFTER
Building Background and Vocabulary

Apply Vocabulary Strategies

Use spelling patterns. Write the word *clustered* on chart paper and underline the letters *ed*. Tell children that they can sometimes figure out the meaning of the word by looking for spelling patterns that they know.

MODEL The letter combination *ed* is familiar to me because I have seen it in words like *walked*. I know that the *ed* ending means that the word tells about something that happened in the past.

Guide children in using a similar procedure to decode the words *raced* and *gathered*.

RETEACH lesson vocabulary. Have children listen to each of the following riddles. Tell them to hold up the word card that answers each riddle. Reread the riddle aloud with the correct answer. Then discuss how children made their choices.

1. I walked around, but I didn't know where I was going. How did I walk? (*wandered*)
2. I am very special and fantastic. What am I? (*amazing*)
3. I was not a slow poke! How did I move? (*raced*)
4. I got my pals to bunch all together around the swings. What did we do? (*clustered*)
5. I found shells at the beach and put them in my basket. What did I do with the shells? (*gathered*)

FLUENCY BUILDER Use *Intervention Practice Book* p. 19. Read each word in the first column aloud and have children repeat it. Then have children work in pairs to read the words in the first column aloud to each other. Follow the same procedure with each of the remaining columns. After partners have practiced reading aloud the words in each column separately, have them practice the entire list. (Save *Intervention Practice Book* page 19 to use with pages 51 and 53.)

INTERVENTION PRACTICE BOOK
page 19

Wilson Sat Alone/Just You and Me

BEFORE
Reading "Wilson Sat Alone"
pages 124–145

USE SKILL CARD 5A

Narrative Elements: Character

PRETEACH the skill. Tell children that characters are the people or animals in a story. Point out how they can tell what a character is like by paying attention to what a character says, his or her words, and what a character does, his or her actions. Discuss how readers can also use their own personal experience to understand why characters talk and act the way they do.

Have children look at **side A of Skill Card 5: Narrative Elements (Character)**. Read the definition of *character*. Next read the story and have children read it with you.

Now call attention to the chart and have volunteers take turns reading the information aloud. Ask:

- **What would happen if Martin were crying?** (*Possible response: The information in the chart would be different.*)

- **Why is it helpful to pay attention to what characters say and do?** (*Possible response: to understand what characters are like*)

Prepare to Read: "Wilson Sat Alone"

Preview. Tell children that they are going to read a selection entitled "Wilson Sat Alone." Explain that this is a story that could really happen. Explain to children that "Wilson Sat Alone" tells about a boy who does everything alone. Then preview the selection.

JUST FOR YOU
pages 124–145

- **Pages 126–127:** I see the title, "Wilson Sat Alone," and the name of the author. I see a picture of children playing and a boy all alone. I think that the boy who is alone must be Wilson.

- **Pages 128–129:** On these pages, I see the children pushing their desks together. Wilson is sitting alone. Wilson does not look happy sitting alone. I think the selection must be about how Wilson feels being alone.

- **Pages 130–131:** In these pictures, I see the children eat together in the cafeteria, all except Wilson, who sits alone. I think something is going to happen to Wilson.

- **Pages 132–133:** On these pages, I see that the children all play together, except Wilson. I wonder if Wilson will get to play with the children.

Set Purpose. Model setting a purpose for reading "Wilson Sat Alone."

MODEL From what I have seen in my preview, I think I will probably find out how Wilson feels about being alone. I will read to find out if Wilson gets to do things with the other children.

Lesson 5 • Intervention Teacher's Guide

AFTER

Reading "Wilson Sat Alone" pages 124–145

Reread and Summarize

Have children reread and summarize "Wilson Sat Alone" in sections, as described below.

> Pages 128–131
>
> **Let's reread pages 128–131 to recall what the children and Wilson do in school.**
>
> Summary: The children study and eat together, but Wilson sits alone in the class and in the cafeteria.
>
> Pages 132–135
>
> **Let's reread pages 132–135 to recall the other things that the children and Wilson did and how Wilson probably felt.**
>
> Summary: The children played games, read, left school, and made snowmen together, but Wilson played, read, and walked home from school alone. He did not laugh and probably felt sad.
>
> Pages 136–139
>
> **Let's reread pages 136–139 to recall what happens when the new girl Sara comes to school.**
>
> Summary: When Sara comes to school, she smiles all the time. She sits, eats, reads, and plays alone only for one day. Then she joined the other children and did everything with them. Wilson watched her and when Sara saw him, she raced over to him and roared a monster roar.
>
> Pages 140–144
>
> **Let's reread pages 140–144 to remember what happened to Wilson at the end of the story.**
>
> Summary: Wilson roared back at Sara, and from that day on, he did everything with the children and was not alone anymore.

FLUENCY BUILDER Be sure children have copies of *Intervention Practice Book* p. 19. Call attention to the sentences on the bottom half of the page. Tell children that their goal is to read each phrase or sentence smoothly. Model appropriate pace, expression, and phrasing as you read each sentence, and have children read it after you. Then have children practice by reading the sentences aloud three times to a partner.

INTERVENTION PRACTICE BOOK
page 19

BEFORE

Making Connections
pages 146–147

Directed Reading: "Just You and Me," pp. 38–43

SOUNDS OF SUNSHINE
pp. 38–43

Ask a volunteer to read aloud the title. Help children to see that the boy is alone and the other children are together. Read pages 38–39 while children listen to find out what the boy does when his parents tell him to make a friend. Ask: **What do the boy's parents mean when they tell him to "make a friend"?** (*Possible response: Play with another child at school.*) **INTERPRETATION**

Ask: **How do the boy's actions tell you what he is like?** (*Possible response: He sits alone and looks sad, so he must be lonely.*)
NARRATIVE ELEMENT (CHARACTER)

Page 40

Have children read page 40 to find out what the boy does with his snow friend. Ask: **How does the boy play with his friend? Do they play together?** (*Possible response: The boy jogs and hops, but Bob only watches; they don't really play together.*) **DRAW CONCLUSIONS**

Page 41

Have children read page 41 to find out how Bob brings the other children over. Ask: **Why do the other children want to come over to Bob?** (*Possible response: He is an amazing snowman.*) **NOTE DETAILS**

Pages 42–43

Read aloud pages 42–43 to children. Model using the Make and Confirm Predictions strategy to help children learn how to be active readers.

> **MODEL** When I read that the boy made a snowman, I predicted that the other children would want to come and look at him. Then I predicted that they would want to play with the boy because he had made such an amazing snowman. Then I read ahead to find out if my prediction was correct, and I was right! **MAKE AND CONFIRM PREDICTIONS**

INTERVENTION PRACTICE BOOK
page 21

Ask: **What happens after the other children ask about Bob?** (*Possible response: They ask the boy to play with them.*) **NOTE DETAILS**

Summarize the selection. Have children summarize the selection by telling what happened at the beginning, middle, and end of the story in three or four sentences.

Answers to *Think About It* Questions

1. The boy makes a friend out of snow. **SUMMARY**
2. Bob can't be there because he is made of snow. He melts when it is hot. **INTERPRETATION**
3. Accept reasonable responses. **TASK**

AFTER
Skill Review
pages 147

USE SKILL CARD 5B

(Focus Skill) Narrative Elements: Character

RETEACH the skill. Have children look at **side B of Skill Card 5: Narrative Elements (Character)**. Read the skill reminder with them, and have a volunteer read the story aloud.

Read aloud the set of directions. Explain that children will work with partners to create their own charts. Guide them to picture the story in their mind as they think about what the characters say and do.

After children have completed their character charts, have them display and explain their work. Point out that the selection "Just You and Me" has characters that say and do many things. Ask volunteers to name some of the things these characters say and do.

(Focus Skill) Review Phonics Skill from "Wilson Sat Alone"

RETEACH phonograms -at, -ate Write the following sentence on the board. *Nate chatted with Matt and Kate by the fence gate.* Have children copy the sentence. Then have them circle the words with *-at* and underline words with *-ate*. Then ask children to tell which words they circled and which words they underlined.

FLUENCY BUILDER Be sure children have copies of *Intervention Practice Book* page 19. Explain that today children will practice the sentences on the bottom half of the page by reading them aloud on tape. Assign new partners. Have children take turns reading the sentences aloud to each other and then reading them on tape.

INTERVENTION PRACTICE BOOK
page 19

Wilson Sat Alone/Just You and Me   **53**

BEFORE
Drafting a Thank-You Note
pages 147A

Writing: Thank-You Note

Build on prior knowledge. Tell children that they are going to talk and write about information they might share in a thank-you note. Explain that a thank-you note is similar to a friendly letter, but it includes a message thanking someone for something they did or gave. Guide children to see that thank-you notes may be written to all sorts of people.

> Yours truly, Wilson
> Thank you for playing with me.
> Thank you for being my friend.
> Dear Sara,
> I hope we can be friends forever.

Construct the text. "Share the pen" with children. Help them to organize the list into a thank-you note. For example:

> Dear Sara,
>
> Thank you for being my friend. Thank you for playing with me. I hope we can be friends forever.
>
> Yours truly,
> Wilson

Revisit the text. Read the thank-you note together. Guide children to see the different parts of the friendly letter. Ask: **How do I know who this thank-you note is for?** (*It is for Sara, because it says "Dear Sara."*)

Ask: **How do I know who wrote this thank-you note?** (*Wilson wrote the thank-you note, because it says "Yours truly, Wilson."*)

- Ask: **How can I combine the first and second sentence to make the thank-you note read more smoothly?** (*Thank you for being my friend and for playing with me.*) Make the appropriate change.

- Have children read the completed thank-you note aloud and then copy it on their papers.

On Your Own
Have children write a list of topics for thank-you notes they would like to write. Encourage them to write who each thank-you note is for.

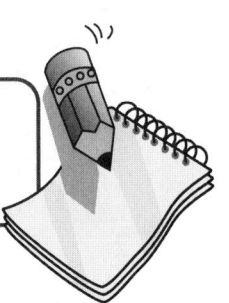

Lesson 5 • Intervention Teacher's Guide

AFTER

*Spelling Lesson
page 145H*

Connect Spelling and Phonics

RETEACH short vowel /o/o. Tell children to number their papers 1–7. Dictate the following words, and have children write them. After each word is written, write it on the board so children can proofread their work. On their papers, they should draw a line through a misspelled word and write the correct spelling below it.

1. hot*	2. top*	3. nod	4. pot*
5. mop*	6. Bob*	7. not*	

* Word appears in "Just You and Me."

Dictate the following sentence and have children write it: *The top on that pot is hot.*

Build and Read Longer Words

Remind children that they have learned how to decode words with the /o/ sound. Explain that now they will use what they have learned to help them read some longer words.

Write the following words on the board: *topping, mopping, pots, logs.*

Remind children that they should look for words they know in longer words. Point to *mopping* and read it aloud. Ask children which part of the word says *mop* and which part says *ping.* Ask children what *mop* and *ping* together say. Have children blend the word parts to form the longer word *mopping.* Help children understand that sometimes a consonant is doubled when the ending *-ing* is added to a word. Repeat this procedure with each word on the board.

INTERVENTION ASSESSMENT BOOK

FLUENCY BUILDER Have children choose a passage from "Just You and Me" to read aloud to a partner. You may have children choose passages that they found particularly interesting, or have them choose one of the following options:

- Read pages 38–39. (From *I had no . . .* through *. . . got a mop.*) Total: 91 words.
- Read pages 40–41. (From *My snow friend . . .* through *. . . It is amazing*) Total: 73 words.

SCALE
1 Not good
2 Pretty good
3 Good
4 Great!

Children should read the selected passage aloud to their partners three times. Have the child rate each reading on a scale from 1 to 4.

Wilson Sat Alone/Just You and Me

BEFORE Weekly Assessments

Review Vocabulary

To revisit Vocabulary Words prior to the weekly assignment, use these sentence frames. Have volunteers take turns reading aloud the sentence stems and choices. Have children identify the correct choice and explain why that choice makes sense in the sentence.

1. If something is **amazing**, it is probably
    a. ordinary.
    b. wonderful.
2. He **wandered** around, and everyone knew that
    a. he had a plan.
    b. he did not have a plan.
3. If your friends **clustered** together, they were
    a. in a group.
    b. far away from each other.
4. After she **gathered** flowers, she had
    a. nothing.
    b. a bunch of flowers.
5. The two friends **raced** home, and got there
    a. very fast.
    b. slowly.

Correct responses: 1. **b**, 2. **b**, 3. **a**, 4. **b**, 5. **a**

You may want to display the Vocabulary Words and definitions on page 49 and have children copy them to use when they study for the vocabulary test.

(Focus Skill) Narrative Elements: Character

To review character before the weekly assessment, distribute *Intervention Practice Book* p. 22. Have volunteers read aloud the first direction line and the sentences. Guide children to think about the things characters say and do.

Review Test Prep

Ask children to turn to page 149 of the *Pupil Edition*. Call attention to the tips for answering the test questions. Tell children that paying attention to these tips can help them answer not only the test questions on this page but also other test questions like these.

Have children follow along as you read each test question and the tip that goes with it. Discuss how good test-takers do their work calmly and quietly.

56 Lesson 5 • Intervention Teacher's Guide

AFTER
Weekly Assessments

Self-Selected Reading

Have children select their own books to read independently. They might choose books from the classroom library shelf, or you may wish to offer a group of appropriate books from which children can choose.

- *Jenny's Wish* by Ted Jamison. See page 149M of the *Teacher's Edition* for an Independent Reading Plan.
- *Leo the Late Bloomer* by Robert Kraus. Windhill, 1971.
- *Snug Bug's Play Day* by Cathy East Dubowski. Grosset & Dunlap, 1997.

After children have chosen their books, give each child a copy of "My Reading Log," which can be found on page R35 in the back of the *Teacher's Edition*. Have children fill in the information at the top of the form. Then have them use the log to keep track of their reading and to record their responses to the literature.

Conduct Student-Teacher Conferences. Arrange time for each child to meet with you individually to discuss his or her self-selected reading. Have children bring their Reading Logs to share with you at the conference. Children might also like to choose a favorite passage to read aloud to you. Ask questions designed to stimulate discussion of the book. For example, you might ask what children like to do when they are alone and how their activities might differ if they are with friends.

FLUENCY PERFORMANCE Have children read aloud to you the passage from "Just You and Me" that they selected and practiced with their partners. Keep track of the number of words the child reads correctly. Ask the child to rate his or her own performance on the 1–4 scale. If children are not happy with their oral reading, give them an opportunity to continue practicing and then to reread the passage again to you.

See *Oral Reading Fluency Assessment* for monitoring progress.

LESSON 6

BEFORE Building Background and Vocabulary

Use with

"The Enormous Turnip"

Review Phonics: Short Vowel /e/e

Identify the sound. Tell children to listen for the /e/ or short e vowel sound as you say the words *men* and *bet*. Then have children repeat the following sentence twice: *Jen will pet a red hen.* Ask them to identify the words that have the /e/ sound. (*Jen, pet, red, hen*)

Associate letters to sound. Write on the board: *Jen will pet a red hen.* Invite a volunteer to underline words with the letter *e*. Explain that in these words, the letter *e* stands for the /e/ sound. Point out that when a word has a vowel in between two consonants, the vowel sound is usually short. Have volunteers identify the CVC pattern in *Jen, pet, red*, and *hen*.

Word blending. Model how to blend and read the word *Jen*. Slide your hand under the letters as you slowly elongate the sounds /jjeenn/. Then say the word naturally—*Jen*. Use the same procedure for *pet, red*, and *hen*.

Apply the skill. *Vowel Substitution* Write the first word in each pair below on the board. Have children read each word aloud. Then make the necessary changes to form the word in parentheses. Have children read the new words.

pan (pen)	**big** (beg)	**rod** (red)	**stop** (step)
tin (ten)	**man** (men)	**mat** (met)	**sit** (set)

INTERVENTION PRACTICE BOOK page 24

Introduce Vocabulary

PRETEACH lesson vocabulary. Tell children that they are going to learn six new words that they will see again when they read "The Enormous Turnip." Teach each Vocabulary Word using the following process.

Use these suggestions or similar ideas to give the meaning or context.

enormous	Relate to dinosaurs, elephants, whales.
granddaughter	Point out the words *grand* and *daughter*. Relate to *grandfather, grandson.*
grew	Relate generally to how many children have grown since kindergarten and first grade.
planted	Point out the *-ed* ending. Explain that to plant something is to put it in the ground.

> Write the word.
> Say the word.
> Track the word and have children repeat it.
> Give the meaning or context.

Lesson 6 • Intervention Teacher's Guide

strong   Relate to people and things that are strong.

turnip   Relate to another root vegetable such as a carrot or a beet.

For vocabulary activities, see Vocabulary Games on pages 2–5.

AFTER
Building Background and Vocabulary

Apply Vocabulary Strategies

Vocabulary Words
- **enormous** very large
- **granddaughter** a daughter of one's son or daughter
- **grew** became larger
- **planted** put in the ground to grow
- **strong** powerful
- **turnip** kind of root vegetable

Use spelling patterns. Write the word *grew* on chart paper. Below *grew* write *grass* and *new*. Use a colored marker to underline *gr* in *grew* and *grass*. Use a second color to underline *ew* in *grew* and *new*. Tell children that they can sometimes figure out the pronunciation of words by looking for letter patterns that they know.

> **MODEL** The letter combination *gr* is familiar to me because I have seen it in words like *grass*. I have also seen the letter combination *ew* in words like *new*. When I blend these two letter patterns I read *grew*.

Guide children in using a similar procedure to decode the word *planted*.

RETEACH lesson vocabulary. Have children listen to each riddle and then hold up the word card that completes the answer. Reread each riddle aloud with the correct answer. Discuss how the children made their choices.

1. I am powerful enough to carry heavy boxes. I am __(strong)__.
2. Who is my daughter's daughter? She is my __(granddaughter)__.
3. I am as tall as a tree and as wide as a house. I am __(enormous)__.
4. How did I get bigger and bigger? I __(grew)__.
5. I grow under the ground and you can eat me. I am a __(turnip)__.
6. I am a seed that was put in the ground to grow. I was __(planted)__.

FLUENCY BUILDER Use *Intervention Practice Book* page 23. Read each word in the first column aloud and have children repeat it. Then have children work in pairs to read the words in the first column aloud to each other. Follow the same procedure with each of the remaining columns. After partners have practiced reading aloud the words in each column, have them listen to each other as they practice the entire list.

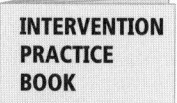

INTERVENTION PRACTICE BOOK
page 23

The Enormous Turnip/A Turnip's Tale

BEFORE

Reading "The Enormous Turnip"
pages 154–166

USE SKILL CARD 6A

Focus Skill: Sequence

PRETEACH the skill. Tell children that events happen in a certain order. Give an example such as waking up, eating breakfast, and then going to school. Discuss why these events do not happen in a different order.

Have children look at **side A of Skill Card 6: Sequence**. Read the definition of sequence. Next, have children look at the pictures and describe what is happening in each one.

Now call attention to the chart. Have volunteers take turns reading the sentences aloud. Ask: **Why does the chart show the events in this order?** (Possible response: Because this is the order in which the events happened.) **What would happen if the sentences were in a different order?** (Possible response: What happened would not make sense.) **Why are the words in the sequence chart important?** (They help children understand how these words give clues to the sequence of events.)

Explain that when events in a story are in time order, they are organized, or set up, according to sequence.

Prepare to Read: "The Enormous Turnip"

Preview. Tell children that they are going to read a story entitled "The Enormous Turnip." Explain that this is a folktale that has been told for many years to Russian children. Tell children that "The Enormous Turnip" makes a turnip seem larger than it usually is in real life. Then preview the selection.

JUST FOR YOU
pages 154–166

- **Pages 154–155:** I see the title "The Enormous Turnip" and the name of the author and illustrator. I also see a big turnip. It must be the enormous turnip. On page 155, I see an old man planting something. I think it must be the turnip.

- **Pages 156–157:** On these pages, I see the old man trying to pull something out of the ground. I think it is the turnip.

- **Pages 158–159:** Now I see a woman helping the man. I think they are pulling hard. I think they need more help.

Set Purpose. Model setting a purpose for reading "The Enormous Turnip."

MODEL From what I have seen in my preview, I know that the old man is having a lot of trouble pulling up the turnip. One purpose for reading is to find out what happens in a story. I will read to find out how the old man finally pulls up the turnip.

60   Lesson 6 • Intervention Teacher's Guide

AFTER

Reading "The Enormous Turnip"
pages 154–167

Reread and Summarize

Have children reread and summarize "The Enormous Turnip" in sections, as described below.

Pages 155–157

Let's reread pages 155–157 to recall how the story begins.

Summary: An old man planted a turnip seed and wished for it to grow. The turnip grew to be so enormous that the man could not pull it up.

Pages 158–159

Now let's reread pages 158–159 to remind us what the old man did when he could not pull up the enormous turnip.

Summary: He called the old woman to help him and they pulled and pulled but still could not pull the turnip from the ground.

Pages 160–164

As we reread pages 160–164, let's remember who came to help the old man and old woman pull up the enormous turnip.

Summary: The old woman called her granddaughter. They could not pull up the turnip. The granddaughter called the black dog. They still could not pull up the turnip, so the black dog called the cat. Still, they could not pull up the turnip.

Pages 165–166

Let's reread pages 165–166 to recall how they finally pulled the enormous turnip.

The cat called the mouse. The mouse pulled the cat; the cat pulled the dog; the dog pulled the granddaughter; the granddaughter pulled the old woman; the old woman pulled the old man; and the turnip came up.

FLUENCY BUILDER Use *Intervention Practice Book* page 23. Point out the sentences on the bottom half of the page. Tell children that their goal is to read each phrase or sentence smoothly. Model appropriate pace, expression, and phrasing as you read each sentence, and have children read it after you. Then have children practice by reading the sentences aloud three times to a partner.

INTERVENTION PRACTICE BOOK
page 23

The Enormous Turnip/A Turnip's Tale

BEFORE

Making Connections
pages 168–169

Directed Reading: "A Turnip's Tale," pp. 46–52

SOUNDS OF SUNSHINE pp. 46–52

Page 46

Ask a volunteer to read aloud the title. Help children identify the turnip in the illustration on page 46. Read aloud page 46 while the children listen to find out why the turnip was so big. Ask: **How did the turnip get to be enormous?** (*Possible response: It grew and grew.*) **CAUSE AND EFFECT**

Page 47

Make sure children understand that the water level in a well goes up and down. Read page 47 aloud while the children listen to find out what happened to the turnip. Ask: **What happened to the turnip? What caused that to happen?** (*Possible response: It fell down the well. Before that, it fell over and rolled down the hill.*) **SEQUENCE**

Page 48–49

Have the children read page 48 to find out what the woman did. Ask: **Why could she not pull the turnip out of the well?** (*Possible response: The turnip was too heavy.*) **DRAW CONCLUSION**

Read aloud the first five paragraphs on page 49 while the children listen to find out who came to help the woman. Model using the summarize strategy to make clear what happened in the story.

> **MODEL** I am confused about what happened. I am going to summarize to help me understand. The granddaughter helped the woman, but they could not get the turnip out of the well. Then some men said they would help. **SEQUENCE EVENTS/SUMMARIZE**

Discuss whether the children agree with your summary. Have a volunteer read aloud the rest of page 49 while the others listen for what happened. Ask: **Who pulled together? What happened?** (*Possible responses: The woman, the granddaughter, and the men all pulled but could not get the turnip out of the well. Then the men called for more help.*) **SEQUENCE EVENTS/SUMMARIZE**

Page 50

Have the children read page 50 to find out who else came to help. Ask: **How does the woman feel about the mouse?** (*Possible responses: She thinks he is not strong. She thinks he is a pest.*) **IDENTIFY CHARACTERS' EMOTIONS**

Have the children look at the illustration on page 50 to find out how the mouse helps. Ask: **Do you think filling the well with water will bring up the turnip?** (*Responses will vary.*) **MAKE PREDICTIONS**

Page 51

INTERVENTION PRACTICE BOOK page 25

Have the children read page 51 to see if their prediction was correct. Ask: **What did the woman learn from the mouse?** (*Possible responses: Help can come from unexpected places. Brainpower is sometimes better than strength.*) **DRAW CONCLUSIONS**

Summarize the Selection. Ask children to think about and retell the events in the story. Then have them complete *Intervention Practice Book* page 25.

Lesson 6 • Intervention Teacher's Guide

Page 52

Answers to *Think About It* Questions

1. The mouse and the others add water to make the turnip come up to the top of the well. **SEQUENCE EVENTS/SUMMARIZE**
2. She said that the mouse was little and not strong. **INTERPRET STORY DETAILS**
3. Accept reasonable responses. **TASK/EXPRESS PERSONAL OPINIONS**

AFTER
Skill Review
page 153A

USE SKILL CARD 6B

Sequence

RETEACH the skill. Have children look at **side B of Skill Card 6: Sequence**. Read the skill reminder with them, and have a volunteer read the paragraph aloud.

Have a volunteer read aloud the set of directions. Explain that the children will work with partners to create their own sequence charts. Remind them to write one event in each box to show the sequence. Have the children create their own graphics that model the one on the skill card.

After children have completed their sequence charts, have them display and explain their work. Point out that "A Turnip's Tale" is organized according to sequence. It tells in time order the events in the story.

Review Phonics Skill from "The Enormous Turnip"

RETEACH phonograms *-ack* and *-ock*. Write this sentence on the board: *In Mack's pack was a rock and a clock.* Read the sentence aloud. Have volunteers point to the words with the *-ack*. (*Mack, pack*) Then have children point to the words with the phonogram *-ock*. (*rock, clock*) Then read this list aloud and have children raise their hands when they hear the phonogram *-ack* and clap their hands when they hear the phonogram *-ock*: *big, men, sack, sock, pen, best, rack, lock.*

FLUENCY BUILDER Use copies of *Intervention Practice Book* page 23. Explain that today the children will practice the sentences on the bottom half of the page by reading them aloud on tape. Assign new partners. Have the children take turns reading the sentences aloud to each other and then reading them on tape.

INTERVENTION PRACTICE BOOK
page 23

BEFORE
Drafting dialogue
pages 171C

Writer's Craft: Dialogue

Build on prior knowledge. Tell children that they are going to talk about and write dialogue. Write on the board:

> The turnip is stuck in the well.
> I can help.

Construct the text. "Share the pen" with the children. Guide them in deciding who might have spoken each of these sentences in "A Turnip's Tale." Help them add a comma and the speaker's name to each sentence. Have them use the word *said* to show the person was speaking.

> The turnip is stuck in the well, said the woman.
> I can help, said the mouse.

Revisit the text. Reread the dialogue together. Ask: **How can I let the reader know which words are spoken?** (*Put quotation marks before and after the spoken words.*) Guide children in adding the quotation marks.

> "The turnip is stuck in the well," said the woman.
> "I can help," said the mouse.

Ask: **In the second sentence, what noun tells who the speaker is?** (*mouse*)

Have children read the completed dialogue aloud and then copy it onto their papers.

On Your Own

Have children write a sentence that tells what someone said to them today. Remind them to use the word *said* and the speaker's name. Have them use a comma to separate what is said from what is read. Remind them to add quotation marks to show which words are spoken.

AFTER

Spelling Lesson
pages 167I

Connect Spelling and Phonics

RETEACH short vowel /e/e. Tell children to number their papers 1–8. Dictate the following words and have children write them. After each word is written, write it on the board so children can proofread their work. Children should draw a line through a misspelled word and write the correct spelling below it.

| 1. men* | 2. set | 3. yes | 4. get* |
| 5. bed | 6. well* | 7. nest | 8. best* |

*Word appears in "A Turnip's Tale."

Dictate the following sentence and have children write it: *Ted let the hen in the pen*.

Build and Read Longer Words

Remind children that they have learned how to decode words with the short e vowel sound spelled e. Explain that now they will use what they have learned to help them read some longer words.

Write the word *bedpost* on the board. Tell children that they can sometimes figure out long words by looking for syllables. Cover *post* and have a volunteer read *bed*. Then cover *bed* and have a volunteer read *post*. Point out that *bed* has the /e/ sound. Have children blend the word parts to read the longer word *bedpost*. Follow a similar procedure with these words: *nesting*, *tender*, *restful*, and *setback*.

INTERVENTION ASSESSMENT BOOK

FLUENCY BUILDER Have children choose a passage from *"A Turnip's Tale"* to read aloud to a partner. You may have children choose passages that they found particularly interesting, or have them choose one of the following options:

- Read pages 46–48. (From *A woman planted . . .* through . . . *called for help*. Total: 81 words)

- Read pages 49–50. (From *"I will help . . .* through . . . *Then all the rest helped*. Total: 116 words)

Children should read the selected passage aloud to their partners three times. Have the child rate each of his or her own readings on a scale from 1 to 4.

The Enormous Turnip/A Turnip's Tale

BEFORE Weekly Assessments

Review Vocabulary

To revisit vocabulary words prior to the weekly assessment, use these sentences. Have volunteers take turns reading aloud the sentences. Children identify whether the statement is true or false and explain how they know.

1. An **enormous** watermelon is very big.
2. My **granddaughter** is my sister's daughter.
3. If a tree **grew**, it became taller.
4. A bicycle is always **planted** in the garden.
5. A **strong** boy cannot lift a pencil.
6. A **turnip** is a vegetable.

Correct responses: 1. true, 2. false, 3. true, 4. false, 5. false, 6. true.

You may want to display the vocabulary words and definitions on page 59 and have children copy them to use when they study for the vocabulary test.

★ Focus Skill Review Sequence

To review sequence before the weekly assessment, distribute *Intervention Practice Book* page 26. Have volunteers read aloud the first direction line and the sentences. Guide children to use signal words and unstated clues to put the sentences in order in the sequence chart.

Review Test Prep

Ask children to turn to page 171 of the *Pupil Edition*. Call attention to the Tips for answering the test questions. Tell children that paying attention to these tips can help them answer not only the test questions on this page but also other test questions like these.

JUST FOR YOU page 171

Have children follow along as you read each test question and the tip that goes with it. Discuss why the signal word *first* is the most important word in Question 1. Then ask what signal word in Question 2 can help them figure out the correct answer to that question. *(last)*

INTERVENTION PRACTICE BOOK page 26

INTERVENTION ASSESSMENT BOOK

AFTER Self-Selected Reading

Weekly Assessments

Have children select their own books to read independently. They might choose books from the classroom library shelf, or you may wish to offer a group of appropriate books such as the following from which children can choose.

- *Jill and the Giant.* See page 17 10 of the *Teacher's Edition* for an Independent Reading Plan.
- *The Three Billy Goats Gruff* by Stephen Carpenter. HarperCollins, 1998.
- *There is a Carrot in My Ear and Other Noodle Tales* by Alvin Schwartz. HarperCollins, 1982.

After children have chosen their books, give each child a copy of "My Reading Log," which can be found on page R35 in the back of the *Teacher's Edition*. Have children fill in the information at the top of the form. Then have them use the log to keep track of their reading and to record their responses to the literature.

Conduct student-teacher conferences. Arrange time for each child to confer with you individually about his or her self-selected reading. Have children bring their Reading Logs to share with you at the conference. Children might also like to choose a favorite passage to read aloud to you. Ask questions about the book to stimulate discussion. For example, you might ask the child to describe the sequence of events in the story. For nonfiction, you might ask what information the child learned from the text, how the author structured the text, or how illustrations helped the child understand the topic.

FLUENCY PERFORMANCE Have children read aloud to you the passage from "A Turnip's Tale" that they selected and practiced earlier with their partners. Keep track of the number of words each child reads correctly. Ask the child to rate his or her own performance on the 1–4 scale. If children are not happy with their oral reading, give them an opportunity to continue practicing and then to reread the passage to you.

See *Oral Reading Fluency Assessment* for monitoring progress.

The Enormous Turnip/A Turnip's Tale

LESSON 7

BEFORE Building Background and Vocabulary

Use with

"Helping Out"

Review Phonics: Digraph /sh/*sh*

Identify the sound. Tell children to listen for the /sh/ sound as you say the words *trash* and *share*. Then have children repeat the following sentence twice: *She sells shells by the shore.* Ask them to identify the three words that have the /sh/ sound. (*she, shells, shore*)

Associate letters to sound. Write on the board: *She sells shells by the shore.* Have a volunteer underline the letters *sh* where they appear. Tell children that when the letters *s* and *h* come together, they usually stand for one sound—the /sh/ sound in *she, shells,* and *shore.*

Word blending. Model how to blend and read the word *ship*. Write the word on the board, then slide your hand under the word as you elongate the sounds: /shiipp/. Then say the word naturally—*ship*. Follow a similar procedure for the word *shine*.

Apply the skill. *Consonant Substitution* Write the following words on the board, and have children read each one aloud. Then have children substitute each underlined letter to form the words in parentheses. Have a volunteer read aloud each new word.

| be**d** (shed) | po**p** (shop) | ca**b** (cash) | cu**t** (shut) |
| **b**in (shin) | **h**ip (ship) | wi**n** (wish) | r**an** (rash) |

INTERVENTION PRACTICE BOOK page 28

Introduce Vocabulary

PRETEACH **lesson vocabulary.** Tell children that they are going to learn six new words that they will see again when they read a story called "Helping Out." Teach each Vocabulary Word using the following process.

Use the following suggestions or similar ideas to give the meaning or context for each word.

alongside	Point out the words *along* and *side*. Relate to *next to*.
chores	Relate to jobs that children may do at home.
engine	Relate to different machines that have engines, such as a car or lawn mower.
simple	Relate to things that are easy to do such as wave your hand and things that are plain like a hotdog without ketchup, mustard, or relish.

> Write the word.
> Say the word.
> Track the word and have children repeat it.
> Give the meaning or context.

Lesson 7 • Intervention Teacher's Guide

sprout	Relate to tiny plants just starting to grow.
tool	Relate to a tool such as a screwdriver or a hammer.

For vocabulary activities, see Vocabulary Games on pages 2–7.

> **Vocabulary Words**
> **alongside** by the side of
> **chores** jobs that have to be done regularly
> **engine** motor
> **simple** not difficult, fancy or complicated
> **sprout** begin to grow
> **tool** an object that makes a job easier

AFTER
Building Background and Vocabulary

Apply Vocabulary Strategies

Use Familiar Patterns. Write the word *chores* on chart paper. Then write *chew* and *more*. Use a colored marker to underline *ch* in *chores* and *chew*. Use a second color to underline *or* in *chores* and *more*. Tell children that they can sometimes figure out how to pronounce a word by looking for letter patterns that they know.

> **MODEL** The letter combination *ch* is familiar to me because I have seen it in words like *chew*. I have also seen the letter combination *or* in words like *more*. When I blend the familiar letter patterns with the remaining letters, I read *chores*.

Guide children in using a similar procedure to decode the words *sprout* and *tool*.

RETEACH lesson vocabulary. Have children listen to each of the following sentences. Tell them to hold up the word card that completes each sentence. Reread each sentence aloud with the correct word choice. Then discuss how the meaning of the vocabulary word fits the sentence.

1. Sweeping floors is one of my __(chores)__.
2. To drive this invention, we need an __(engine)__.
3. The tiny plant coming out was just starting to __(sprout)__.
4. Dad was taking a fast drive when a policeman pulled __(alongside)__.
5. To fix the stool, the handyman used a __(tool)__.
6. Smile to make a dimple—it's that __(simple)__.

FLUENCY BUILDER Use *Intervention Practice Book* p. 27.
Read each word in the first column aloud and have children repeat it. Then have children work in pairs to read the words in the first column aloud to each other. Follow the same procedure with each of the remaining columns. After partners have practiced reading aloud the words in each column separately, have them practice the entire list. (Save *Intervention Practice Book* page 27 to use with pages 71 and 73.)

INTERVENTION PRACTICE BOOK
page 27

Helping Out/Tools That Help

BEFORE
Reading "Helping Out"
pages 174–186

USE SKILL CARD 7A

(Focus Skill) Main Idea

PRETEACH the skill. Point out to children that the main idea of a story is the most important idea. Discuss that knowing which idea is the main idea helps readers understand what the story is about.

Have children look at **side A of Skill Card 7: Main Idea**. Read the definition of *main idea*. Next read the paragraph aloud and then have children reread it with you. Ask:

- Why is the main idea that Tim likes to help people? (*Possible response: Because it is the most important idea.*)

- Why isn't the main idea that Tim helps his father clean the garage? (*Possible response: This idea tells just one of the ways that Tim likes to help.*)

- What other ideas tell how Tim helps? (*Possible response: He helps his mother wash the dishes. He helps his little sister put her toys away.*)

Explain that other ideas in a story usually tell something about the main idea.

Prepare to Read: "Helping Out"

Preview. Tell children that they are going to read a selection entitled "Helping Out." Explain that this selection is a photo essay that tells about a topic using photographs and words. Tell children that "Helping Out" gives information about how children can help others do many kinds of jobs. Then preview the selection.

JUST FOR YOU
pages 174–186

- **Pages 174–175:** I see the title, "Helping Out," on page 174 and the name of the photographer on page 175. The picture on these pages shows a girl and a man. I think she is helping him.

- **Pages 176–177:** On these pages I see a girl handing a man a hammer. I think this selection must be about ways children can help others.

- **Pages 178–179:** Now I see kids working in a garden and washing a car. They look like they are having fun working. I think these pages must tell how helping can be fun.

Set Purpose. Tell children that they can use what they have learned from the preview to set a purpose for reading. Model setting a purpose for reading "Helping Out."

MODEL From what I have seen in my preview, I think I will learn more about ways that children can help others. One purpose for reading is to learn important ideas about a topic. I will look for photographs that give important ideas about the topic. I will read to learn about the ideas in the photographs.

AFTER
Reading
"Helping Out"
pages 174–186

Reread and Summarize

Have children reread and summarize "Helping Out" in sections, as described below.

Pages 174–177

Let's reread pages 174–177 to remember some ways kids can help out.

Summary: Kids can help out by holding something for someone to work on or by handing the person they are helping a tool.

Pages 178–181

As we reread pages 178–181, let's find out about more kinds of jobs kids can help with.

Summary: In the spring kids can help by planting seeds in the garden. On a hot day some chores, such as washing a car, can be fun. Some jobs, such as helping change the oil in a car engine, can be dirty.

Pages 182–183

Now let's reread pages 182–183 to recall what we learned from these pages about helping out.

Summary: Kids can help their teacher keep the classroom neat or help an adult paint. Working with an adult and doing a good job can make you feel pretty special.

Pages 184–186

Let's reread pages 184–186 to recall the best things about helping out.

Summary: After you learn to do things well, you can get paid for your work, but the best thing about helping out is that it can bring two people closer together.

FLUENCY BUILDER Be sure children have copies of *Intervention Practice Book* p. 27. Call attention to the sentences on the bottom half of the page. Tell children that their goal is to read each phrase or sentence smoothly. Model appropriate pace, expression, and phrasing as you read each sentence, and have children read it after you. Then have children practice by reading the sentences aloud three times to a partner.

INTERVENTION PRACTICE BOOK
page 27

Helping Out/Tools That Help

BEFORE

Making Connections
pages 190–191

Directed Reading: "Tools That Help," pp. 54–61

Sounds of Sunshine pp. 54–61

Pages 54–55

Ask a volunteer to read aloud the title. Help children understand from the illustration that this selection is told by two children who interviewed other kids about the chores they do. Read pages 54–55 aloud while children listen to find out what the interviewers learned about Ted. Ask: **What is the most important thing you learned about Ted?** (*Possible response: Ted likes helping his mom.*) **MAIN IDEA**

Pages 56–57

Have a volunteer read aloud page 56 while other children listen to find out about Jim's chore. Write the word *simple* on the board. Model using the Decoding/Phonics strategy to decode this word.

> **MODEL** When I read this page, some of the words on it are new to me. I look for vowel sounds or consonant sounds that I know to help me figure out these new words. I also use blending to put the different sounds together. I look at the letters in the word *simple* and think about the sounds the letters stand for. (Slide your hand under the letters on the board as you slowly elongate the sounds.) I say the word slowly to myself /ssiimmppll/. Then I say the word again quickly-simple.
> **DECODING/PHONICS**

Discuss the strategies children use to help them figure out how to pronounce unfamiliar words. Have a volunteer read aloud page 57. Ask: **How did you know what the word *engine* should sound like?** (*Possible response: I looked at the letters and thought about the sounds the letters stand for.*) **DECODING/PHONICS**

Pages 58–59

Read aloud page 58 while children listen and look at the illustrations to find out what job Ben just finished. Ask: **What work did Ben do?** (*Possible response: He painted the fence.*) **DRAW CONCLUSIONS**

Have a volunteer read aloud page 59 while children listen to find out about Pat's chore. Ask: **What is Pat's chore?** (*Possible response: walking her dog, Shep*) **NOTE DETAILS**

Have children look at the illustrations on page 59 to find out what tool helps Pat walk Shep. Ask: **What tool helps Pat walk Shep?** (*Possible response: a leash*) **NOTE DETAILS**

Page 60

INTERVENTION PRACTICE BOOK
page 29

Read aloud page 60 while children listen for questions they can answer. Ask: **Which chores do you most like doing? What tools do you like to use?** (*Accept reasonable responses.*) **EXPRESS PERSONAL OPINIONS**

Summarize the selection. Ask children to think about the events in the story. Have them tell you the events in the story in order. Then have them complete *Intervention Practice Book* page 29.

Answers to *Think About It* Questions

1. Possible response: The kids wash dishes, help fix an engine, and walk the dog. **SUMMARIZE**
2. Possible response: Pat walks the dog, Shep, but you can also play with dogs during walks. **INTERPRET STORY DETAILS**
3. Accept reasonable responses. **TASK**

AFTER
Skill Review
page 173A

USE SKILL CARD 7B

Focus Skill Main Idea

RETEACH the skill. Have children look at **side B of Skill Card 7: Main Idea**. Read the skill reminder with them, and have a volunteer read the paragraph aloud.

Read aloud the next direction. Remind children to think about all the ideas in the story before they decide which one is the most important.

After children have identified and written the main idea, have them share their answer with the class. Point out that the selection "Tools That Help" has a main idea and other ideas that tell something about the main idea.

Review Phonics Skill from "Helping Out"

RETEACH r-controlled vowels /ûr/ *ear* Write this sentence on the board: *The girl yearned to learn more about earning money.* Read the sentence aloud. Have volunteers point to the words with the /ûr/ sound. Then have children use each word with *-ear* in a different sentence.

FLUENCY BUILDER Be sure children have copies of *Intervention Practice Book* page 27. Explain that today children will practice the sentences on the bottom half of the page by reading them aloud on tape. Assign new partners. Have children take turns reading the sentences aloud to each other and then reading them on tape.

INTERVENTION PRACTICE BOOK
page 27

Helping Out/Tools That Help

BEFORE
Drafting a
Personal Story
page 193C

Writer's Craft: Using Colorful Words

Build on prior knowledge. Tell children that they are going to talk and write about something that happened to them. Point out that they can use colorful words to describe their experience to make it more descriptive and interesting. Invite a volunteer to name a personal experience he or she would like to write about. Write it on the board. Then list some ideas for colorful words that might be used to describe the experience.

> Experience: The time I caught a fish
>
> Idea 1: What the lake looked like when I went fishing: *calm*
>
> Idea 2: What my line did when the fish took the bait: *jerked*
>
> Idea 3: What the fish felt like after I caught it: *slippery*

Construct the text. "Share the pen" with children. Guide them in using the colorful words to write sentences that describe catching a fish. For example:

> When I went fishing, the lake was calm. I put my line in the water. My line jerked. I caught a fish. The fish felt slippery.

Revisit the text. Go back and read the sentences together. Ask: **What can I do to make sure the reader has a picture of what happened in the story?** (*Add colorful words*)

- Guide children in adding colorful words for details. For example: First I put my long pole in the clear water. Then my line jerked. Finally I caught a slippery fish. Explain that interesting words like these give details to an audience.

- Ask: **What pronoun can we use to replace the words *the fish*?** (*it*) Make the appropriate change.

- Have children read the descriptive paragraph aloud and then copy it on their own papers.

On Your Own

Have children write a paragraph about something that happened to them. Remind them to use colorful words to describe the experience.

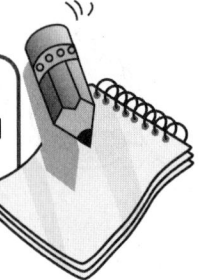

Lesson 7 • Intervention Teacher's Guide

AFTER

Spelling Lesson
page 187I

Connect Spelling and Phonics

RETEACH digraph /sh/ *sh.* Write the word *shop* on the board. Explain that you will say more words in which the /sh/ sound is spelled *sh.* Have volunteers write each word on the board. Check for misspelled words and help children correct each one by drawing a line through the word and writing the correct spelling above it.

| 1. shop | 2. shed | 3. ship | 4. shin |
| 5. cash | 6. wish* | 7. dishes* | 8. push |

*Word appears in "Tools That Help."

Dictate the following sentence and have children write it:
Set the trash can in the shed.

Build and Read Longer Words

Remind children that they have learned how to decode words with the /sh/ sound spelled *sh.* Explain that now they will use what they have learned to help them read some longer words.

Write the word *wishing* on the board. Tell children that they can sometimes figure out long words by looking for syllables. Cover *-ing* and have a volunteer read the word *wish.* Then cover *wish* and have a volunteer read the syllable *–ing.* Point out that *wish* has the /sh/ sound spelled *sh.* Have children blend the word parts to read the longer word *wishing.* Follow a similar procedure with these words: *shopping, dishwasher, shipshape,* and *fishing.*

INTERVENTION ASSESSMENT BOOK

FLUENCY BUILDER Have children choose a passage from "Tools That Help" to read aloud to a partner. You may have children choose passages that they found particularly interesting, or have them choose one of the following options:

- Read pages 55–56. (From *Ted likes helping . . .* through *. . . helps me do the job.* Total: 63 words)

- Read pages 58–59. (From *Ben helped do . . .* through *. . . This tool helps!* Total: 46 words)

Encourage children to read their passages aloud to their partners three times. Have the child rate his or her own reading on a scale from 1 to 4.

Helping Out/Tools That Help **75**

BEFORE Weekly Assessments

Review Vocabulary

To revisit vocabulary words prior to the weekly assessment, use these sentence frames. Have volunteers take turns reading aloud the sentence stems and choices. Children identify the correct choice and explain why that choice makes sense in the sentence.

1. If you walk **alongside** your friend, you are walking
   a. by her side.
   b. behind her.
2. A child doing **chores** is probably
   a. busy working.
   b. sleeping.
3. If the **engine** is running, you could be
   a. peddling a bicycle.
   b. riding in a car.
4. A **simple** chore might be to
   a. wash the dishes
   b. build a house.
5. When flowers **sprout**, they
   a. bloom.
   b. begin to grow.
6. You need a **tool** to help you
   a. build a birdhouse
   b. wave at your friend.

Correct responses: 1. **a**, 2. **a**, 3. **b**, 4. **a**, 5. **b**, 6. **a**.

You may want to display the vocabulary words and definitions on **page 69** and have children copy them to use when they study for the vocabulary test.

Focus Skill — Review Main Idea

To review main idea before the weekly assessment, distribute *Intervention Practice Book* p. 30. Have volunteers read aloud the directions and then the paragraph. Guide children to think about the most important thing that they read.

INTERVENTION PRACTICE BOOK page 30

Review Test Prep

Ask children to turn to page 193 of the *Pupil Edition*. Call attention to the tips for answering the test questions. Tell children that paying attention to these tips can help them answer not only the test questions but also other test questions like these.

JUST FOR YOU page 193

Have children follow along as you read each test question and the tip that goes with it. Discuss how the first, third, and fourth sentences in question 1 tell something about the second sentence. Remind children to think about which sentence in question 2 is not as important as the others.

INTERVENTION ASSESSMENT BOOK

Lesson 7 • Intervention Teacher's Guide

AFTER
Weekly Assessments

Self-Selected Reading

Have children select their own book to read independently. They might choose a book from the classroom library shelf, or you may wish to offer a group of appropriate books from which children can choose.

- *Help!* by Kathryn Corbett (See page 193O of the *Teacher's Edition* for an Independent Reading Plan.)
- *Wonderful Worms* by Linda Glaser. Millbrook, 1992.
- *The Sun's Family of Planets* by Allan Fowler. Children's Press, 1992

After children have chosen their books, give each child a copy of "My Reading Log," which can be found on page R35 in the back of the *Teacher's Edition.* Have children fill in the information at the top of the form. Then have them use the log to keep track of their reading and to record their responses to the literature.

Conduct student-teacher conferences. Arrange time for each child to meet with you individually to discuss his or her self-selected reading. Have children bring their Reading Logs to share with you at the conference. Children might also like to share a favorite passage to read aloud to you. Ask questions designed to stimulate discussion of the book. For example, you might ask what information the child learned from a nonfiction text or how illustrations helped him or her better understand the topic.

FLUENCY PERFORMANCE Have children read aloud to you the passage from "Tools That Help" that they selected and practiced with their partners. Keep track of the number of words the child reads correctly. Ask the child to rate his or her own performance on the 1–4 scale. If children are not happy with their oral reading, give them an opportunity to continue practicing and then to reread the passage again to you.

See *Oral Reading Fluency Assessment* for monitoring progress.

Helping Out/Tools That Help

LESSON 8

BEFORE
Building Background and Vocabulary

Use with

"Mr. Putter and Tabby Fly the Plane"

Review Phonics: Short Vowel /u/u

Identify the sound. Tell children to listen for the /u/ or short *u* vowel sound as you say the words *tug* and *cut*. Then have children repeat the following sentence twice: *A bug in the mud cannot run.* Ask them to identify the three words that have the /u/ sound. (*bug, mud, run*)

Associate letters to sound. Write on the board: *A bug in the mud cannot run.* Have volunteers underline the words that contain the letter *u*. Tell children that in these words, the letter *u* stands for the /u/ sound. Remind children that when a word has a vowel between two or more consonants, the word usually has the short vowel sound.

Word blending. Model how to blend and read the word *bug*. Slide your hand under the word as you elongate the sounds /bbuugg/. Then say the word naturally—*bug*. Follow a similar procedure with the word *run*.

Apply the skill. *Vowel Substitution* Write the following words on the board and have children read each aloud. Make the changes necessary to form the words in parentheses. Have a volunteer read aloud each new word.

not (nut)	**ham** (hum)	**bog** (bug)	**tag** (tug)
mesh (mush)	**rib** (rub)	**fan** (fun)	**bat** (but)

Introduce Vocabulary

PRETEACH lesson vocabulary. Tell children that they are going to learn five new words that they will see again when they read a story called "Mr. Putter and Tabby Fly the Plane." Teach each Vocabulary Word using the following process.

Use the following suggestions or similar ideas to give the meaning or context.

> Write the word.
> Say the word.
> Track the word and have students repeat it.
> Give the meaning or context.

cranes   This is a multiple-meaning word. Relate to machines that are often used to lift heavy things during construction of a tall building.

directions   Point out the base word *direct*. Explain that *direct* means "to order or command," as in this sentence: *I direct you to wet the dog and then open the shampoo bottle.* Explain that these are directions for washing a dog.

promise   Relate to any promise you may have made to the children.

INTERVENTION PRACTICE BOOK
page 32

78   Lesson 8 • Intervention Teacher's Guide

twitch	Demonstrate by making your arm twitch.
worry	Explain that when we are afraid, we worry about what might happen.

For vocabulary activities, see Vocabulary Games on pages 2–7.

Vocabulary Words
cranes machines with long, movable arms used to lift things
directions instructions for how to do something
promise statement made by a person telling that he or she will do something
twitch to move with a sharp, quick movement
worry to think that bad things may happen

AFTER
Building Background and Vocabulary

Apply Vocabulary Strategies

Use familiar patterns. Write the word *directions* on chart paper, and underline the letters *-tion*. Tell children that they can sometimes figure out how to pronounce a word by looking for familiar letter patterns.

MODEL The letter pattern *-tion* is familiar to me because I have heard it in other words like *motion* and *connection*. When I blend the first part of the word with the familiar letter pattern *-tion* plus *s*, I read *directions*.

Guide children in using a similar procedure to decode the words *promise* and *worry*.

RETEACH lesson vocabulary. Have children listen to each of the following riddles. Tell them to hold up the word card that answers each riddle. Reread the riddle aloud with the correct word choice. Then discuss how the meaning of the Vocabulary Word fits the riddle.

1. We can lift heavy things up to the tops of tall buildings. We are <u>(cranes)</u>.
2. I move quickly and jerk a lot. What do I do? I <u>(twitch)</u>.
3. I can tell you how to bake a cake or make a birdhouse. I am a set of <u>(directions)</u>.
4. I always think that bad things are going to happen. I <u>(worry)</u>.
5. When someone gives me to you, you can be sure they will do what they say. I am a <u>(promise)</u>.

FLUENCY BUILDER Using *Intervention Practice Book* page 31, read each word in the first column aloud and have children repeat it. Then have children work in pairs to read the words in the first column aloud to each other. Follow the same procedure with each of the remaining columns. After partners have practiced reading aloud the words in each column separately, have them practice the entire list. (Save *Intervention Practice Book* page 31 to use on pages 81 and 83.)

INTERVENTION PRACTICE BOOK
page 31

Mr. Putter and Tabby Fly the Plane/The Promise

BEFORE
Reading "Mr. Putter and Tabby Fly the Plane"
pages 196–219

USE SKILL CARD 8A

(Focus Skill) Predict Outcomes

PRETEACH the skill. Tell children that they can use what they already know and clues in a story to predict what will happen. Hold a piece of fruit and say "Yum". Discuss how the word *yum* is a clue that you will enjoy eating the fruit.

Have children look at **side A of Skill Card 8: Predict Outcomes.** Read the introduction about how readers predict outcomes. Next read the paragraph aloud, and then have children reread it with you.

Now call attention to the diagram and have volunteers take turns reading the clues aloud. Then read the prediction aloud. Ask:

- **How do the clues help us figure out that Tuffy chases the squirrel?** (*Possible response: The clues tell us that Tuffy likes to chase squirrels and that a squirrel comes near Tuffy.*)

- **What do you already know about dogs that could help you make a prediction?** (*Possible response: Some dogs chase squirrels.*)

Explain that identifying clues as you read a text and predicting what will happen next can help you better understand the story.

Prepare to Read: "Mr. Putter and Tabby Fly the Plane"

Preview. Tell children they will read the selection "Mr. Putter and Tabby Fly the Plane." Explain that this story is realistic fiction. The people and places seem real, but the story is made up. Then preview the selection.

JUST FOR YOU pages 196–219

- **Pages 196–197:** I see the title, "Mr. Putter and Tabby Fly the Plane." I see a picture of a man with a cat. That must be Mr. Putter and Tabby. I see a plane. I think that is the plane they fly.

- **Pages 198–199:** On page 198 I see Mr. Putter and Tabby looking in a toy shop. I think Mr. Putter looks interested.

- **Pages 200–201:** I see Tabby with the toys. Tabby looks afraid. I see Mr. Putter smiling at a fire engine. Mr. Putter must like toys.

- **Pages 202–203:** On these pages I see Mr. Putter playing with a plane. I see a boy with planes in his room. I think the boy could be Mr. Putter when he was young. I think Mr. Putter has always liked airplanes.

Set purpose. Model setting a purpose for reading "Mr. Putter and Tabby Fly the Plane."

MODEL From what I have seen in my preview, I think that I will find out more about Mr. Putter and Tabby and toy airplanes. One purpose for reading is to find out what happens to the characters in a story. I will read to find out what happens to Mr. Putter and Tabby.

80 Lesson 8 • Intervention Teacher's Guide

AFTER

Reading "Mr. Putter and Tabby Fly the Plane"
pages 196–219

Reread and Summarize

Have children reread and summarize "Mr. Putter and Tabby Fly the Plane" in sections, as described below.

Pages 198–202

Let's reread pages 198–202 to remember how the story begins.

Summary: Mr. Putter loves toys, but they make Tabby nervous. She loves Mr. Putter, and so she puts up with it. At the toy store, Mr. Putter plays with everything, especially the airplanes. Anything that flies makes Tabby hiccup.

Pages 203–207

Now let's reread pages 203–207 to recall why Mr. Putter buys the plane.

Summary: Mr. Putter has loved planes since he was a boy but never got to fly one. At the store he buys a plane with a radio control that a person could fly. Tabby hiccups all the way home. Mr. Putter promises her some tea.

Pages 208–212

As we reread pages 208–212, let's remember what happens when Mr. Putter and Tabby get home.

Summary: Mr. Putter gives Tabby tea and a muffin, and then they go outside to fly the plane. First the plane does not start, then it falls on its nose, and finally a wing falls off. Tabby purrs and purrs and purrs.

Pages 213–217

Let's reread pages 213–217 to remember how the story ends.

Summary: Mr. Putter is so sad. He says he is not good at flying planes. Tabby feels sad, too. She makes Mr. Putter feel better, and then he fixes the plane and tries again. The plane flies high in the sky. Tabby purrs and hiccups.

FLUENCY BUILDER Be sure children have copies of *Intervention Practice Book* page 31, which you used for the previous Fluency Builder activity. Call attention to the sentences on the bottom half of the page. Tell children that their goal is to read each phrase or sentence smoothly. Model appropriate pace, expression, and phrasing as you read each sentence and have children read it after you. Then have children practice by reading the sentences aloud three times to a partner.

INTERVENTION PRACTICE BOOK
page 31

BEFORE

Making Connections pages 222–223

Directed Reading: "The Promise" pp. 62–69

Sounds of Sunshine pp. 62–69

Ask a volunteer to read aloud the title. Make sure children understand what a promise is. Help children identify the setting in the illustration as a toy shop. Read page 62 aloud while children listen to find out more about the picture. Ask: **Who is the boy in the picture?** (*Possible response: Lun*) **DRAW CONCLUSIONS**

Ask: **What do Lun and his mom buy?** (*a toy plane*) **NOTE DETAILS**

Page 63

Read aloud page 63 while children look at the picture and listen to find out what Bud buys. Ask: **Which crane does Bud buy?** (*Possible response: the one Mr. Crump is pointing to*) **INTERPRET STORY EVENTS**

Ask: **Why does he buy that one?** (*Possible response: because it works and has directions*) **CAUSE AND EFFECT**

Pages 64–65

Read aloud page 64 while children listen to find out what Muffin does. Ask: **What do you think Muffin will do next?** (*Possible response: I think she will chase the bug because she likes bugs.*) **PREDICT OUTCOMES**

Have a volunteer read aloud page 65 while children listen to find out if their prediction was correct. Ask: **What can Muffin do? What can the bug do?** (*Possible response: Muffin can run and jump. The bug can fly.*) **NOTE DETAILS**

Page 66

Read aloud the first four paragraphs on page 66 while children listen for what happens. Write the word *spilled* on the board. Model using word bits and parts to understand this word.

> **MODEL** When I see a word I do not know, I look for parts of the word that I do know. I look at the word *spilled* and see the smaller word *spill*. I know that *spill* means "to fall out of something." Now I know that the toys fell out all over.

Discuss the strategies children use to help them figure out unfamiliar words. Read aloud the rest of page 66 while children listen to find out what Muffin did. Ask: **What word part do you recognize in the word *looked*?** (*Possible response: look*) **LOOK AT WORD BITS AND PARTS**

Page 67

Have a volunteer read aloud page 67 while children listen to find out what happens to the bug. Ask: **What happens to the bug?** (*Mr. Crump lets it go and it flies away.*) **INTERPRET STORY EVENTS**

Page 68

Read aloud page 68 while children listen to find out what happens next. Ask: **What do you think Muffin will do next? Why?** (*Possible response: She will probably chase the bug, because she likes to hunt for bugs.*) **PREDICT OUTCOMES**

Lesson 8 • Intervention Teacher's Guide

INTERVENTION PRACTICE BOOK *page 33*

Page 69

AFTER
Skill Review *page 225C*

USE SKILL CARD 8B

Summarize the selection. Ask children to think about the events in the story. Then have them complete *Intervention Practice Book* 33.

Answers to *Think About It* Questions

1. Mr. Crump promised that Muffin would get her bug. **SUMMARIZE**
2. Possible response: No, because some bugs may move faster than Muffin. **INTERPRET STORY EVENTS**
3. Accept reasonable responses. **DRAW A PICTURE**

(Focus Skill) Predict Outcomes

RETEACH the skill. Have children look at **side B of Skill Card 8: Predict Outcomes**. Read the skill reminder and first direction line with them. Have a volunteer read the story aloud.

Read aloud the next set of directions. Explain that children will work with partners to create their own diagrams. Remind them to look in the story for important ideas that could be clues.

After children have completed their diagrams, have them display and explain their work. Point out that predicting outcomes as they read can help them better understand a story.

Review Phonics Skill from "Mr. Putter and Tabby Fly the Plane"

RETEACH **Common Abbreviations.** On the board, make two columns. In the first column, write the abbreviations *Mr., Sept., Tues., Ave., ft.,* and *Dr.* In the second column, write in random order the words *Mister, September, Tuesday, Avenue, feet,* and *Doctor*. Ask volunteers to draw a line between each abbreviation and the word it stands for. Remind children that when they see an abbreviation, the abbreviation is to be read aloud just as if the entire word was written.

FLUENCY BUILDER Be sure that children have copies of *Intervention Practice Book* page 31. Explain that today children will practice the sentences on the bottom half of the page by reading them aloud on tape. Assign new partners. Have children take turns reading the sentences aloud to each other and then reading them on tape.

INTERVENTION PRACTICE BOOK *page 31*

Mr. Putter and Tabby Fly the Plane/The Promise

BEFORE

Drafting a Paragraph That Describes
page 223A

Writing Process: Descriptive Sentences

Build on prior knowledge. Tell children that they are going to talk and write about one of their favorite places. Explain that by using descriptive words, they can help others better imagine the place. Write on the board:

> My room is small.
> My room is messy.
> My room has interesting things in it.

Construct the text. "Share the pen" with children. Guide them to think of descriptive words to add to each of the sentences. Ask them to describe just how small the room is. Have them tell how messy the room is. Ask them to name what kinds of interesting things are in the room. Write new sentences that include their ideas. For example:

> *My room is so small that only one person can visit me at a time.*
>
> *There are open drawers with clothes hanging out.*
>
> *There is an aquarium in the corner.*

Revisit the text. Go back and read the sentences together. Ask: **How can I make the second and third sentences even more descriptive?** (*add more descriptive words*)

- Guide children in adding more descriptive words to each sentence. For example: *There are open drawers with clothes hanging out and model airplane parts on the desk. There is an aquarium in the corner with colorful tropical fish.*

- Ask: **What sentence could we add to tell how you feel about your room?** (*Accept reasonable responses.*) Add an appropriate sentence such as: *It is the best room a child could have.* Have children read the completed sentences aloud and then copy them onto their papers.

On Your Own

Have children write descriptive sentences about the classroom. Remind them to use descriptive words.

Lesson 8 • Intervention Teacher's Guide

AFTER

Spelling Lesson
page 219H

Connect Spelling and Phonics

RETEACH Short Vowel /u/u. Write the word *rut* on the board. Explain that you will say more words in which the /u/ sound is spelled *u*. Have volunteers write each word on the board. Check for misspelled words and help children correct them.

1. fun*   2. dug*   3. tub   4. plug
5. jump*   6. hugged* 7. tugging*

*Word appears in "The Promise."

Dictate the following sentence and have children write it: *The bug had fun in the tub.*

Build and Read Longer Words

Remind children that they have learned how to decode words with the short sound of /u/ spelled *u*. Explain that now they will use what they have learned to help them read some longer words.

Write the word *button* on the board. Tell children that they can sometimes figure out long words by looking for syllables or word parts. Cover *ton* and have a volunteer read the word *but*. Then cover *but* and have a volunteer read *ton*. Point out that *but* has the short sound of /u/ spelled *u*. Have children blend the word parts to read the longer word *button*. Follow a similar procedure with these words: *junkyard, funny, jumper, tugboat,* and *muffin*.

INTERVENTION ASSESSMENT BOOK

FLUENCY BUILDER Have children choose a passage from "The Promise" to read aloud to a partner. You may have children choose passages that they found particularly interesting, or have them choose one of the following options:

- Read pages 62–63. (From "*Mr. Crump, will . . .* through *. . . dad bought that one.* Total: 68 words)

- Read pages 64–66. (From *Muffin jumped up . . .* through *. . . spilled all over.* Total: 84 words)

Children should read the selected passage aloud to their partners three times. Have the child rate each reading on a scale of 1 to 4.

Mr. Putter and Tabby Fly the Plane/The Promise **85**

BEFORE Weekly Assessments

Review Vocabulary

To revisit Vocabulary Words prior to the weekly assessment, use these sentence frames. Have volunteers take turns reading aloud the sentence stems and choices. Children should identify the correct choice and explain why that choice makes sense in the sentence.

1. If I **promise** you something, I
   a. can forget all about it.
   b. have to do what I promised.
2. Sam began to **worry** that
   a. something bad might happen.
   b. he was going to have fun.
3. The men used **cranes** to help them
   a. lift heavy beams.
   b. dig a hole.
4. When I **twitch**, I
   a. jerk.
   b. sleep.
5. Jeff read the **directions** to help him
   a. sneeze.
   b. put together a model plane.

Correct responses: 1b, 2a, 3a, 4a, 5b

You may want to display the Vocabulary Words and definitions on page 79 and have children copy them to use when they study for the vocabulary test.

Review Predict Outcomes

To review predict outcomes before the weekly assessment, distribute *Intervention Practice Book* page 34. Have volunteers read aloud the first direction line and the paragraph. Guide children to look for clues as they read to help them predict the outcome.

INTERVENTION PRACTICE BOOK page 34

Review Test Prep

Write on the board:

My Aunt Agatha screams when she sees a cat.

One day at my house our cat ran right over her foot!

Aunt Agatha

a. picked up the cat.

b. petted the cat.

c. screamed.

d. said "Nice kitty."

JUST FOR YOU page 225

Read the text and question aloud. Guide children to look for clues in the text to help them answer the question.

INTERVENTION ASSESSMENT BOOK

Lesson 8 • Intervention Teacher's Guide

AFTER
Weekly Assessments

Self-Selected Reading

Have children select their own books to read independently. They might choose books from the classroom library shelf, or you may wish to offer a group of appropriate books from which children can choose.

- *Fly Ladybug, Fly.* (See page 225S of the *Teacher's Edition* for a Lesson Plan.)
- *Kit and Kat* by Tomie dePaola. Grosset & Dunlap, 1986.
- *Contrary Mary* by Anita Jeram. Candlewick, 1995.

After children have chosen their books, give each child a copy of My Reading Log, which can be found on page R35 in the back of the *Teacher's Edition*. Have children fill in the information at the top of the form. Then have them use the log to keep track of their reading and to record their responses to the literature.

Conduct student-teacher conferences. Arrange time for each child to confer with you individually about his or her self-selected reading. Have children bring their Reading Logs to share with you at the conference. Children might also like to share a favorite passage to read aloud to you. Ask questions designed to stimulate discussion about the book. For example, you might ask what the children learned about the characters in the stories or have them give a brief summary of the story.

FLUENCY PERFORMANCE Have children read aloud to you the passage from "The Promise" that they selected and practiced with their partners. Keep track of the number of words each child reads correctly. Ask the child to rate his or her own performance on the 1–4 scale. If children are not happy with their oral reading, give them an opportunity to continue practicing and then to reread the passage to you again.

See *Oral Reading Fluency Assessment* for monitoring progress.

LESSON 9

BEFORE Building Background and Vocabulary

Use with

"Hedgehog Bakes a Cake"

Review Phonics: Digraphs /th/ th, /hw/ wh

Identify the sound. Have children listen as you say the following sentence. *I whacked the ball with a thick bat.* Have children identify the words with the /th/ sound. (*with, thick*) Then have them identify the words with the /hw/ sound. (*whacked*)

Associate letters to sound. Write on the board: *I whacked the ball with a thick bat.* Have a volunteer underline the letters *th* where they appear. Tell children that the letters *th* usually stand for the /th/ sound they hear in *thumb, thin,* and *path.* Have a volunteer underline the letters *wh* in *whacked.* Explain that the letters *wh* can stand for the /hw/ sound in *whacked.* Write other words with /hw/ *wh* on the board: *when, what, white, whisper.*

Word blending. Model how to blend and read the word *thick.* Slide your hand under the word as you elongate the sounds /thiik/. Then say the word naturally—*thick.* Follow a similar procedure with the word *when.*

Apply the skill. *Consonant Substitution* Write each of the following words on the board and have children read each aloud. Make the changes necessary to form the words in parentheses. Have a volunteer read aloud each new word.

| **tin** (thin) | **hen** (when) | **wit** (with) | **mop** (moth) |
| **tick** (thick) | **bite** (white) | **pat** (path) | **mat** (math) |

INTERVENTION PRACTICE BOOK page 36

Introduce Vocabulary

PRETEACH **lesson vocabulary.** Tell children that they are going to learn six words that they will see again when they read "Hedgehog Bakes a Cake." Teach each Vocabulary Word using the following process.

Use the following suggestions or similar ideas to give the meaning or context.

batter	This is a multiple-meaning word. Children may be more familiar with a meaning from baseball. Related to cooking, mixing ingredients into a thick liquid.
buttery	Point out the *-y* ending. Relate to a muffin covered with lots of butter or a cake made with lots of butter.
perfect	Relate to a paragraph written with no mistakes.
recipe	Relate to cooking.

> Write the word.
> Say the word.
> Track the word and have students repeat it.
> Give the meaning or context.

Lesson 9 • Intervention Teacher's Guide

smeared Explain that *smear* means "to spread something sticky" as to smear peanut butter on bread. Point out the *-ed* ending.

yellow cake Point out the familiar words *yellow* and *cake*.

For vocabulary activities, see Vocabulary Games on pages 2–7.

Vocabulary Words

batter thick liquid mixture used in cooking
buttery full of or covered with butter
perfect as good as something can be
recipe set of instructions, or steps, used when cooking or baking
smeared spread something sticky or greasy
yellow cake cake that is yellow because it contains egg yolks

AFTER
Building Background and Vocabulary

Apply Vocabulary Strategies

Use familiar word parts. Write the word *buttery* on chart paper and underline the word *butter* in one color and the ending *y* in another color. Tell children that they can sometimes figure out the meaning of a word by looking for word parts that they know.

MODEL I already know what butter is. So the word *buttery* must mean "something made with lots of butter" or "something that tastes like butter."

Guide children in using a similar procedure to figure out the meanings of *smeared* and *yellow cake*.

RETEACH lesson vocabulary. Write the following sentences on the board. After reading each sentence aloud, have children tell the Vocabulary Word that could be used in place of each underlined part. Reread the sentence with the Vocabulary Word.

1. Jim <u>spread</u> peanut butter on bread. (smeared)
2. Sara got a <u>five stars</u> score on her test. (perfect)
3. Mom read the <u>directions</u> for making muffins. (recipe)
4. Ted combined flour, milk, and eggs and stirred the <u>thick mixture</u>. (batter)
5. The blueberry muffin tasted <u>like butter</u>. (buttery)
6. Kim used lots of egg yolks to bake a <u>golden birthday dessert</u>. (yellow cake)

FLUENCY BUILDER Using *Intervention Practice Book* page 35, read each word in the first column aloud and have children repeat it. Then have children read the words in the first column aloud to a partner. Follow the same procedure with the remaining columns. After partners have practiced reading the words in each column separately, have them practice the entire list.

Save *Intervention Practice Book* page 35 to use on pages 91 and 93.

INTERVENTION PRACTICE BOOK
page 35

Hedgehog Bakes a Cake/Too Many Cupcakes

BEFORE

Reading "Hedgehog Bakes a Cake"
pages 228–245

USE SKILL CARD 9A

(Focus Skill) Synonyms

PRETEACH the skill. Explain that synonyms are words that have the same or almost the same meanings. Give the example of *sick* and *ill*. Discuss the concept that knowing synonyms can help readers better understand what they are reading.

Have children look at **side A of Skill Card 9: Synonyms.** Read the definition of synonyms. Next read the two sentences aloud. Point out that the underlined words have synonyms. Now call attention to the exercise and have volunteers take turns reading the sentences aloud. Have children read the sentences with the synonyms for the underlined words. Ask:

- How can you figure out the meaning of the underlined word?
- How can you find the synonym for the underlined word?
- Why do the sentences keep the same meaning when the underlined word is changed?

Have children think of new word pairs that are synonyms.

Prepare to Read: "Hedgehog Bakes a Cake"

Preview. Tell children that they are going to read a story called "Hedgehog Bakes a Cake." Explain that the story has made-up characters and events that happen in order (beginning, middle, end). Then preview the selection.

JUST FOR YOU
pages 228–245

- **Pages 228–229:** I see the title, "Hedgehog Bakes a Cake," and the names of the author and the illustrator. I see a picture of a spiny animal stirring something in a bowl. I think that is Hedgehog mixing up a cake.

- **Pages 230–231:** On page 230, I see Hedgehog reading a book. I think he is looking at a recipe for the cake. On page 231, I see him getting out the ingredients to bake the cake.

- **Pages 232–237:** A rabbit comes in. I think the rabbit is trying to help, but he is messy. Then a squirrel comes to help.

Set Purpose. Model setting a purpose for reading "Hedgehog Bakes a Cake."

MODEL I can see that this is a story about Hedgehog, who bakes a cake. His friends come to help him. One purpose for reading a story is to find out what happens. I want to find out how the cake turns out.

90 Lesson 9 • Intervention Teacher's Guide

AFTER

Reading "Hedgehog Bakes a Cake"
pages 228–245

Reread and Summarize

Have children reread and summarize "Hedgehog Bakes a Cake" in sections, as described below.

Pages 230–233

Let's reread pages 230–233 to remember how the story begins.

Summary: Hedgehog was getting ready to bake a cake when Rabbit came over. Rabbit said he would show Hedgehog what to do. Rabbit dumped the flour into the bowl and made a mess.

Pages 234–237

Now let's reread pages 234–237 to recall what happened next.

Summary: Rabbit mixed the batter. It was lumpy. Squirrel came over and added eggs. Eggshells fell into the lumpy batter. Hedgehog mixed, and the batter was more lumpy.

Pages 238–239

Let's reread pages 238–239 to find out what Owl did to help.

Summary: Hedgehog did not want any more help, but he let Owl butter the pan. Owl smeared butter around with her wing and turned the oven up too high. Squirrel and Owl had gotten very messy, so they went home to clean up.

Pages 240–245

Let's reread pages 240–245 to find out how Hedgehog finally baked his cake.

Summary: Hedgehog threw away the batter. He locked his door and carefully followed the recipe to make a cake. Then he cleaned the kitchen. When his friends came back, the cake was done. They all thought it was the best cake they had ever had. Each one thought it was because of what they had done to help.

FLUENCY BUILDER Be sure children have copies of *Intervention Practice Book* page 35, which you used for the previous Fluency Builder activity. Call attention to the sentences on the bottom of the page. Tell children that their goal is to read each phrase or sentence smoothly. Model appropriate pace, expression, and phrasing as you read each sentence. Have children read it after you. Then have children read the sentences to a partner three times.

INTERVENTION PRACTICE BOOK
page 35

BEFORE
Making Connections
pages 250–251

Directed Reading: "Too Many Cupcakes" pp. 70–75

Ask a volunteer to read aloud the title. Point out Rabbit and Possum in the picture. Read aloud page 70 while children listen to find out what Rabbit and Possum will do. Ask: **Why might Possum think cupcakes are grand?** (*Accept reasonable responses.*) **EXPRESS OPINIONS**

SOUNDS OF SUNSHINE
pp. 70–75

Page 71

Have a volunteer read aloud page 71 while children follow along. Ask what happened to the bowl. Then ask: **What synonym can you use for the word cracked?** (*Possible response: broke*) **SYNONYMS**

Pages 72–73

Have children read page 72 to find out what happens when the batter is mixed. Model making inferences as you read.

> **MODEL** When I read that Possum added this and that, I wondered why he would do that. Then I remembered that on page 71 it said that he got out the bowl for Rabbit. I like to help in the kitchen, so I think Possum wanted to help. **MAKE INFERENCES**

Discuss how using what readers learn from the text and what they already know can help them figure out things the author does not say directly. Have a volunteer read aloud page 73. Ask: **Why do you think Possum said he took a bath in the batter?** (*Possible response: Because he had batter smeared all over him.*) **NOTE DETAILS**

Page 74

Read page 74 with children to find out why the oven door is open. Ask: **How does Rabbit feel about the baking? How do you know?** (*Possible response: He is happy; he says "Perfect!"*) **MAKE INFERENCES**

Page 75

Have a volunteer read aloud page 75 while children follow along. Ask: **How might Possum feel at the end of the story?** (*Possible response: He is happy because Rabbit says it is okay and that he will be a whiz at eating the cupcakes.*) **DRAW CONCLUSIONS**

Summarize the selection. Remind children to focus on the most important events in the story.

INTERVENTION PRACTICE BOOK
page 37

Lesson 9 • Intervention Teacher's Guide

Page 76

Answers to *Think About It* Questions

1. Rabbit mixed the cake batter in the bathtub because Possum dropped the bowl that Rabbit had planned to use. **SUMMARIZE**
2. Possum was sad because he was not much help in the kitchen. **INTERPRET STORY DETAILS**
3. Accept reasonable responses. Children's responses should reflect an understanding of story concepts. **TASK**

AFTER
Skill Review
page 25 II

USE SKILL CARD 1B

(Focus Skill) Synonyms

RETEACH the skill. Have children look at **side B of Skill Card 9: Synonyms.** Read the skill reminder with them. Then read aloud the directions. Have a volunteer read aloud the sentences and word choices. Explain that children will complete the exercise.

After children have finished, have them explain why their word choice makes sense. Explain that a word can have more than one synonym. Display children's papers in the classroom.

Review Phonics Skill from "Hedgehog Bakes a Cake"

RETEACH *r*-controlled vowel /ôr/*our*. Create word cards for the following words: *pour, your, four, court, course,* and *source*. In a small group, have children take turns picking a card, reading the word, and using the word in a sentence. Then display all the word cards. Have children tell what letters stand for the /ôr/ sound in each word. (*our*)

FLUENCY BUILDER Be sure that children have copies of *Intervention Practice Book* page 35. Explain that today children will practice the sentences on the bottom half of the page by reading them onto a tape. Assign new partners. Have children take turns reading the sentences aloud to each other and then recording them.

INTERVENTION PRACTICE BOOK
page 35

Hedgehog Bakes a Cake/Too Many Cupcakes   **93**

BEFORE
Drafting a Story
page 251A

Writing Process: Story

Build on prior knowledge. Tell children that they are going to talk about and write the beginning of a story. Display the following information:

> Characters: Frog, Mouse
> Setting: a water park on a summer day
> Events: (a) Frog wants to go on all the rides.
> (b) Mouse makes excuses to not go on rides.

Construct the text. "Share the pen" with children. Guide them to use the ideas on the board to write the beginning of a story. For example:

> Frog and Mouse went to Splash Time Water Park. Frog wanted to go on all the rides. Mouse said the Slide Ride was too high and the Wave Craze had water that was too cold. Frog thought Mouse was afraid of the water.

Revisit the text. Go back and read the story beginning. Ask: **How can I tell the readers why Frog wants to go on the rides?** (*Make up a reason and add it to the story.*)

- Guide children to revise the second sentence to tell why Frog wants to go on the rides. For example: *He was hot and all the rides were exciting.*

- Ask: **How can I let the reader know what Frog and Mouse said to each other?** (*Add dialogue.*)

- Have children read the story beginning and then suggest ideas for how the story could be continued.

On Your Own

Have children fill out a story map for a story of their own. Have them think about characters, setting, and the problem the characters might face and solve. Have children then begin to draft their stories.

Lesson 9 • Intervention Teacher's Guide

AFTER
Spelling Lesson
page 247H

Connect Spelling and Phonics

RETEACH **digraphs /th/ th, /hw/ wh.** Write the word *whiz* on the board. Explain that you will say two more words in which the sound /hw/ is spelled *wh*. Have volunteers write each word on the board. Then write the word *think* on the board, explain that you will say five words in which the /th/ sound is spelled *th*, and repeat the process.

| 1. whiz* | 2. when | 3. whisk | 4. thud* |
| 5. thick* | 6. bath* | 7. math | 8. cloth |

* Word appears in "Too Many Cupcakes."

Dictate the following sentence and have children write it: *When will a moth take a bath?*

Build and Read Longer Words

Remind children that they have learned how to decode words with *th* and *wh*. Tell them that now they will use what they have learned to help them read some longer words.

Write the word *bathtub* on the board. Tell children that they can sometimes figure out long words by looking at the syllables. Cover *tub* and have a volunteer read the word *bath*. Then cover *bath* and have a volunteer read the word *tub*. Point out that *bath* has the /th/ sound spelled *th*. Have children blend the word parts to read the longer word *bathtub*. Follow a similar procedure with *thumbtack*, *thankful*, *wherever*, *whispering*, and *thunder*.

INTERVENTION ASSESSMENT BOOK

FLUENCY BUILDER Have children choose a passage from "Too Many Cupcakes" to read aloud to a partner. You may have children choose passages that they found interesting, or have them choose one of the following options:

- Read pages 71–72. (From *Rabbit was a whiz . . . through . . . What a mess!* Total: 88 words)

- Read pages 73–75. (From *Possum had batter . . . through . . . I just make a mess."* Total: 84 words)

Children should read the selected passage aloud to their partners three times. Have children rate each reading on a scale from 1 to 4.

Hedgehog Bakes a Cake/Too Many Cupcakes **95**

BEFORE Weekly Assessments

Review Vocabulary

To revisit Vocabulary Words prior to the weekly assessment, use these sentences. Have volunteers take turns reading aloud a sentence stem and the choices. Children identify the correct choice and explain why that choice makes sense in the sentence.

1. Something that you need to make a **yellow cake** is
   a. egg yolks.　　　　　　　b. chocolate.
2. You can use a **recipe** to help you
   a. put up a tent　　　　　　b. make a pie.
3. Something that is often **smeared** on bread is
   a. milk.　　　　　　　　　b. jelly.
4. If you wash a dirty shirt and it comes out **perfect** it
   a. has some spots.　　　　　b. is completely clean.
5. This cookie tastes **buttery** because
   a. it has a lot of butter in it.　b. it is yellow.
6. Cake **batter** is
   a. thick and gooey.　　　　b. thin and runny.

Correct responses: 1a, 2b, 3b, 4b, 5a, 6a.

You may want to display the vocabulary words and definitions on page 89 and have children copy them to use when they study for the vocabulary test.

(Focus Skill) Review Synonyms

To review synonyms before the weekly assessment, distribute *Intervention Practice Book* page 38. Have volunteers read aloud the first direction line and the sentences. Guide children to use the information in each sentence to help them understand the meaning of the underlined word.

Review Test Prep

Ask children to turn to page 253 of the *Pupil Edition*. Call attention to the Tips for answering the test questions. Tell children that these tips can help them answer the questions on the page as well as other test questions like them.

JUST FOR YOU page 253

Have children follow along as you read each question and the tip that goes with it. Discuss that they should answer each question about the underlined word.

INTERVENTION PRACTICE BOOK page 38

INTERVENTION ASSESSMENT BOOK

Lesson 9 • Intervention Teacher's Guide

AFTER Weekly Assessments

Self-Selected Reading

Have children select their own books to read independently. They might choose books from the classroom library shelf, or you may wish to offer a group of appropriate books from which children can choose.

- *Birthday Cookies.* See page 2530 of the *Teacher's Edition* for an Independent Reading Plan.
- *Mean Soup* by Betsy Everitt. Harcourt, 1992.
- *The Cake That Mack Ate* by Rose Robart. Little, Brown, 1986.

After children have chosen their books, give each child a copy of My Reading Log, which can be found on page R35 in the back of the *Teacher's Edition*. Have children fill in the information at the top of the form. Then have them use the log to keep track of their reading and to record their responses to the literature.

Conduct student-teacher conferences. Arrange time for each child to confer with you individually about his or her self-selected reading. Have children bring their Reading Logs to share with you at the conference. Children might also like to choose a favorite passage to read aloud to you. Ask questions about the book designed to stimulate discussion. For example, you might ask what information the child learned from a nonfiction text, or how the pictures added to a fiction story.

FLUENCY PERFORMANCE Have children read aloud to you the passage from "Too Many Cupcakes" that they selected and practiced with their partners. Keep track of the number of words the child reads correctly. Ask the child to rate his or her own performance on the 1–4 scale. If children are not happy with their oral reading, give them a chance to practice more and to read the passage to you again.

See *Oral Reading Fluency Assessment* for monitoring progress.

Hedgehog Bakes a Cake/Too Many Cupcakes

LESSON 10

BEFORE Building Background and Vocabulary

Use with

"Lemonade for Sale"

Review Phonics: *R*-Controlled Vowel: /är/*ar*

Identify the sound. Tell children to listen for the /är/ sound as you say the words *yard* and *bar*. Then have children repeat the following sentence twice: *It is hard to park a car in the dark.* Ask them to identify the four words that have the /är/ sound. (*hard, park, car, dark*)

Associate letters to sound. Write on the board: *It is hard to park a car in the dark*. Underline the letters *ar* in *hard, park, car* and *dark*. Explain that this letter combination stands for the /är/ sound.

Word blending. Model how to blend and read the word *car*. Slide your hand under the word as you elongate the sounds /käärr/. Then say the word naturally—*car*. Follow a similar procedure with the word *dark*.

Apply the skill. *Letter Substitution* Write the following words on the board, and have children read each aloud. Make the changes necessary to form the words in parentheses. Have a volunteer read aloud each new word.

INTERVENTION PRACTICE BOOK
page 40

| **had** (hard) | **lad** (lard) | **ham** (harm) | **ban** (barn) |
| **pack** (park) | **cat** (cart) | **pat** (part) | **mat** (mart) |

Introduce Vocabulary

PRETEACH **lesson vocabulary.** Tell children that they are going to learn five new words that they will see again when they read a realistic fiction story called "Lemonade for Sale." Teach each Vocabulary Word using the following process.

Use these suggestions or similar ideas to give the meaning or context.

> Write the word.
> Say the word.
> Track the word and have children repeat it.
> Give the meaning or context.

announced Point out the base word *announce*. Have volunteers announce something to the class. Point out that when a word ends in *-ed*, it means it happened in the past.

arrived Point out the base word *arrive*. Relate to *came*. Tell what time you arrived at school.

glum Relate to feeling sad. Point out the *gl* and *um* letter combinations. Then blend the word.

members Relate to children who belong to a scout troop or a team.

rebuild Demonstrate by building a stack of blocks. Knock them down; then rebuild the stack.

For vocabulary activities, see Vocabulary Games on pages 2–7. *(Intervention Teachers Guide)*

AFTER
Building Background and Vocabulary

Apply Vocabulary Strategies

Use Synonyms. Write the words *glum* and *sad* on chart paper and explain that these words are synonyms. Tell children that recognizing synonyms can help them figure out the meanings of words.

> **MODEL** I know that synonyms are words that have the same or almost the same meaning. If I know that *glum* and *sad* are synonyms, it will help me to remember what each word means.

Guide children in a similar procedure to understand the meaning of *arrived* and *announced*. Synonyms they could suggest are *came* and *told*.

RETEACH lesson vocabulary. Have children listen to each of the following sentences. Tell them to hold up the word card that completes each rhyme. Reread the sentence aloud with the correct word choice. Then discuss how the meaning of the vocabulary word fits the sentence.

1. Vera cried when the big gift __(arrived)__.
2. "The basketball bounced," the loudspeaker __(announced)__.
3. The birdhouse fell apart when we drilled so we have to __(rebuild)__.
4. Lynn knew that her chum felt sad and __(glum)__.
5. "We've marched for five Novembers," said the marching band __(members)__.

Vocabulary Words
announced made something known to many people
arrived came to a place
glum gloomy; sad
members those who belong to a group
rebuild make something again; build again

FLUENCY BUILDER Using *Intervention Practice Book* page 39, read aloud each word in the first column and have children repeat it. Then have children work in pairs to read the words in the first column aloud to each other. Follow the same procedure with each of the remaining columns. After partners have practiced reading aloud the words in each separate column, have them read aloud the entire list.

(Save *Intervention Practice Book* page 39 to use on pages 101 and 103.)

INTERVENTION PRACTICE BOOK
page 39

Lemonade for Sale/A Lemonade Surprise

BEFORE
Reading "Lemonade for Sale"
pages 256–274

USE SKILL CARD 10A

Focus Skill: COMPARE AND CONTRAST

PRETEACH the skill. Explain to children that when you compare things you tell how they are the same and when you contrast things you tell how they are different. For example: two children may be alike because they are girls and different because one has a dog and the other has a cat. Discuss why it helps readers to compare and contrast as they read.

Have children look at **side A of Skill Card 10: Compare and Contrast**. Read the definition of compare and contrast. Next, read the paragraphs aloud and then have children reread them with you. Ask: **How do you know that Jeremy and Fred are both 12 years old?** (*Possible response: because it tells their ages in the paragraphs.*) **How do you know that Jeremy and Fred like different sports?** (*Possible response: because the last sentence says that Jeremy likes football and the last sentence says that Fred likes soccer.*) **Why are *12 years old* and *has a dog* in the middle circle?** (*Possible response: These are ways that Jeremy and Fred are alike.*)

Explain that when we compare and contrast characters in different stories, it helps us to understand both characters better.

Prepare to Read: "Lemonade for Sale"

Preview. Tell children that they are going to read a selection entitled "Lemonade for Sale." Explain that it is realistic fiction. The people and places seem real, but the story is made-up. Then preview the selection.

JUST FOR YOU
pages 256–274

- **Pages 256–257:** I see the title, "Lemonade for Sale," and the names of the author and illustrator. The picture shows some children in a hammock. I think two of them are drinking lemonade.

- **Pages 258–259:** On these pages, I see a clubhouse that looks like it might fall down. I see children looking at an empty piggybank. I think they don't have money to fix their clubhouse.

- **Pages 260–261:** On these pages, I see the children talking. I think they are talking about how to earn money. I see a bar graph. I think they are going to use it to keep track of something.

- **Pages 262–263:** On page 262, I see a stand with a sign that says "Lemonade 25 cents." I think the children are selling lemonade to earn money for the clubhouse. On page 263, I see the days of the week on the bar graph. I think they will chart how much money they make each day.

Set Purpose. Model setting a purpose for reading "Lemonade for Sale."

MODEL From what I have seen in my preview, I think I will find out if the children earn enough money to fix their clubhouse. One purpose for reading is to learn what happens in a story. I will read to find out how the story turns out.

100 Lesson 10 • Intervention Teacher's Guide

AFTER

Reading "Lemonade for Sale"
pages 256–274

Reread and Summarize

Have children reread and summarize "Lemonade for Sale" in sections, as described below.

Pages 258–261
Let's reread pages 258–261 to remember how the story begins.

Summary: The members of the Elm Street Kid's Club were glum because their clubhouse was falling down. They decided to sell lemonade to make money to fix the clubhouse. Sheri made a bar graph to keep track of sales.

Pages 262–267
Let's reread pages 262–267 to remind ourselves of what happened at the lemonade stand.

Summary: The children made lemonade. On Monday, they sold 30 cups. On Tuesday, they sold 40 cups. Wednesday they sold 56 cups. Each day, Sheri entered the number of cups on the bar graph. Things were going great.

Pages 268–271
Now let's reread pages 268–271 to find out what happened next.

Summary: On Thursday, they only sold 24 cups. The bar graph was low. Matthew noticed that all the people were down the street. They went, too, and discovered that everyone was watching a juggler. Sheri had an idea.

Pages 272–274
Let's reread pages 272–274 to find out if the children made enough money to fix their clubhouse.

Summary: On Friday, Sheri brought Jed to juggle next to the lemonade stand. More people came than ever before. The children sold so many cups of lemonade that they had enough money to rebuild their clubhouse.

FLUENCY BUILDER Use *Intervention Practice Book* page 39. Point out the sentences on the bottom half of the page. Remind students to pay attention to the slashes and to read each phrase or unit smoothly. Model appropriate pace, expression, and phrasing as you read each sentence, and have students read it after you. Then have students practice by reading the sentences aloud three times to a partner.

INTERVENTION PRACTICE BOOK
page 39

Lemonade for Sale/A Lemonade Surprise **101**

Directed Reading: "A Lemonade Surprise," pp. 78–84

BEFORE
Making Connections
pages 278–279

SOUNDS OF SUNSHINE
pp. 78–84

Page 78

Ask a volunteer to read aloud the title. Explain that children will find out what the surprise is as they read the story. Read page 78 aloud while children listen to find out why Barb is glum. Ask: **Why is Barb glum?** (*Possible response: She has moved and misses her friends.*) **IDENTIFY CHARACTERS' EMOTIONS/DRAW CONCLUSIONS**

Page 79

Read aloud the first two words on page 79 while children listen. Write the word *spotted* on the board. Model using the Read Ahead strategy to find the meaning for this word.

> **MODEL** I am not sure what the word *spotted* means. I am going to read ahead to see if the rest of the sentence will help me figure out the meaning. It says Barb spotted some children in the next yard. This tells me that she saw the children. *Spotted* must mean "saw." **READ AHEAD**

Discuss how reading ahead can help readers figure out the meaning of a difficult word. Have a volunteer read aloud the words *She grabbed*. Then have them finish reading the sentence. Ask: **How does reading about the cups and the jug help you figure out what *grabbed* means?** (*Possible response: If she was holding cups and a jug, then she must have picked them up. So* grabbed *must mean "picked up."*)

Pages 80–81

Have a volunteer read these pages aloud while children listen to find out what problem Mark, Kim, and Karl have. Ask: **How is what happened so far in this story like what happened in "Lemonade for Sale?"** (*Possible responses: Children have a clubhouse that needs to be rebuilt but they don't have enough money. In both stories they sell lemonade to earn money.*) **COMPARE AND CONTRAST**

Pages 82–83

Ask a volunteer to read aloud page 82 while children listen to find out how the club members got started. Ask: **What do Kim and Karl do?** (*Possible response: set up the stand*) **NOTE DETAILS**

Page 84

Read aloud page 84 while children listen to find out how the story ends. Ask: **How does Barb feel at the end? Why?** (*Possible response: She is happy because she is a friend, and all friends are club members.*) **INTERPRET STORY EVENTS**

Summarize the selection. Ask children to focus on the most important events in the story. Then have them complete *Intervention Practice Book* page 41.

INTERVENTION PRACTICE BOOK
page 41

Lesson 10 • Intervention Teacher's Guide

Answers to *Think About It* Questions

1. Barb brings lemonade to the children next door. She helps them make money for a new clubhouse. **SUMMARIZE**
2. Barb misses her friends, and her mother says that she will make new friends at school. **INTERPRET STORY DETAILS**
3. Accept reasonable responses. **TASK**

AFTER
Skill Review
page 281C

USE SKILL CARD 10B

(Focus Skill) Compare and Contrast

RETEACH the skill. Have children look at side B of Skill Card 10: Compare and Contrast. Read the skill reminder aloud with them and have a volunteer read the paragraphs aloud.

Read the next set of directions. Explain that children will work with partners to create their own diagrams. Remind them to reread both paragraphs to find out how the settings are alike and how they are different.

After children have completed their compare and contrast diagrams, have them display and explain their work. Point out that "A Lemonade Surprise" has a plot that is quite like the plot in "Lemonade for Sale."

Review Phonics Skill from "Lemonade for Sale"

RETEACH Phonograms ar, arm, ark. Write these sentences on the board: *Barb saw the dog in the yard. The dog barked and ran to the farm.* Read the sentences aloud. Have volunteers point to the words with the /är/ sound. Then read the following list aloud and have children raise their hands when they hear the /är/ sound: *part, rub, far, start, star, silly, hard, charming, marker, stop, shark.*

FLUENCY BUILDER Be sure that children have copies of *Intervention Practice Book* page 39. Explain that today children will practice the sentences on the bottom half of the page by reading them aloud on tape. Assign new partners. Have the children take turns reading the sentences aloud to each other and then reading them on tape.

INTERVENTION PRACTICE BOOK
page 39

Lemonade for Sale/A Lemonade Surprise

BEFORE
Drafting a Good Ending
page 281G

Writing: Good Endings

Build on prior knowledge. Tell children that they are going to talk about and write a good ending for a story. Display the following:

> It was Bret's first day at his new school. He missed his old friends. At recess, he stood alone. He watched the other boys play ball. One of the boys hit the ball hard, and it flew toward Bret.

Construct the text. "Share the pen" with children. Help them get ideas for a good ending to the story. Write the ideas on the board in the order they might happen in the story. For example:

- Bret catches the ball.
- Bret gives the ball to the boys.
- The boys ask Bret to play ball.
- Bret is happy.

Revisit the text. Go back and read the ideas together. Ask: **How can we use these ideas to write a good ending?** (*make them into sentences that fit the story*)

- Guide children into combining the ideas into sentences. For example: *Bret caught the ball and threw it back to the boys. The boys asked Bret to join their game. Bret was happy.*

- Ask: **What information could we add to show why Bret was happy?** (*because he had found new friends*) Make the appropriate change.

- Have children read the paragraph aloud with the ending. Have them copy the paragraph onto their own papers.

On Your Own

Have children write a new ending for "A Lemonade Surprise." Remind them that a good ending shows how the problem was solved.

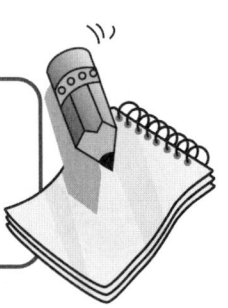

104 Lesson 10 • Intervention Teacher's Guide

AFTER
Spelling Lesson
page 275H

Connect Spelling and Phonics

RETEACH **R-Controlled Vowel: /är/ar.** Write the word *yard* on the board. Explain that you will say more words in which the /är/ sound is spelled *ar*. Have volunteers write each word on the board. Check for misspelled words and help children correct each one by drawing a line through the word and writing the correct spelling above it.

| 1. yard* | 2. yarn | 3. card* | 4. star |
| 5. park | 6. start | 7. farm | |

*Word appears in "A Lemonade Surprise."

Dictate the following sentence and have children write it: *The car is parked in the barn.*

Build and Read Longer Words

Remind children that they have learned how to decode words with *r*-controlled vowel /är/ spelled *ar*. Explain that now they will use what they have learned to help them read some longer words.

Write the word *farming* on the board. Tell children that they can sometimes figure out long words by looking for syllables. Cover the *-ing* and have a volunteer read the word *farm*. Then cover *farm* and have a volunteer read the syllable *-ing*. Point out that *farm* has the /är/ sound spelled *ar*. Have children blend the word parts to read the longer word *farming*. Follow a similar procedure with these words: *cardboard*, *parked*, *barnyard*, *harmful*.

INTERVENTION
ASSESSMENT
BOOK

FLUENCY BUILDER Have children choose a passage from "A Lemonade Surprise" to read aloud to a partner. You may have children choose passages that they found particularly interesting, or have them choose one of the following options:

- Read pages 80–81. (From *"Thanks for the Lemonade,"*... through ... *members yelled*. Total: 75 words)

- Read pages 83–84. (From *"Come and get it!"*... through ... *members of this club."* Total: 95 words)

Children should read the selected passage aloud to their partners three times. Have children rate each of their own readings on a scale from 1 to 4.

Lemonade for Sale/A Lemonade Surprise **105**

BEFORE Weekly Assessments

Review Vocabulary

To revisit vocabulary words prior to the weekly assessment, use these sentence frames. Have volunteers take turns reading aloud the sentence stems and choices. Children identify the correct choice and explain why that choice makes sense in the sentence.

1. If Aunt Vera **arrived** at 6 P.M., she probably
   a. got to your home then.   b. answered the phone then.
2. If you had to **rebuild** your sand castle, it had probably
   a. lasted forever.   b. fallen down.
3. Someone who is feeling **glum** is
   a. sad.   b. tired.
4. One of the **members** of your family is
   a. your sister.   b. your bike.
5. If Sally **announced** her plans, she probably wanted
   a. no one to know.   b. everyone to know.

Correct responses: 1**a**, 2**b**, 3**a**, 4**a**, 5**b**.

You may want to display the vocabulary words and definitions on page 99 and have children copy them to use when they study for the vocabulary test.

(Focus Skill) Review Compare and Contrast

To review compare and contrast before the weekly assessment, distribute *Intervention Practice Book* page 42. Have volunteers read aloud the first direction line and the two stories. Guide children to reread the stories before filling in the graphic organizer.

Review Test Prep

Ask children to turn to page 281 of the *Pupil Edition*. Call attention to the tips for answering test questions. Tell children that paying attention to these tips can help them answer not only the test questions on this page but also other test questions like these.

Have children follow along as you read each test question and the tip that goes with it. Discuss why it is important to break the word into syllables. (Possible response: *It may help you sound it out.*) Discuss why it is important to read all the choices before you pick one. (Possible response: *The best answer may be the last answer.*)

INTERVENTION PRACTICE BOOK page 42

INTERVENTION ASSESSMENT BOOK

106 Lesson 10 • Intervention Teacher's Guide

AFTER Self-Selected Reading

Weekly Assessments

Have children select their own books to read independently. They might choose books from the classroom library shelf, or you may wish to offer a group of appropriate books such as the following from which children can choose.

- *The Tree House* by Daniel Barnes. See page 28 IS of the *Teacher's Edition* for an Independent Reading Plan.
- *The Day I Had to Play with My Sister* by Crosby Bonsall. HarperCollins, 1988.
- *Rex and Lilly Family Time* by Laurie Krasny Brown. Little, Brown, 1995.

After children have chosen their books, give each child a copy of My Reading Log, which can be found on page R35 in the back of the *Teacher's Edition*. Have children fill in the information at the top of the form. Then have them use the log to keep track of their reading and to record their responses to the literature.

Conduct student-teacher conferences. Arrange time for each child to confer with you individually about his or her self-selected reading. Have children bring their Reading Logs to share with you at the conference. Children might also like to choose a favorite passage to read aloud to you. Ask questions designed to stimulate discussion about the book. For example, ask how a favorite character in the book compares or contrasts with a character in "A Lemonade Surprise."

FLUENCY PERFORMANCE Have children read aloud to you the passage from "A Lemonade Surprise" that they selected and practiced with their partners. Keep track of the number of words each child reads correctly. Ask the child to rate his or her own performance on the 1–4 scale. If children are not happy with their oral reading, give them an opportunity to continue practicing and then to reread the passage to you again.

See *Oral Reading Fluency Assessment* for monitoring progress.

Lemonade for Sale/A Lemonade Surprise

LESSON 11

BEFORE Building Background and Vocabulary

Use with

"Johnny Appleseed"

Review Phonics: Digraphs /ch/*ch, tch*

Identify the sound. Have children repeat the following sentence three times: *Charlie Chimp can catch Chuck Chick*. Ask children which words in the sentence have the /ch/ sound. (*Charlie, Chimp, catch, Chuck, Chick*)

Associate letters to sound. Write the sentence *Charlie Chimp can catch Chuck Chick* on the board. Tell children that the letters *ch* and *tch* often stand for the /ch/ sound. Ask a volunteer to underline the letters *ch* or *tch* in each word.

Word blending. Model how to blend and read the word *chat*. Write the word on the board, and slide your hand under the word as you elongate the sounds /chaatt/. Then say the word naturally. Repeat the activity for the words *chip, chop, itch, patch*.

Apply the skill. *Consonant Substitution* Write the following words on the board, and have children read each one aloud. Make the changes necessary to form the word in parentheses. Have volunteers read aloud each new word.

| **cat** (chat) | **mop** (chop) | **map** (match) | **swim** (switch) |
| **tin** (chin) | **west** (chest) | **hat** (hatch) | **pin** (pitch) |

INTERVENTION PRACTICE BOOK
page 44

Introduce Vocabulary

PRETEACH lesson vocabulary. Tell children that they are going to learn six words that they will see again in the play "Johnny Appleseed." Teach every Vocabulary Word, using the following process.

Provide children with the meaning of each word or a context for the word.

> Write the word.
> Say the word.
> Track the word and have children repeat it.
> Give the meaning or context.

frontier — Point out the small word *front*. Explain that a *frontier* is a place out in front of you where you have not been yet.

nearby — Show two things that are close to each other. *The playground is near the school. It is nearby.*

orchards — Point to trees outside or to pictures in a book. Using a fruit as an example, tell children that fruit is grown in *orchards* which have many fruit trees.

survive — Relate to staying alive. Explain that people need water, food, and shelter to *survive*.

108 Lesson 11 • Intervention Teacher's Guide

tame   Tell children that to *tame* something means to bring it under control. Relate to an animal trainer at a zoo.

wild   Explain that *wild* is the opposite of *tame*. Something *wild* has not been changed from its natural state.

For vocabulary activities, see Vocabulary Games on pages 2–7.

> ### Vocabulary Words
> **frontier** the part of the country at the edge of a settled area
> **nearby** not far away
> **orchards** areas of land where fruit trees are grown
> **survive** stay alive
> **tame** to bring under control or make more gentle
> **wild** in a natural state; not controlled by humans

AFTER — Building Background and Vocabulary

Apply Vocabulary Strategies

Use synonyms/antonyms. Write the words *close* and *nearby* on chart paper and explain that these words mean almost the same thing and are called *synonyms*. Explain that knowing that two words have almost the same meaning can help you remember what a word means when you read it.

MODEL I know that *synonyms* are words that mean almost the same thing. If I know that *close* and *nearby* are synonyms, I can remember what each word means.

Provide a similar example for *survive* (live) and *orchard* (trees).

RETEACH lesson vocabulary. Create synonym triplets with children. Have children make a word card for each vocabulary word. Then print the following word pairs on the board and read them aloud. Tell children to hold up the word card that completes the synonym triplet. Reread the words and discuss how children made their choices.

1. settled area/prairie (*frontier*)
2. close/not far (*nearby*)
3. forests/trees (*orchards*)
4. live/struggle (*survive*)
5. control/train (*tame*)
6. natural/uncontrolled (*wild*)

FLUENCY BUILDER Using *Intervention Practice Book* p. 43, read each word in the first column aloud and have children repeat it. Then have children read the words in the first column aloud to a partner. Use the same procedure with the remaining columns. After partners have practiced reading aloud the words in each column separately, have them read the entire list.

INTERVENTION PRACTICE BOOK
page 43

(Save *Intervention Practice Book* page 43 to use on pages 111 and 113.)

Johnny Appleseed/Anna's Apple Doll

BEFORE

Reading "Johnny Appleseed"
pages 286–304

USE SKILL CARD 11A

(Focus Skill) Details

PRETEACH the skill. Explain that details are small parts that make up the main idea of a sentence or story. Discuss how details help give readers a richer picture of what is happening in a story and understand it better.

Have children look at **side A of Skill Card 11: Details**. Read the explanation of *details*. Next, read the paragraph and have children reread it with you.

Call attention to the web and ask children to give details about the topic. Ask:

- What would happen if Mom made a pizza instead of an apple pie? (*Possible response: The details would be different.*)
- What details help you better imagine the pie? (*Its golden crust, small chunks of apple, brown sugar and cinnamon.*)

Prepare to Read: "Johnny Appleseed"

Preview. Tell children that they are going to read a play entitled "Johnny Appleseed." Explain that a play can be acted out. Tell children that "Johnny Appleseed" tells about a real man who lived long ago. His name was John Chapman. Then preview the selection.

Just for You
pages 286–304

- **Pages 286–287:** I see where it says that this story is a legend. It has been told again and again for many years. On page 287, it tells where and when the play begins. It will begin long ago in the woods.
- **Pages 288–289:** On these pages I see lots of people. I see a baby with an apple. That might be Johnny.
- **Pages 290–297:** It looks like Johnny has grown up. He is wearing a pot on his head and he is planting seeds. It looks like he is having an adventure.
- **Pages 298–304:** I see animals and an old man. There are apples in most of the pictures.

Set purpose. Model setting a purpose for reading "Johnny Appleseed."

MODEL From my preview, I think I will find out the life of John Chapman. I want to find out how he got the name *Johnny Appleseed*.

110 Lesson 11 • Intervention Teacher's Guide

AFTER Reading "Johnny Appleseed" pages 286–304

Reread and Summarize

Have children reread and summarize "Johnny Appleseed" in sections, as described below.

Pages 286–289

Let's reread pages 286–289 to recall what John Chapman's life was like when he was young.

Summary: John Chapman had ten half-brothers and half-sisters and lived on the frontier. He wanted to plant apple seeds, and people called him Johnny Appleseed.

Pages 290–295

Let's reread pages 290–295 to remember what Johnny did when he left home and why he wanted to plant seeds.

Summary: He walked the countryside and planted appleseeds and grew apple trees. He wanted to help people by having apple trees growing for them as they moved around the country. He lived outdoors.

Pages 296–299

Let's reread pages 296–299 to remember what happened when he met new friends and wild animals.

Summary: Johnny made many new friends who invited him to stay with them. He liked to live outdoors. He slept with the animals. All he needed was his cooking pot. He wanted to keep moving and plant more apple trees.

Pages 300–303

Let's reread pages 300–303 to recall what happened when Johnny Appleseed grew old.

Summary: He kept planting trees and living on the frontier. Having apples ready for people who moved to new places made him happy.

FLUENCY BUILDER Be sure children have copies of *Intervention Practice Book* p. 43, which you used for the previous Fluency Builder activity. Call attention to the sentences on the bottom half of the page. The slashes break the sentences into phrases to allow children to work on phrasing. Tell children that their goal is to read each phrase or sentence smoothly. Model appropriate pace, expression and phrasing as you read each sentence. Then have children read it after you. Have children practice reading the sentences aloud to a partner three times.

INTERVENTION PRACTICE BOOK
page 43

Johnny Appleseed/Anna's Apple Doll

BEFORE
Making Connections
pages 308–309

Directed Reading: "Anna's Apple Doll," pp. 86–92

Read aloud the title. Tell children that the selection is a play that takes place in the west. Discuss how the picture on page 87 helps children imagine the play's setting. Ask how paying attention to the details in the play and illustrations will help them understand it better.

SOUNDS OF SUNSHINE
pp. 86–92

Ask: **Where is Anna going to play? What will she do there?** (*She will play in the orchard and pick apples.*) **DETAILS**

Pages 88–89

Read aloud page 89. Have children listen to find out what happens between Anna and her brothers. Model using the Create Mental Images strategy. Draw children's attention to the words in parentheses. Tell them that this text tells the characters what movements to make.

> **MODEL** When I read a play, I try to picture in my mind what is happening. I think about who the characters are, and how they feel about what is happening. I try to imagine myself in a character's place.
> **CREATE MENTAL IMAGES**

Pages 90–91

Have children read page 91 to find out what Anna does with an apple. Ask: **What does Anna do with one of the apples?** (*She makes it into an apple doll.*) **STORY EVENTS**

Ask: **How does Anna make the doll's legs and feet?** (*She uses sticks.*) **DETAILS**

Page 92

Have children read page 92 to find out how Anna's family responds to the apple doll. Ask: **What does Anna's family think about her doll?** (*They like it.*) **DRAW CONCLUSIONS**

Ask: **How are Anna's brothers different to her at the end of the story than they were at the beginning?** (*First they teased her. Now they are being nice to her and complimenting her.*) **INTERPRET CHARACTER'S ACTIONS**

Summarize the selection. Ask children what happened at the beginning, in the middle, and at the end of "Anna's Apple Doll."

Page 93

INTERVENTION PRACTICE BOOK
page 45

Answers to *Think About It* Questions

1. She makes a doll out of the apple. She uses sticks for legs and feet. **DETAILS**
2. They think she is too young to do anything useful. They tease her. **DRAW CONCLUSIONS**
3. Accept reasonable responses. **FOLLOWING DIRECTIONS**

Lesson 11 • Intervention Teacher's Guide

AFTER

Skill Review
pages 285A

USE SKILL CARD 11B

Focus Skill: Details

RETEACH the skill. Have children look at **side B of Skill Card 11: Details.** Read the skill reminder with them, and have a volunteer read the paragraph aloud.

Read aloud the set of directions. Explain that children will work with partners to create their own web of details. When they have completed their webs, have them explain and display their work.

Review Phonics Skill from "Johnny Appleseed"

RETEACH *r*-**Controlled Vowels /ir/ *ear, eer.*** Create sets of word cards for partners or small groups to use. Use the words *year, deer, dear, beard, fear, hear, cheer,* and *ear.* Have children sort the word cards by how /ir/ is spelled. Then children can take turns choosing a card and saying a sentence that uses the word.

FLUENCY BUILDER Be sure that children have copies of *Intervention Practice Book* page 43. Explain that today children will practice the sentences on the page by reading them onto a tape. Help children choose new partners. Have partners take turns reading the sentences aloud to each other and then recording them.

INTERVENTION PRACTICE BOOK
page 43

Johnny Appleseed/Anna's Apple Doll

BEFORE
Drafting an Informative Paragraph
pages 311G

Informative Paragraph: Giving Facts and Reasons

Build on prior knowledge. Tell children that they are going to talk and write about giving detailed information about something. Discuss that when you share information, you want to include details so that your meaning is clear. Guide children to see that good informative sentences should include a clear topic or main idea. Display and read aloud a list like the following list:

> Sentence Topic: A wolf
>
> Detail 1: A wolf looks a lot like a dog.
>
> Detail 2: A wolf is not tame.
>
> Detail 3: A wolf would not make a good pet.

Construct the text. "Share the pen" with children. Guide them in writing informative sentences based on the topic *A wolf* and a list of details. For example:

- A wolf looks a lot like a dog, but is not a dog. It is a wild animal. A wolf would not make a good pet.

Revisit the text. Go back and read aloud the sentences. Ask: **How do the details tell about the wolf?** (*They tell how a wolf is like a dog and how it is different.*)

- Ask: **Where can I add another detail to make the sentence more interesting?** (*Responses will vary.*)
- Have children read the new sentences aloud and then copy their favorite sentences to their papers.

On Your Own

Have children choose a favorite weekend hobby or activity and write a sentence about it. Ask them to take turns reading the sentence to a partner, checking to see that the details and meaning are clear. Then have them revise their sentences as needed and share them aloud with a group.

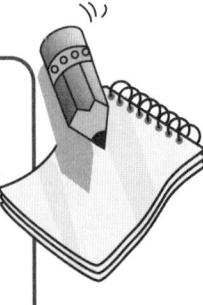

AFTER

Spelling
page 305H

Connect Spelling and Phonics

RETEACH **digraphs /ch/ ch, tch.** Tell children to number their papers 1–8. Dictate the following words, and have children write them. After each word is written, write it on the board so children can proofread their work. Direct them to draw a line through a misspelled word and write the correct spelling below it or to the side.

| 1. chin * | 2. chop* | 3. chest | 4. chart |
| 5. chick | 6. chat | 7. such | 8. much |

* Word appears in "Anna's Apple Doll."

Dictate and have children write the following sentence: *Mitch can catch a chicken.*

Build and Read Longer Words

Remind children that they have learned how to decode words with the /ch/ *ch*, *tch* sound. Explain that now they will use what they have learned to help them read some longer words.

Write the word *childish* on the board. Tell children that they can sometimes figure out long words by looking for syllables and word parts. Cover the letters *ish* and select a volunteer to read *child*. Point out that *child* has the /ch/ sound. Then cover *child-* and have a volunteer read *ish*. Have children blend the word parts to read the longer word *childish*. Follow a similar procedure with these words: *hatching*, *chipmunk*, *chocolate*, *chapter*, *chatter*. Encourage children to build other long words.

INTERVENTION ASSESSMENT BOOK

FLUENCY BUILDER Have children choose a passage from "Anna's Apple Doll" to read aloud to a partner. You may have children choose passages that they found interesting, or give one of the following options:

- Read page 89. (From *Charles: Well, look . . . through . . . fun picking apples*. Total: 112 words.)
- Read pages 91–92. (From *Garth: Anna, let's go . . . through . . . Anna . . . will be fun!* Total: 108 words.)

Children should read the selected passage aloud to a partner three times. Have the child rate each reading on a scale from 1 to 4.

SCALE
1 Not good
2 Pretty good
3 Good
4 Great!

Johnny Appleseed/Anna's Apple Doll

BEFORE Weekly Assessments

Review Vocabulary

To revisit the Vocabulary Words prior to the weekly assessment, use the following sentence frames. Have volunteers take turns reading aloud a sentence frame and answer choices. Children should identify the correct answer and explain why that choice makes sense in the sentence.

1. The **frontier** is like
   a. the country.
   b. the city.
2. Since my school is **nearby**, I
   a. get there by plane.
   b. can walk there.
3. An **orchard** is a place where you will see many
   a. fruit trees.
   b. car washes.
4. To **survive**, your body must have
   a. water.
   b. pizza.
5. When you **tame** an animal, you make it
   a. more gentle.
   b. more wild.
6. A **wild** animal might live in
   a. the kitchen.
   b. the woods.

Correct responses: 1a, 2b, 3a, 4a, 5a, 6b

You may want to display the Vocabulary Words and definitions on page 109, and have children copy them to study for the vocabulary test.

Review Details

(Focus Skill)

To review details before the weekly assessment, distribute *Intervention Practice Book* p. 46. Have volunteers read aloud the first direction line and the sentences. Guide children to look for the main idea and important details to help them create a mental image of what they are reading.

INTERVENTION PRACTICE BOOK
page 46

Review Test Prep

Ask children to turn to page 311 of the *Pupil Edition*. Call attention to the Tip for answering the test questions. Tell children that paying attention to the tip can help them answer not only these questions but other test questions like them.

JUST FOR YOU
page 311

Print the following sentence on the board: *The apple was red, hard, juicy, and ripe*. Print the following sample test question on the board and have children follow along as you read it: *The apple will taste: a) scary. b) good. c) spicy.* Discuss how knowing that the apple is juicy and ripe helps children know that it will taste good. Tell them that a good test-taking tip is to read all the answer choices before selecting a response.

INTERVENTION ASSESSMENT BOOK

Lesson 11 • Intervention Teacher's Guide

AFTER Weekly Assessments

Self-Selected Reading

Have children select their own books to read independently. They might choose books from the classroom library shelf, or you may wish to offer a group of appropriate books from which children can choose.

- *On the Wild Frontier.* (See page 311S of the *Teacher's Edition* for an Independent Reading Plan.)
- *Not Now! Said the Cow* by Joanne Oppenheim. Bantam, 1989.
- *Why the Sun and the Moon Live in the Sky* by Elphinstone Dayrell. Houghton Mifflin, 1968.

After children have chosen their books, give each child a copy of My Reading Log, which can be found on page R35 in the back of the *Teacher's Edition*. Have children fill in the information at the top of the form and then use the log to keep track of their reading and record responses to the literature.

Conduct student-teacher conferences. Arrange time for each child to conference with you individually about his or her self-selected reading. Have children bring their Reading Logs to share at the conference. Children might also like to share a favorite passage to read aloud to you. Ask questions about the book designed to stimulate discussion. For example, you might ask if there are any similarities between the book and "Johnny Appleseed."

FLUENCY PERFORMANCE Have children read aloud to you the passage from "Anna's Apple Doll" that they selected and practiced with their partners. Keep track of the number of words the child reads correctly. Ask the child to rate his or her own performance on the 1–4 scale. If children are not happy with their oral reading, give them a chance to practice more and reread the passage to you again.

See *Oral Reading Fluency Assessment* for monitoring progress.

LESSON 12

BEFORE
Building Background and Vocabulary

Use with

"From Seed to Plant"

Review Phonics: R-controlled Vowel /ôr/ *or, ore, our*

Identify the sound. Read aloud the following sentence: *Mort went to the store at four.* Ask children to repeat the sentence three times, identifying the words that have the /ôr/ sound. (*Mort, store, four*)

Associate letters to sound. Write on the board the sentence *Mort went to the store at four.* Tell children that the letters *or, ore,* and *our* often stand for the /ôr/ sound. Select a volunteer to underline the words that contain the /ôr/ sound.

Word blending. Model how to blend and read the word *sport.* Write *sport* on the board and slide your hand under the word as you elongate the sounds /ssp ôô rrt/. Then say the word naturally—*sport.* Follow a similar procedure for the words *corn, more,* and *pour.*

Apply the skill. *Vowel Substitution* Write the following words on the board, and have children read each word aloud. Make the changes necessary to form the word in parentheses. Have volunteers read aloud the new word.

INTERVENTION PRACTICE BOOK
page 48

| **can** (corn) | **pet** (port) | **spot** (sport) | **far** (four) |
| **star** (store) | **par** (pour) | **bin** (born) | **hen** (horn) |

Introduce Vocabulary

PRETEACH **lesson vocabulary.** Tell children that they are going to learn five new words that they will see again when they read a story called "From Seed to Plant." Teach each Vocabulary Word using the following process.

Use these suggestions or similar ideas to give the meaning or context.

beautiful — Relate the word to a flower or something very pretty.

nutrition — Give an example of a food that is healthful, such as an apple. Explain that junk food is low in food value and that it is not healthful to eat much of it.

protects — Model protecting your head by covering yourself with your arms. Put on sunglasses to show how to protect your eyes from the sun.

> Write the word.
> Say the word.
> Track the word and have children repeat it.
> Give the meaning or context.

Lesson 12 • Intervention Teacher's Guide

ripens	Show two bananas, one green and one yellow. Explain that the green one *ripens* and becomes ready to eat, as the yellow one is.
streams	Relate to water. Explain that a *stream* is a narrow path of water that moves. Use a faucet to demonstrate, or slowly pour a stream of water from a cup.

For vocabulary activities, see Vocabulary Games on pages 2–7.

> **Vocabulary Words**
> **beautiful** very pretty
> **nutrition** food part that is needed for life and growth
> **protects** keeps safe from harm
> **ripens** matures and becomes ready to eat
> **streams** small rivers; brooks

AFTER
Building Background and Vocabulary

Apply Vocabulary Strategies

Use familiar words parts. Write the words *beauty* and *beautiful* on the board, and explain that they are nearly the same. Tell children that noticing words that come from each other will help them figure out the meaning of words.

> **MODEL** I know that *beauty* has to do with being pretty or nice-looking. I can tell that *beauty* and *beautiful* are related or mean almost the same thing.

Guide children in a similar procedure to find the meaning of *protection* and *ripe*.

RETEACH lesson vocabulary. Have children listen to each of the following word groups and meaning clues. Tell them to hold up the word card that belongs with each group. Discuss how children made their choices.

1. beauty—full of beauty (*beautiful*)
2. nutritious—healthful (*nutrition*)
3. protect, protection—keeps safe (*protects*)
4. ripe—fully ready (*ripens*)
5. stream, streaming—flowing water (*streams*)

FLUENCY BUILDER Using *Intervention Practice Book* p. 47, read aloud each word in the first column and have children repeat it. Then have children work in pairs to read aloud to each other the words in the first column. Follow the same procedure with the words in each of the remaining columns. After partners have practiced reading aloud the words in each column separately, have them practice the entire list.

INTERVENTION PRACTICE BOOK
page 47

(Save *Intervention Practice Book* page 47 to use on pages 121 and 123.)

From Seed to Plant/A Day in the Life of a Seed

BEFORE

Reading "From Seed to Plant"
pages 314–331

USE SKILL CARD 12A

(Focus Skill) Read Diagrams

PRETEACH the skill. Point out to children that diagrams are pictures with labels that give information. Tell them that diagrams help give a clear picture of what a selection is about and help readers learn the right words to name the parts of something.

Have children look at **side A of Skill Card 2: Read Diagrams.** Read the definition of *diagrams*. Next, read the paragraph and then have children reread it with you.

Now call attention to the diagram and have volunteers take turns reading the labels aloud. Ask:

- **What would the diagram look like if the main idea of this paragraph was about building a house instead of planting a seed?** (*Possible response: The diagram would show parts of a house.*)

- **Why would a diagram be helpful to include in your writing?** (*Possible response: It would help the reader understand what you are writing about.*)

Prepare to Read: "From Seed to Plant"

Preview. Tell children that they are going to read a selection entitled "From Seed to Plant." Explain that this is an informational selection. Tell children that "From Seed to Plant" gives facts about how plants are grown. Then preview the selection.

JUST FOR YOU
pages 314–331

- **Pages 314–317:** I see the title of the selection, "From Seed to Plant," and I see many pictures of plants and flowers. I think this will tell how plants and flowers grow.

- **Pages 318–321:** I see different kinds of plants and flowers and there are words printed in the drawings. I think I will learn what different parts of the flowers and plants are called.

- **Pages 322–327:** On these pages, I notice different animals. They must have something to do with how things grow. I also see rain, and I think I will learn how things like animals and weather help plants and flowers grow.

- **Pages 328–331:** I see big plants and I see kids eating apples. Maybe I will learn how things like apples are grown.

Set Purpose. Model setting a purpose for reading "From Seed to Plant."

MODEL Judging from my preview, I think I will learn how plants and flowers are grown from seeds. I think I will learn new names for parts of plants. I will read the words and look at the diagrams to find out how a seed turns into a plant or flower.

Lesson 12 • Intervention Teacher's Guide

AFTER
Reading "From Seed to Plant"
pages 314–331

Reread and Summarize

Have children reread and summarize "From Seed to Plant" in sections, as described below.

Pages 314–317

Let's reread pages 314–317 to recall how plants begin and what some of the parts of flowers are called.

Summary: Seeds grow into the same kind of plant that made them. Most seeds begin as flowers. The parts of a flower are petal, stigma, stamen, pistil, ovules, sepal, and stem.

Pages 318–323

Let's reread pages 318–323 to remember what pollination is and how seeds are made and how they travel.

Summary: The wind and other things like birds and water help move pollen from one plant to another. If pollen from one kind of flower lands on the pistil of the same kind of flower, a new seed may begin. When new seeds ripen, they become new plants.

Pages 324–325

Let's reread pages 324–325 to recall how people can plant.

Summary: Seeds come in packets that have directions on them. The food that the plant needs to grow is already in the seed!

Pages 326–329

Let's reread pages 326–329 to remember how the plant grows and what it needs to be big and strong.

Summary: Plants need water and sunlight. Germination is the name for when the seed begins to grow. The root stays in the soil and the leaves grow up. The leaves make food for the plant. Buds open into flowers, where new seeds grow.

FLUENCY BUILDER Be sure children have copies of *Intervention Practice Book* p. 47. Call attention to the sentences on the bottom half of the page. The slashes break the sentences into phrases to allow you to work on natural phrasing. Tell children that their goal is to read each phrase or sentence smoothly. Model appropriate pace, expression, and phrasing as you read each sentence, and have children read it after you. Then have children practice by reading the sentences aloud three times to a partner.

INTERVENTION PRACTICE BOOK
page 47

BEFORE
Making Connections
pages 334–335

Directed Reading:
"A Day in the Life of a Seed," pp. 94–100

Select a volunteer to read aloud the title. Help children see that the selection will focus on what is happening to the seed of a flower. Tell them to look at the picture on pages 94–95 to find out what is happening in the sunflowers. Ask: **What is happening in the sunflowers?** (*Possible response: Seeds are forming in them.*) **DETAILS**

SOUNDS OF SUNSHINE
pages 94–101

Ask: **How would you label the picture of the flower to show the different parts, such as the seeds, pod, petals, and soil?** (*Accept reasonable responses.*) (Focus Skill) **READ DIAGRAMS**

Ask: **What happens when the pod splits?** (*Possible response: A sunflower seed pops out.*) **SEQUENCE**

Page 96

Have children read page 96 to find out what happens to the seed. Ask: **What happens to the seed?** (*Possible response: A mouse picks it up and drops it into a stream.*) **DETAILS**

Ask: **What do you think will happen to the seed now?** (*Accept reasonable responses.*) **MAKE PREDICTIONS**

Page 97

Have children read page 97 to find out what happens to the seed.
Ask: **What happens to the seed next?** (*Possible response: It floats down the stream and then gets stuck in the grass and thorns.*) **DETAILS**

Ask: **What will happen to the seed now?** (*Accept reasonable responses.*) **MAKE PREDICTIONS**

Reread page 97 aloud for children, modeling the Reread Aloud strategy to clarify words or ideas.

> **MODEL** When I reread part of a story, it helps me understand what is happening. Sometimes it helps me remember facts or it helps me understand a new word or idea. When I reread this page, I remember that the *seed is stuck in grass and thorns*, so I don't think that the *seed will travel in the stream* anymore. (Focus Strategy) **REREAD ALOUD**

Page 98

Have children read page 98. Ask: **What happens to the seed now?** (*Possible response: It falls into the soil when a rabbit pulls the grass out by the roots.*) **DETAILS**

Ask: **What do you think will happen next?** (*Accept reasonable responses.*) **MAKE PREDICTIONS**

Page 99

Have children read to find out the answer to the question. Ask: **What will happen now?** (*Possible response: The seed will sprout; roots will form; a stem and leaves will grow.*) **SUMMARIZE**

Lesson 12 • Intervention Teacher's Guide

Page 100

INTERVENTION PRACTICE BOOK page 49

Have children look at the picture on page 100. Ask: **What do you think the seed will grow into and what will happen after it does?** (*Accept reasonable responses.*) **MAKE PREDICTIONS**

Have children read the page to find out if they were right. **UNDERSTAND STORY EVENTS**

Summarize the selection. Ask children to think about the trip the seed in this story takes. Then have them summarize the story in a few sentences.

Page 101

Answers to *Think About It* Questions

1. A mouse drops it into a stream. It floats away and then gets stuck in the grass. It falls into the soil when a rabbit pulls the grass out by the roots. **DETAILS**
2. The seed will sprout, roots will form, and a stem and leaves will grow. **SUMMARIZE**
3. Accept all reasonable responses. **WRITE A STORY**

AFTER

Skill Review *pages 335I*

USE SKILL CARD 12B

(Focus Skill) Read Diagrams

RETEACH the skill. Have children look at **side B of Skill Card 12: Read Diagrams**. Read the skill reminder with them, and have a volunteer read the paragraph aloud.

Read the directions. Explain that children will work with partners to label the parts of the sports shoe. Tell them that once the picture has labels, it is called a diagram.

After children have labeled their drawings and added color and other details, have them display their diagrams. Point out that the selection "A Day in the Life of a Seed" has pictures that could be labeled to become diagrams. Ask volunteers to give some examples from the story illustrations.

Review Phonics Skill from "From Seed to Plant"

RETEACH Consonant Blends: *spr, str, thr.* Write the following sentence on the board: **Do you want to stroll or sprint through the park?** Read the sentence aloud, and ask children to identify the word with the /str/ sound. Then ask which letters make this sound. Have a volunteer underline these letters. Do the same for the /spr/ and /thr/ words.

FLUENCY BUILDER Be sure that children have copies of *Intervention Practice Book* page 47. Explain that today children will practice the sentences on the bottom half of the page by reading them aloud on tape. Assign partners. Have children take turns reading the sentences aloud to each other and then reading them on tape.

INTERVENTION PRACTICE BOOK page 47

From Seed to Plant/A Day in the Life of a Seed

BEFORE
Drafting an Informative Paragraph
page 337C

Writer's Craft: Informative Sentence

Build on prior knowledge. Tell children that they are going to talk about and write a sentence that informs or tells someone about something. Explain that it is important to stay focused on the topic. Provide the following example on the board:

> Sentence topic: A food plant's worst enemies
> Detail 1: Bugs hurt them.
> Detail 2: Animals nibble on them.
> Detail 3: Dry days make them droop.

Construct the text. "Share the pen" with children. Guide them in writing an informative sentence based on the topic and the list of details. For example:

A food plant's worst enemies are bugs, animals, and dry days.

Revisit the text. Reread the informative sentence. Ask: **If I included facts about another topic, such as the tallest trees or favorite pets, what would happen to my sentence?** (*It would not make sense.*)

- Have children discuss what they could write about in a paragraph that started with the sentence above.

On Your Own

Have children write possible topics for an informative sentence. Ask them to choose one topic and write a list of details about it. Then have children write an informative sentence that focuses on one topic.

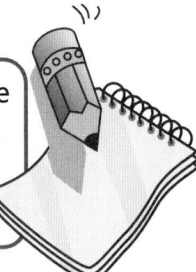

AFTER

Spelling Lesson
pages 33 II

Connect Spelling and Phonics

RETEACH **R-controlled vowel /ôr/*or, ore, our.*** Tell children to number their papers 1–8. Dictate the following words, and have children write them. After each word is written, write it on the board so children can proofread their work. They should draw a line through a misspelled word and write the correct spelling below it.

| 1. for* | 2. sport | 3. porch | 4. morning* |
| 5. forming* | 6. short* | 7. corn* | 8. fork |

* Word appears in "A Day in the Life of a Seed."

Dictate the following sentence and have children write it: *It began to pour some more on Gordon.*

Build and Read Longer Words

Remind children that they have learned how to decode words with /ôr/*or, ore, our.* Explain that now they will use what they have learned to help them read some longer words.

Write the word *forgot* on the board. Remind children that they can often figure out longer words by looking for shorter words in them. Cover *got* and have children read the word *for.* Then cover *for* and have a volunteer read *got.* Point out that *for* has the sound of /ôr/. Have children blend the word parts to read the longer word *forgot.* Follow a similar procedure to have children blend smaller words to read these longer words: *shortstop* and *corncob.*

INTERVENTION ASSESSMENT BOOK

FLUENCY BUILDER Have children choose a passage from "A Day in the Life of a Seed" to read aloud to a partner. You may have children choose passages that they found particularly interesting, or have them choose one of the following options:

- Read pages 96–97. (From *A mouse . . .* through *. . . and thorns.* Total: 46 words.)
- Read pages 99–100. (From *What will . . .* through *. . . sunflower garden.* Total: 72 words.)

SCALE
1 Not good
2 Pretty good
3 Good
4 Great!

Children should read the selected passage aloud to their partners three times. Have the reader rate each reading on a scale from 1 to 4.

From Seed to Plant/A Day in the Life of a Seed

BEFORE Weekly Assessments

Review Vocabulary

To revisit Vocabulary Words prior to the weekly assessment, use the following synonym pair format. Have volunteers take turns reading the given word. Ask them to identify the correct choice to create a synonym pair and then explain why the two belong together.

1. **beautiful**
   a. spicy
   b. pretty
2. **nutrition**
   a. food part
   b. weakness
3. **protects**
   a. burns
   b. keeps safe
4. **ripens**
   a. rolls
   b. matures
5. **streams**
   a. small rivers
   b. libraries

Correct responses: 1b, 2a, 3b, 4b, 5a

You may want to display the Vocabulary Words and definitions on page 119, and have children copy them to use when they study for the vocabulary test.

(Focus Skill) Review Read Diagrams

To review reading diagrams before the weekly assessment, distribute *Intervention Practice Book* p. 50. Have volunteers read aloud the first direction line and the sentences. Guide children to look closely at what words are used to label the picture and where they are printed.

INTERVENTION PRACTICE BOOK page 50

Review Test Prep

Ask children to turn to page 337 of the *Pupil Edition*. Call attention to the tips for answering the test questions. Tell children that paying attention to these tips can help them answer not only the test questions on this page but also other test questions like these.

JUST FOR YOU page 337

Have children follow along as you read each test question and the tip that goes with it. Discuss how each choice in question 1 asks about the words used to label the diagram. Tell them to look closely at the line connecting the word and the picture for a clue about what the diagram is showing. Then have them read each choice and ask themselves if it makes sense in the diagram. Remind them to look back at the diagram when they answer question 2.

INTERVENTION ASSESSMENT BOOK

Lesson 12 • Intervention Teacher's Guide

AFTER Self-Selected Reading

Weekly Assessments

Have children select their own books to read independently. They might choose books from the classroom library shelf, or you may wish to offer a group of appropriate books from which children can choose.

- *The Seed Surprise.* (See page 337O of the *Teacher's Edition* for a Lesson Plan.)
- *Mushroom in the Rain* by Mirra Ginsburg. Macmillan, 1974.
- *Wonderful Worms* by Linda Glaser. Millbrook, 1992.

After children have chosen their books, give each child a copy of My Reading Log, which can be found on page R35 in the back of the *Teacher's Edition*. Have children fill in the information at the top of the form. Then have them use the log to keep track of their reading and to record their responses to the literature.

Conduct student-teacher conferences. Arrange time for each child to confer with you individually about his or her self-selected reading. Have children bring their Reading Logs to share with you at the conference. Children might also like to share a favorite passage to read aloud to you. Ask questions designed to stimulate discussion about the book. For example, you might ask if there were any diagrams included in the selections, or if they learned enough information to draw a diagram of the focus topic.

FLUENCY PERFORMANCE Have children read aloud to you the passage from "A Day in the Life of a Seed" that they selected and practiced with their partners. Keep track of the number of words the child reads correctly. Ask the child to rate his or her own performance on the 1–4 scale. If children are not happy with their oral reading, give them an opportunity to continue practicing and then to reread the passage to you.

See *Oral Reading Fluency Assessment* **for monitoring progress.**

LESSON 13

BEFORE Building Background and Vocabulary

Use with

"The Secret Life of Trees"

Review Phonics: R-controlled Vowel /ûr/*ir, er, ur*

Identify the sound. Read aloud the following sentence: *Vern has a bird and a turtle.* Ask children to repeat the sentence three times, identifying the words that have the /ûr/ sound. (*Vern, bird, turtle*)

Associate letters to sound. Write the sentence *Vern has a bird and a turtle* on the board and read it aloud with children. Tell them that the letters *er*, *ir*, and *ur* often stand for the /ûr/ sound. Select a volunteer to circle the words that contain the /ûr/ sound.

Word blending. Model how to blend and read the word *shirt*. Print *shirt* on the board and slide your hand under the word as you elongate the sounds /shûrt/. Then say the word naturally—*shirt*. Follow a similar procedure for the words *turn, herd, surf,* and *firm*.

Apply the skill. *Vowel Substitution* Write the following words on the board, and have children read each aloud. Make the changes necessary to form the words in parentheses. Have volunteers read aloud each new word.

| **hard** (herd) | **cub** (curb) | **hut** (hurt) | **torn** (turn) | **park** (perk) |
| **far** (fur) | **skit** (skirt) | **star** (stir) | **dart** (dirt) | **bud** (bird) |

INTERVENTION PRACTICE BOOK page 52

Introduce Vocabulary

PRETEACH lesson vocabulary. Tell children that they are going to learn five new words that they will see again when they read a story called "The Secret Life of Trees." Teach each Vocabulary Word using the process shown in the box.

Use these suggestions or similar ideas to give the meaning or context.

discover	Relate to finding something that was lost or learning how to do something in school.
energy	This is a multiple-meaning word. Point to a light or something electrical and explain that it takes power, or energy, to make it work. Children may be more familiar with the energy they get from food or rest.
forecast	Relate to the weather and the predicting of what will happen.

> Write the word.
> Say the word.
> Track the word and have children repeat it.
> Give the meaning or context.

128 Lesson 13 • Intervention Teacher's Guide

shed   Relate to a dog, snake, or other animal that gets rid of its hair or skin.

source   Point out that water from the faucet comes from a river, lake, or ocean. Point out that fruit comes from trees. Explain that the *source* is where something comes from.

Vocabulary Words
discover find out; learn for the first time
energy the power to do things
forecast predict
shed throw off
source place from which something comes

For vocabulary activities, see Vocabulary Games on pages 2–7.

AFTER
Building Background and Vocabulary

Apply Vocabulary Strategies

RETEACH lesson vocabulary. Write the words *discover* and *find out* on chart paper and explain that these words are *synonyms*. Tell them that recognizing *synonyms* will help them remember the meanings of words.

MODEL I know that *synonyms* are words that mean almost the same thing. If I know that discover and find out are *synonyms*, then I will understand and remember what each word means.

Guide children in a similar procedure to understand the meaning of *forecast* and *shed*.

Vocabulary Activity. Have children listen to each of the following clues. Tell them to hold up the card that shows the correct match. Reread the clue aloud and say the correct answer. Have children verify their words and discuss how they made their choices.

1. When you learn something for the first time, you __(discover)__ something new.
2. Eating a good breakfast gives me __(energy)__ for the day.
3. The weather reports __(forecast)__ a storm for tomorrow.
4. Many dogs __(shed)__ their hair in the spring.
5. A tree is a __(source)__ of paper, wood, and food.

FLUENCY BUILDER Using *Intervention Practice Book* page 51, read aloud each word in the first column aloud and have children repeat it. Then have children work in pairs to read aloud to each other the words in the first column. Follow the same procedure with each of the remaining columns. After partners have practiced reading aloud the words in each column separately, have them practice the entire list.

Save *Intervention Practice Book* page 51 to use on pages 131 and 133.

INTERVENTION PRACTICE BOOK
page 51

The Secret Life of Trees/The Old Tree   **129**

BEFORE

Reading "The Secret Life of Trees"
pages 340–359

USE SKILL CARD 13A

⭐ Focus Skill: Fact and Fiction

PRETEACH the skill. Point out to children that a fact gives information about a real thing or event and that fiction tells a story that is meant to entertain. Explain that books with facts often have photographs, diagrams, and charts. Discuss how fiction tells stories that are made up.

Have children look at **side A of Skill Card 13: Fact and Fiction.** Read the definition of *fact* and *fiction*. Next read the paragraph and then have children reread it with you.

Now call attention to the chart and have volunteers take turns reading the information aloud. Ask:

- **Would this story be fact or fiction?** (*Possible response: Even though there are some facts, it would be fiction since it has things that are made up.*)

- **How will you be able to tell if what you are reading is fact or fiction?** (*Possible response: Look for photographs, diagrams, or charts and things that are true for factual selections. Look for things that are imaginary for fiction.*)

Prepare to Read: "The Secret Life of Trees"

Preview. Tell children that they are going to read a selection entitled "The Secret Life of Trees." Explain that this is a non-fiction selection that gives factual information about trees. Then preview the selection.

JUST FOR YOU
pages 340–359

- **Pages 340–341:** I see the title, "The Secret Life of Trees." I see photographs of trees. I think this story will be about real trees.

- **Pages 342–347:** I notice that there are different sections with photos and information on each page. I see headings that let me know what each section tells about. The information on these pages seems to tell about tree life.

- **Pages 348–350:** These pages show different kinds of trees. The heading on page 348, "Kinds of Trees," gives me a clue. I see photos of leaves and branches from different trees.

- **Pages 351–353:** I see trees from fall and winter. Maybe these pages will tell about what happens to trees in the different seasons.

- **Pages 354–359:** I see pictures of pinecones and coconuts. This selection will remind me of things that come from trees.

Set Purpose. Set a purpose for reading "The Secret Life of Trees."

MODEL From what I have seen in my preview, I think that I will probably learn facts about kinds of trees and tree life. I will read to find out what happens to trees and what things come from them.

Lesson 13 • Intervention Teacher's Guide

AFTER

"The Secret Life of Trees"
pages 340–359

Reread and Summarize

Have children reread and summarize sections of "The Secret Life of Trees" as described below.

> Pages 341–345
>
> **Let's reread pages 341–345 to recall facts about tree life, such as how old and how big trees get.**
>
> Summary: The tallest tree is over 360 feet high. Part of the tree is underground. These are the roots. Trees can live for hundreds, even thousands, of years. The oldest tree is 4,900 years old.
>
> Pages 346–347
>
> **Let's reread pages 346–347 to remember the different living things that make trees their home.**
>
> Summary: Animals live on and in trees. Birds build nests up high. Insects bury themselves in the bark.
>
> Pages 348–355
>
> **Let's reread pages 348–355 to recall some of the different types of trees.**
>
> Summary: The two main types of trees are broad-leaved and conifers.
>
> Pages 356–359
>
> **Let's reread pages 356–359 to recall different things that come from trees.**
>
> Summary: Many things, such as fruits and nuts come from trees. Trees are the source of wood and paper. Other things made from trees are tables, chairs, swings, and books.

FLUENCY BUILDER Be sure children have copies of *Intervention Practice Book* page 51, which you used for the previous Fluency Builder activity. Call attention to the sentences on the bottom half of the page. Tell children that their goal is to read each phrase or sentence smoothly. Model appropriate pace, expression and phrasing as you read each sentence, and have children read it after you. Then have children practice by reading the sentences aloud three times to a partner.

INTERVENTION PRACTICE BOOK

page 51

BEFORE
Making Connections
pages 362–363

Directed Reading: "The Old Tree"

Ask a volunteer to read aloud the title. Help children see that the selection tells about a tree and that it is nonfiction. Read pages 102–103 while children listen for factual clues.

SOUNDS OF SUNSHINE
pp. 102–108

Ask: **What is the main idea of these pages?** (*Possible response: They tell about a tall tree and some of the things that happen to it and that live on it.*) **SUMMARIZE**

Ask: **Do you think this selection is fact or fiction? Why?** (*Possible response: It is fact, because it tells true things about the tree, like what happens in the fall and spring, and what the tree is used for by animals.*) **FACT AND FICTION**

Pages 104–105

Ask: **What happens when the wind knocks a tree to the ground?** (*Possible response: Moss begins to grow on it, and ants and other bugs make it their home. Then animals come to eat the bugs.*)

Model using the Look at Word Bits and Parts strategy to decode the meaning of an unfamiliar word. Write the word *rotting* on the board, and underline *rot*.

MODEL When I see a new word, I look for clues about what it might mean. I look at *rotting* and see a word that I know: *rot*. I know that this means "to fall apart and die or to decay." Then I look at the *-ing*, and I know that *rotting* means "decaying." **LOOK AT WORD BITS AND PARTS**

Pages 106–107

Ask children to read pages 106–107 to find out why the old tree is important to other living things. Ask: **How is this old tree, which has fallen to the ground and lost its leaves, still important?** (*Possible response: It has given a home to plants, insects, and animals.*) **DRAW CONCLUSIONS**

Ask: **How do you know if this is fact or fiction?** (*Possible response: It is fact because it tells true things about the tree. It does not have make-believe things happening, such as animals or plants talking.*) **INTERPRET STORY EVENTS**

INTERVENTION PRACTICE BOOK
page 53

Summarize the selection. Ask children to think about how all living things are important. Then have them complete *Intervention Practice Book* page 53.

Lesson 13 • Intervention Teacher's Guide

Answers to *Think About It* Questions

1. The old tree has become a source of shelter for other living things. **DETAILS**
2. Possible response: It is good for forests to have some dead trees so plants and animals have a place to eat, work and live. **CRITICAL THINKING**
3. Accept reasonable responses. **TASK**

AFTER
Skill Review
pages 363I

USE SKILL CARD 13B

(Focus Skill) Review Fact and Fiction

RETEACH the skill. Have children look at **side B of Skill Card 13: Fact and Fiction**. Read the skill reminder with them, and select a volunteer to read the paragraph aloud.

Read aloud the directions. Explain that children will work with partners to complete the chart. Remind them to look for clues that tell if something could really happen or if it is pretend.

After children have completed their charts, have them share them with other partner groups. Tell them to compare the details that they recorded. Ask volunteers to give reasons why they labeled the paragraph *fact* or *fiction*.

Review Phonics Skill from "The Secret Life of Trees"

RETEACH Vowel Digraph: /$\overline{oo}$/*oo*. Say the /$\overline{oo}$/ sound. Remind children that the mouth should be round and open when making the sound /$\overline{oo}$/. Then say: *The roof of the igloo was smooth and cool.* Have children listen for the /$\overline{oo}$/ sound. Then read this list aloud and have children raise their hands when they hear the sound /$\overline{oo}$/: *zoo, loose, goose, corner, pool, shampoo, tooth.*

FLUENCY BUILDER Be sure children have copies of *Intervention Practice Book* page 51. Explain that today children will practice the sentences on the bottom half of the page by reading them aloud on tape. Assign new partners. Have children take turns reading the sentences aloud to each other and then reading them on tape.

INTERVENTION PRACTICE BOOK
page 51

The Secret Life of Trees/The Old Tree

BEFORE
Drafting a Research Report
page 365C

Research Report: Writing a Factual Paragraph

Build on prior knowledge. Tell children that they are going to write a paragraph that contains facts about one topic. Discuss with them examples of factual texts they have read, such as the two selections about trees. Guide them to see that the paragraph has one focus or main idea and that the facts give detailed information about the topic. Display and read aloud the following list:

> Topic: Birds' Nests
> Fact 1: Made from twigs and grass
> Fact 2: Built in trees
> Fact 3: Used to hatch eggs and care for their young

Construct the text. "Share the pen" with children. Guide them in writing a factual paragraph based on the topic *Birds' Nests* and the list of facts. For example:

> A bird's home is its nest. Birds build their nests from twigs and grass. They usually build their nests in trees. Birds hatch their eggs and make a home for their young in the nests.

Revisit the text. Read the paragraph aloud together. Ask: **If I did not have one topic, what would happen to the facts in my paragraph?** (*They would tell about different things.*)

- Guide children to be sure that all the sentences are about the same topic. Have them omit any sentences that stray from this topic.

On Your Own

Have children write a short factual paragraph about a topic that interests them. Urge them to include two or three important facts in their writing.

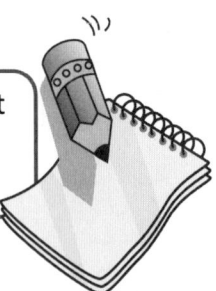

134 Lesson 13 • Intervention Teacher's Guide

AFTER
Spelling Lesson
page 359H

Connect Spelling and Phonics

RETEACH **R-controlled vowel: /ûr/ir, er, ur.** Tell children to number their papers 1–8. Dictate the following words, and have children write them. After each word is written, write it on the board so children can proofread their work. They should draw a line through a misspelled word and write the correct spelling below it.

| 1. dirt* | 2. turn* | 3. paper | 4. discover |
| 5. energy* | 6. chirp* | 7. hurls* | 8. bird* |

* Word appears in "The Old Tree."

Dictate the following sentence and have children write it: *Her cat will perch near the curtain to watch birds.*

Build and Read Longer Words

Remind children that they have learned how to decode words with /ûr/. Explain that now they will use what they have learned to help them read some longer words.

Write the word *perfect* on the board. Tell children that they can often figure out longer words by looking for word parts that they know. Cover *fect*, and have children read *per*. Follow a similar procedure to have them read *fect*. Model how to blend the word parts to read aloud the longer word *perfect*. Follow a similar procedure to have children blend the word parts to read these longer words: *stirring* and *sister*.

INTERVENTION ASSESSMENT BOOK

FLUENCY BUILDER Have children choose a passage from "The Old Tree" to read aloud to a partner. You may have children choose passages that they found particularly interesting, or have them choose one of the following options:

- Read pages 103–104. (From *The tree . . . through . . . around the log.* Total: 96 words.)
- Read pages 106–107. (From *A mother rabbit . . . through . . . living things.* Total: 115 words.)

Children should read the selected passage aloud to their partners three times. Have the partner rate each reading on a scale from 1 to 4.

SCALE
1 Not good
2 Pretty good
3 Good
4 Great!

The Secret Life of Trees/The Old Tree

BEFORE Weekly Assessments

Review Vocabulary

To revisit Vocabulary Words prior to the weekly assessment, use these sentence frames. Have volunteers take turns reading aloud the sentence stems and choices. Children identify the correct choice and explain why that choice makes sense in the sentence.

1. The word **discover** is in the same word family as
   a. *uncover* and *recover*.
   b. *hide* and *seek*.
2. People get **energy** from
   a. shoes.
   b. food.
3. The weather report may **forecast**
   a. a bad storm.
   b. a car accident.
4. **Shed** rhymes with
   a. *fed* and *Ted*.
   b. *cart* and *part*.
5. A good **source** of information about trees is
   a. a stream.
   b. a book.

Correct Responses: 1a, 2b, 3a, 4a, 5b

⭐ Focus Skill Fact and Fiction

To review fact and fiction before the weekly assessment, distribute *Intervention Practice Book* p. 54. Have volunteers read aloud the first direction line and the sentences. Guide children to remember that a fact tells about a real thing or event. Tell them to look for clues to decide if something is fiction, or made up.

Review Test Prep

Ask children to turn to page 365 of the *Pupil Edition*. Call attention to the tips for answering the test questions. Tell children that paying attention to these tips can help them answer not only the questions on this page but other test questions.

JUST FOR YOU page 365

Have children follow along as you read the directions, each test question, and the tip. Discuss the clues to what each book is about. Then discuss the kind of book each question is asking for: a book of facts or a book of fiction. Then make sure that children choose the book title that matches what they are looking for.

INTERVENTION PRACTICE BOOK page 54

INTERVENTION ASSESSMENT BOOK ✓

136 Lesson 13 • Intervention Teacher's Guide

AFTER Self-Selected Reading

Weekly Assessments

Have children select their own books to read independently. They might choose books from the classroom library shelf, or you may wish to offer a group of appropriate books from which children can choose.

- *The Giant of the Desert.* (See page 365O of the *Teacher's Edition* for an Independent Reading Plan.)
- *Spider Spider* by Kate Banks. Sunburst, 2000.
- *Owl Babies* by Martin Waddell. Candlewick, 1995.

Using "My Reading Log" After children have chosen their books, give each child a copy of My Reading Log, which can be found on page R35 in the back of the *Teacher's Edition*. Have children fill in the information at the top of the form. Then have them use the log to keep track of their reading and to record their responses to the literature.

Conduct Student-Teacher Conferences. Arrange time for each child to confer with you individually about his or her self-selected reading. Have children bring their Reading Logs to share with you at the conference. Children might also like to choose a favorite passage to read aloud to you. Ask questions designed to stimulate discussion about the book. For example, you might ask whether the selection is fiction or nonfiction, and what details in the story are fact or made-up.

FLUENCY PERFORMANCE Have children read aloud to you the passage from "The Old Tree" that they selected and practiced with their partners. Keep track of the number of words the child reads correctly. Ask the child to rate his or her own performance on the 1–4 scale. If children are not happy with their oral reading, give them an opportunity to continue practicing and then to reread the passage to you.

See Oral Reading Fluency Assessment for monitoring progress.

The Secret Life of Trees/The Old Tree

Lesson 14

BEFORE Building Background and Vocabulary

Use with

"Watermelon Day"

Introduce: /ou/ *ou, ow*

Identify the sound. Read aloud the following sentence *How did a brown sprout come out of the ground?* Ask children to repeat the sentence three times, identifying the words that have the /ou/ sound. (*How, brown, sprout, out, ground*)

Associate letters to sound. Write on the board the sentence *How did a brown sprout come out of the ground?* Invite a volunteer to underline the words that contain the letters *ou* or *ow*. Tell children that in these words, the letters *ou* and *ow* stand for the /ou/ sound.

Word blending. Model how to blend and read the word *shout*. Slide your hand under the word as you slowly elongate the sounds—/shout/. Then read the word naturally—*shout*. Follow a similar procedure for the words *round, clown, now*.

Apply the skill. *Vowel Substitution* Write the following words on the board, and have children read each aloud. Make the changes necessary to form the words in parentheses. Have volunteers read aloud each new word.

we (wow)	**led** (loud)	**den** (down)	**moth** (mouth)	**clan** (clown)
car (cow)	**put** (pout)	**pond** (pound)	**sand** (sound)	**fund** (found)

INTERVENTION PRACTICE BOOK
page 56

Introduce Vocabulary

PRETEACH lesson vocabulary. Tell children that they are going to learn six words that they will see again when they read the story "Watermelon Day." Teach each Vocabulary Word using the following process.

Use the following suggestions or similar ideas to give the meaning or context.

> Write the word.
> Say the word.
> Track the word and have children repeat it.
> Give the meaning or context.

beneath — Use two books and place one on top of the other. Point to the bottom one and say that it is *beneath* the other one.

knelt — Have a volunteer demonstrate by bending down on one knee. Explain that *knelt* is the past tense of *kneel*.

relay race — If possible, arrange a short relay race between teams of children on the playground or in the gym.

shimmered — Use a shiny object, such as a shiny stone. Hold it up to the sunlight under an electric light and show how it shines and reflects the light.

snug	Wrap a coat or a blanket around yourself and explain that you are cozy, or *snug*, inside it.
wrinkled	Crumple a piece of paper, open it, and point to the folds.

For vocabulary activities, see Vocabulary Games on pages 2–7.

Vocabulary Words
beneath under
knelt got down on knees
relay race running contest in which team members take turns running
shimmered shone
snug tight or cozy
wrinkled had many small folds

AFTER
Building Background and Vocabulary

Apply Vocabulary Strategies

Use context. Explain that many times, we can figure out the meaning of a word from the words around it. Write the following sentence on the board and read it aloud. *I knelt down to look under the bed for my shoe.* Point to the word *knelt* and model how context can help figure out its meaning.

MODEL If I didn't know the word *knelt*, I could think about what I do to look under a bed. I bend or kneel; the word must be *knelt*.

RETEACH lesson vocabulary. Tell children that there will be a word missing in each of the following sentences. Tell them to figure out the missing Vocabulary Word.

1. The carpet _____ my bare feet felt soft. (beneath)
2. Sally felt _____ in the warm blanket. (snug)
3. Our class won the _____! (relay race)
4. Mr. Martinez _____ down to weed the garden. (knelt)
5. The sun _____ on the water. (shimmered)
6. I had to iron my shirt because it was _____. (wrinkled)

FLUENCY BUILDER Using *Intervention Practice Book* page 55, read each word in the first column aloud and have children repeat it. Then have children read the words in the first column aloud to a partner. Follow the same procedure with each of the remaining columns. Have partners practice reading the entire list.

INTERVENTION PRACTICE BOOK
page 55

(Save *Intervention Practice Book* page 55 to use on pages 141 and 143.)

Watermelon Day/Mr. Carver's Carrots

BEFORE
Reading
"Watermelon Day"
pages 368–389

USE SKILL CARD 14A

Make Inferences

PRETEACH the skill. Tell children that we often use something we know to understand things as we read.

Have children look at **side A of Skill Card 14: Make Inferences**. Read the definition of an inference. Next, read the paragraph, and have children read it with you.

Call attention to the chart and select volunteers to take turns reading the clues aloud. Ask:

- **How do you know that Jimmy is feeling sick?** (*Possible response: He is in bed shivering and sneezing.*)

- **What if the author did not give us detailed information about how Jimmy is feeling today?** (*Possible response: We might not know how sick Jimmy feels.*)

Prepare to Read: "Watermelon Day"

Preview. Tell children that they are going to read a story called "Watermelon Day." Explain that it is a piece of realistic fiction; it is about characters that are like people in real life. Then preview the selection.

JUST FOR YOU
pages 368–388

- **Pages 368–373:** The story is called "Watermelon Day." It is about a girl named Jesse. The man in the hat is her father. On page 372, it looks like the people are having a party. There is a big slice of watermelon in the picture.

- **Pages 374–379:** I see pictures of the girl, Jesse, taking care of a watermelon plant. It seems to keep growing until her dad cuts the watermelon from the vine.

Set purpose. Model setting a purpose for reading "Watermelon Day."

MODEL From what I have seen in my preview, I think that the story will tell how Jesse grows a watermelon. I will read to find out who the other people are and if they had a party. I also want to know if Jesse gets a prize for her watermelon.

Lesson 14 • Intervention Teacher's Guide

AFTER Reading "Watermelon Day" pages 368–388

Reread and Summarize

Have children reread and summarize "Watermelon Day" in sections, as described below.

Pages 368–371

Let's reread these pages to recall the characters and why there is a watermelon in the story.

Summary: The girl is named Jesse, and Pappy is her dad. Jesse found a watermelon that will be grown for a Watermelon Day.

Pages 372–377

Let's reread pages 372–377 to remember what a Watermelon Day is and what Jesse does for Watermelon Day.

Summary: A Watermelon Day is a big party with lots of food and games. Jesse wants her watermelon to be picked, but it has to grow bigger first. She takes care of it all summer.

Pages 378–383

Let's recall what happened when the Watermelon Day finally came.

Summary: The relatives were coming. Pappy cut the watermelon free from the vine. It had to float in icy water all day to be cold enough to eat. Jesse was very excited and had a hard time waiting.

Pages 384–387

Let's reread pages 384–387 to recall what happened when the watermelon was ready to be opened.

Summary: Pappy hit the melon and split it open. It was juicy, cold, and sweet. Jesse was so happy to be eating her cold watermelon, she sang and danced.

FLUENCY BUILDER Be sure children have copies of *Intervention Practice Book* page 55, which you used for the previous Fluency Builder activity. Call attention to the sentences at the bottom of the page. The slashes break the sentences into phrases to allow you to work on natural phrasing. Tell children that their goal is to read each phrase or sentence smoothly. Model appropriate pace, expression, and phrasing as you read each sentence. Have children read it after you. Then have children read the sentences aloud to a partner three times.

INTERVENTION PRACTICE BOOK
page 55

Watermelon Day/Mr. Carver's Carrots

BEFORE
Making Connections
pages 390–391

Directed Reading: "Mr. Carver's Carrots," pp. 110–115

SOUNDS OF SUNSHINE
pp. 110–115

Page 110

Ask a volunteer to read aloud the title. Point out Mr. Carver and Ben in the illustration. Read page 110 aloud, having children listen for clues to help them make predictions about what Mr. Carver and Ben might do. Say: **Think about what you know. The characters are hot. Mr. Carver is hungry for carrots, and Ben wants to plant carrots. What will they do?** MAKE PREDICTIONS

Page 111

Have children read page 111 to find out what Mr. Carver and Ben do. Ask them if their predictions were correct. Model sequencing events and summarizing.

MODEL When I am reading a story, I keep in mind the order in which things happen. Keeping story events in order helps me make inferences and predictions about the rest of the story.

Ask: **What has happened so far?** (*Possible response: Mr. Carver wanted carrots and decided to plant some. They work together to plant seeds.*)
SEQUENCE/SUMMARIZE

Pages 112–114

Have children read pages 112–114 to find out what the characters do to care for their carrots. Ask: **What do Ben and Mr. Carver do to take care of their carrots?** SEQUENCE/SUMMARIZE

Ask: **Were Mr. Carver and Ben anxious to eat the carrots? How do you know?** (*Possible response: Yes, they had been waiting for the day the carrots were ready to eat. They crunched and munched them happily.*)
MAKE INFERENCES

Page 115

Have children read page 115 to find out how the end of the story is like the beginning. Ask: **What is Mr. Carver hungry for now?** (*Possible response: watermelon*) DETAILS

INTERVENTION PRACTICE BOOK
page 57

Ask: **How are the end and the beginning of the story alike?** (*Possible response: Mr. Carver is hungry at the beginning and end. Ben asks what they are waiting for.*) COMPARE AND CONTRAST

Summarize the selection. Ask children to think about what happened at the beginning, in the middle, and at the end of "Mr. Carver's Carrots." Help them summarize the story in two or three sentences.

Page 116

Answers to *Think About It* Questions

1. They dig up the ground and put carrot seeds in the soil. Then they water the plants and wait for them to grow. **SEQUENCE/SUMMARIZE**
2. They water them during a heat wave. **INTERPRET STORY DETAILS**
3. Accept reasonable responses. **TASK**

AFTER
Skill Review
page 391I

USE SKILL CARD 14B

(Focus Skill) Make Inferences

RETEACH **the skill.** Have children look at **side B of Skill Card 14: Make Inferences**. Read the skill reminder with them, and have a volunteer read the paragraph aloud.

Read aloud the directions. Have children work with partners to create their own charts. Remind them to use what they know to help them make an inference.

After children have completed their charts, have them share their charts with other children and compare the inference they made and supporting details.

Review Phonics Skill from "Watermelon Day"

RETEACH **consonant digraphs /n/ gn, kn; /r/ wr.** Write the following word pairs on the board or on chart paper. Have volunteers read both words aloud. Talk about the differences in meaning between the words in each pair.

ring/wring	**gnaw/naw**	**knew/new**
knight/night	**knot/not**	**wrap/rap**

Discuss the silent first letter in some of the words.

FLUENCY BUILDER Be sure that children have copies of *Intervention Practice Book* page 55. Explain that today children will read the sentences at the bottom of the page on tape. Assign new partners. Have children take turns reading the sentences aloud to each other and recording them on tape.

INTERVENTION PRACTICE BOOK
page 55

Watermelon Day/Mr. Carver's Carrots **143**

BEFORE
Drafting a Paragraph of Explanation
page 391A

Writing Process: Paragraph of Explanation

Build on prior knowledge. Tell children that you are going to work together to write sentences that explain something. Remind them that an explanation tells **why** or **how** something happens. Display and read aloud the following outline:

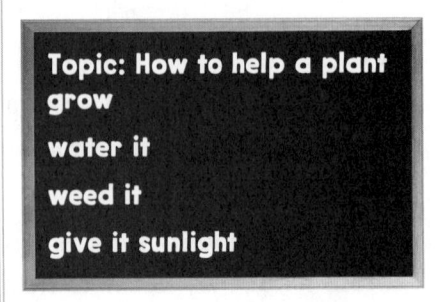

> Topic: How to help a plant grow
> water it
> weed it
> give it sunlight

Construct the text. "Share the pen" with children. Use the following steps to guide children through the process.

- Begin by writing one or two sentences about things to do to take care of a plant.

- As they contribute ideas, encourage children to include reasons why it is important to do these things. For example, *Keep the plant where it will get enough light. Water it when it gets dry. Otherwise, the plant will not grow.*

Revisit the text. Go back and read the sentences. Ask: **Does our writing tell why and how to care for a plant?**

- Ask: **How did the outline help you?**

On Your Own

Have children write a list of things that they feel they can explain. Ask them to outline the details that help tell why or how. Then have children write an opening sentence.

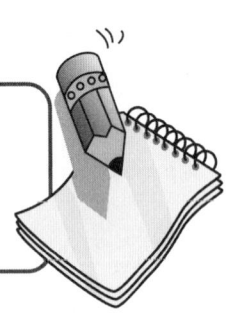

Lesson 14 • Intervention Teacher's Guide

AFTER
Spelling
page 389I

Connect Spelling and Phonics

RETEACH /ou/ou, ow. Have children number their papers 1–8. Explain that you will say words that have the /ou/ sound, and that children will write the words. Dictate the following words for children to write. After each word, write it on the board so children can proofread their work. They should draw a line through a misspelled word and write the correct spelling above or beside it.

| 1. loud | 2. shout | 3. sounds* | 4. cower |
| 5. ground* | 6. sprouts* | 7. proud | 8. power |

* Word appears in "Mr. Carver's Carrots."

Then dictate the following sentence for children to write. *The brown cow went down to town.*

Build and Read Longer Words

Tell children that they will use what they have learned about *ou* and *ow* to read longer words.

Write the word *shouting* on the board. Remind children that they can often figure out longer words by looking for word parts that they know. Cover the *-ing* ending and have children read *shout*. Then have them read the ending *-ing*. Model how to blend the parts to read aloud the whole word—*shouting*. Follow a similar procedure to have children read these words: *plowing, frowning, downtown, underground, cloudy*.

INTERVENTION ASSESSMENT BOOK

FLUENCY BUILDER Have children choose a passage from "Mr. Carver's Carrots" to read aloud to a partner. You may have children choose passages that they found particularly interesting, or have them choose one of the following options:

- Read pages 110–111. (From *The summer day . . .* through *. . . the dark soil.* Total: 86 words.)

- Read pages 112–113. (From *One day a storm . . .* through *. . . lugged them around the garden.* Total: 84 words.)

Children should read the selected passage aloud to a partner three times. Have children rate each reading on a scale from 1 to 4.

BEFORE Weekly Assessments

Review Vocabulary

To revisit the Vocabulary Words prior to the weekly assessment, use these sentence beginnings. Read aloud each sentence beginning and answer choices. Have children identify the correct choice and explain why that choice makes sense.

1. If something is **beneath** something else, it is
   a. under it.
   b. driving it.
2. If he **knelt** to pick up a penny, his knee
   a. felt itchy.
   b. touched the ground.
3. At the end of the **relay race**, you will find
   a. the store.
   b. the finish line.
4. The moonlight **shimmered** on the water and
   a. looked bright.
   b. made everything dark.
5. If you are **snug** in bed, you are probably
   a. under the covers.
   b. reading a book.
6. A **wrinkled** shirt needs
   a. a stove.
   b. an iron.

Correct responses: 1a, 2b, 3b, 4a, 5a, 6b

You may want to display the Vocabulary Words and definitions on page 139 and have children copy them to study for the vocabulary test.

(Focus Skill) Review Make Inferences

INTERVENTION PRACTICE BOOK page 58

To review making inferences before the weekly assessment, distribute *Intervention Practice Book* page 58. Have volunteers read aloud the first direction line and the sentences. To help children make a reasonable inference, guide them to notice details and think about what is happening.

Review Test Prep

INTERVENTION ASSESSMENT BOOK ✓

Ask children to turn to page 393 of the *Pupil Edition*. Call attention to the tips for answering the test questions. Tell children that paying attention to these tips can help them answer the test questions on this page as well as other questions like them.

JUST FOR YOU page 393

Have children follow along as you read each test question and the tip that goes with it. Discuss how the tips are helpful. Have children complete the test questions. Encourage discussion about using the tips and how children chose the correct answer.

AFTER Weekly Assessments

Self-Selected Reading

Have children select their own books to read independently. They might choose books from the classroom library shelf, or you may wish to offer a group of appropriate books from which children can choose.

- *Picnic in the Park.* (See page 393M of the *Teacher's Edition* for an Independent Reading Plan.)
- *Farmer Duck* by Martin Waddell. Candlewick, 1996.
- *Mean Soup* by Betsy Everitt. Harcourt, 1992.

After children have chosen their books, give each child a copy of My Reading Log, which can be found on page R35 in the back of the *Teacher's Edition*. Have children fill in the information at the top of the form. Then have them use the log to keep track of their reading and to record their responses to the literature.

Conduct student-teacher conferences. Arrange time for each child to conference with you individually about his or her self-selected reading. Have children bring their Reading Logs to share with you at the conference. Children might also choose a favorite passage to read aloud to you. Ask questions about the book to stimulate discussion. For example, you might ask if the child made inferences while reading the story, and what information helped him or her make the inferences.

FLUENCY PERFORMANCE Have children read aloud to you the passage from "Mr. Carver's Carrots" that they selected and practiced with their partners. Keep track of the number of words each child reads correctly. Ask the child to rate his or her own performance on the 1–4 scale. If children are not happy with their oral reading, give them an opportunity to practice more and then to read the passage to you again.

See *Oral Reading Fluency Assessment* for monitoring progress.

LESSON 15

BEFORE
Building Background and Vocabulary

Use with

"Pumpkin Fiesta"

Review Phonics: Long Vowel /ā/ *a-e*

Identify the sound. Read aloud the following sentence: *Dave can bake a cake for Pat.* Ask children to repeat the sentence three times, identifying the words that have the /ā/ sound. (*Dave, bake, cake*)

Associate letters to sound. Write the sentence *Dave can bake a cake for Pat* on the board, and have a volunteer underline the words that contain the CVCe pattern *a-e*. Tell children that in these words the vowel sound is /ā/, and the *e* is silent.

Word blending. Model how to blend and read the word *plane*. Write the word *plane* on the board. Slide your hand under the word as you elongate the sounds /ppllāānn/. Then say the word naturally—*plane*. Follow a similar procedure for the words *gate, cape,* and *name*.

INTERVENTION PRACTICE BOOK page 60

Apply the skill. *Vowel Addition* Write the following words on the board and have children read each aloud. Make the changes necessary to form the words in parentheses. Have volunteers read aloud each new word.

can (cane)   **cap** (cape)   **plan** (plane)   **Jan** (Jane)   **Sam** (same)
mad (made)   **mat** (mate)   **hat** (hate)   **man** (mane)   **pan** (pane)

Introduce Vocabulary

PRETEACH **lesson vocabulary.** Tell children that they are going to learn five new words that they will see again when they read a story called "Pumpkin Fiesta." Teach each Vocabulary Word using the process shown in the box.

Use these suggestions or similar ideas to give the meaning or context.

boasted	Relate to bragging about how good you are at a sport or other activity.
crept	Demonstrate by moving slowly around the room in a very quiet way.
crown	Draw and describe what a king or queen wears on his or her head as a sign of royalty.
village	Relate to a group of homes similar to a neighborhood.
vines	Point out the stems of a plant; explain that vines are long stems that hang down or grow along the ground.

> Write the word.
> Say the word.
> Track the word and have children repeat it.
> Give the meaning or context.

AFTER

Building Background and Vocabulary

For vocabulary activities, see Vocabulary Games on pages 2–7.

Apply Vocabulary Strategies

RETEACH lesson vocabulary. Write the words *boasted* and *bragged* on chart paper and explain that these words are synonyms. Tell children that recognizing synonyms will help them figure out the meanings of words.

MODEL I know that synonyms are words that mean almost the same thing. If I know that *boasted* and *bragged* are synonyms, it will help me remember what each word means. Guide children in a similar procedure to help them understand the meaning of the word *crept*. Relate it to *sneaked* and *prowled*.

Vocabulary Words
- **boasted** bragged
- **crept** moved slowly
- **crown** a pretty head covering, often with points
- **village** a group of houses that is not as large as a town
- **vines** plants with long stems that need to be held up

Vocabulary Activity Have children listen to each of the following sentences. Tell them to hold up the word card that completes each rhyme. Reread the sentence aloud with the correct word choice. Then discuss how the meaning of the Vocabulary Word fits the sentence.

1. Do not frown if you wear the __(crown)__.
2. "I eat only bread that is toasted," the silly child __(boasted)__.
3. The water is in bottles so there's no spillage in the __(village)__.
4. They look like lines, so I know they are __(vines)__.
5. Out the door the cat stepped and away it __(crept)__.

FLUENCY BUILDER Use *Intervention Practice Book* p. 59. Read aloud each word in the first column and have children repeat it. Then have children work in pairs to read the words in the first column aloud to each other. Follow the same procedure with each of the remaining columns. After partners have practiced reading aloud the words in each column separately, have them practice the entire list.

INTERVENTION PRACTICE BOOK
page 59

Save *Intervention Practice Book* p. 59 to use on pages 151 and 153.

BEFORE
Reading "Pumpkin Fiesta"
pages 396–419

USE SKILL CARD 15A

Focus Skill: Predict Outcomes

PRETEACH the skill. Point out to children that readers use what they learn at the beginning of a story to predict what will happen later on. Explain that it is important to pay attention to clues in the story because it will help them make predictions.

Have children look at **side A of Skill Card 15: Predict Outcomes**. Read the description of *predicting*. Then read the paragraph with children. Now call attention to the web and have volunteers take turns reading the prediction and clues aloud. Ask:

- **What would happen if you did not have the information that last year's winner practiced for an hour every morning before school?** (*Possible response: You would not know why it is a clue that she set her clock for 6:00 A.M.*)

- **Do you think Melba will win the contest? Why?** (*Possible response: Yes. She has the will to win and is doing everything she can to make it happen.*)

Prepare to Read: "Pumpkin Fiesta"

Preview. Tell children that they are going to read a selection entitled "Pumpkin Fiesta." Explain that "Pumpkin Fiesta" is a story. Tell them that a story has characters, a setting, and a plot. Then preview the selection.

JUST FOR YOU
pages 396–419

- **Pages 396–397:** I see the title, "Pumpkin Fiesta," and the author's name. I see a woman and a man with a pumpkin. I know that fiesta means "party" or "celebration" in Spanish. I think the story will be about a pumpkin party.

- **Pages 398–408:** It looks like the woman is caring for plants on vines. Maybe they are pumpkins. Then I see a new character. He is a funny little man with a pointy chin. He has a sneaky smile on his face. Maybe he is not friendly.

- **Pages 409–413:** The little man is by the plants now. Maybe he is tending the woman's plants. Then I see pictures that show that the plants are pumpkins, and that they are getting bigger.

Continue the picture walk to preview pages 414–418.

Set purpose. Model setting a purpose for reading "Pumpkin Fiesta."

MODEL Judging from my preview, I think that I will probably find out if the little man helps the woman care for the pumpkins. I will also discover why pumpkins are important and if they have something to do with the party.

150 Lesson 15 • Intervention Teacher's Guide

AFTER

Reading "Pumpkin Fiesta" pages 396–419

Reread and Summarize

Have children reread and summarize "Pumpkin Fiesta" in sections, as described below.

Pages 398–402

Let's reread pages 398–402 to recall what Old Juana does with pumpkins and who the man might be.

Summary: Old Juana usually wins the contest for growing the best pumpkins. The man's name is Foolish Fernando. He wants to win the pumpkin contest, too.

Pages 403–412

Let's reread pages 403–412 to remember what Old Juana and Foolish Fernando do to get ready for the contest.

Summary: Old Juana watered and talked kindly to her pumpkins. Foolish Fernando spied on her and tried to copy what she did. When Foolish Fernando's pumpkins are not growing well, he sneaks to the hill and steals Old Juana's.

Pages 413–419

Let's reread pages 413–419 to recall what happens at the fiesta.

Summary: Old Juana is heartbroken when she sees that her pumpkins are missing, but she still goes to the fiesta. At the fiesta, the mayor announces the winning pumpkins, and Old Juana sees that they are hers. She is crowned the winner and promises to teach Foolish Fernando how to grow beautiful pumpkins.

FLUENCY BUILDER Be sure children have copies of *Intervention Practice Book* p. 59, which you used for the previous Fluency Builder activity. Call attention to the sentences on the bottom half of the page. The slashes break the sentences into phrases to allow you to work on natural phrasing. Tell children that their goal is to read each phrase or sentence smoothly. Model appropriate pace, expression and phrasing as you read each sentence, and have children read it after you. Then have children practice by reading the sentences aloud to a partner three times.

INTERVENTION PRACTICE BOOK
page 59

Pumpkin Fiesta/Miss Owl's Secret **151**

BEFORE

Making Connections
pages 422–423

Pages 118–119

Page 120

Pages 121–122

Pages 123–124

INTERVENTION PRACTICE BOOK
page 61

Directed Reading: "Miss Owl's Secret," pp. 118–124

Ask a volunteer to read aloud the title. Help children to see that the characters are animals. Read pages 118–119 while children listen to find out who Miss Owl is, and what her secret might be. Ask: **Who are the animals in the garden? Where is Miss Owl?** (Possible response: They are Miss Owl's friends. Miss Owl is old and might be resting. She isn't able to care for her garden like she used to when she was younger.) **SUMMARIZE**

SOUNDS OF SUNSHINE
pp. 118–124

Have children read page 120 to look for clues about what the animals might do to help Miss Owl. Ask: **How do the animals feel about Miss Owl? What might they do to help her?** (Possible responses: The animals care for her. They want her garden to look nice. They have tools. They might clean her garden for her.) **PREDICT OUTCOMES**

Read aloud pages 121–122 to children. Model using the Self-Correct strategy to check your pronunciation and understanding of certain words. Write the word *puttering* on the board.

> **MODEL** When I read some of the words on these pages, I am not sure if I am pronouncing them correctly. One way to make sense of words is to go back and reread words again, sounding them out slowly. Then look at their meaning to see if they make sense. I look at the word *puttering* and think about the sounds the letters make. I sound it out more than once and check meaning clues. Going back to correct words I might have read incorrectly helps me to understand what is happening and make predictions. **SELF-CORRECT**

Have children read pages 123–124 to see how the animals helped and what Miss Owl does when she finds out. Ask: **What does Miss Owl do when she sees how nice and clean her garden is?** (Possible responses: She had watched them clean and was thankful that they helped her. She rewarded them with a watermelon treat.) **INTERPRET STORY EVENTS**

Summarize the selection. Ask children to think about why and how the animals helped Miss Owl and how she felt about it.

Lesson 15 • Intervention Teacher's Guide

Answers to *Think About It* Questions

1. They clean her garden at night. She is an owl and is awake at night and watches them from her tree. **SUMMARIZE**
2. They know she is old and it's hard for her to care for her garden. They must care about her, or they wouldn't want to help her. **DRAW CONCLUSIONS**
3. Accept reasonable responses. **TASK**

AFTER
Skill Review page 425C

USE SKILL CARD 15B

(Focus Skill) Review Predict Outcomes

RETEACH the skill. Have children look at **side B of Skill Card 15: Predict Outcomes**. Read the skill reminder with them, and have a volunteer read the paragraph aloud.

Read aloud the set of directions. Explain that children will work with partners to create their own webs. Remind them to use clues they read to predict the outcome.

After children have completed their webs, have them display them and explain their predicted outcome and the clues they found to help them. Point out that "Miss Owl's Secret" has clues that help them predict what the animals did. Ask volunteers to identify the clues.

Review Phonics Skill from "Pumpkin Fiesta"

RETEACH Inflections: *-s, -es, -ies*. Write the words *vines*, *boxes*, *babies*, and *pumpkins* on the board and read them with children. Ask if each word is singular or plural. Then have children circle the letters that make the word plural.

FLUENCY BUILDER Be sure that children have copies of *Intervention Practice Book* page 59. Explain that today children will practice the sentences on the bottom half of the page by reading them aloud on tape. Assign new partners. Have children take turns reading the sentences aloud to each other and then reading them on tape.

INTERVENTION PRACTICE BOOK page 59

Pumpkin Fiesta/Miss Owl's Secret

BEFORE
Drafting a Book Report
page 394M

Book Report: Identify Story Elements

Build on prior knowledge. Tell children that they are going to prepare notes that will help them write a book report. Explain that a book report tells someone about a book. Remind children of the important parts of a story: character, plot, setting. Explain that these details should be found in the story and written down to include later in the book report.

Construct the text. "Share the pen" with children. Guide them in making notes of what they remember from the story "Watermelon Day" to help them later when they write their book report. Use the following story and notes as an example:

- Mary had a big dog. They were walking down a busy street near the park. A big white truck was coming toward them. The dog ran away from Mary. She was sad.

> Things I remember from story:
>   dog
> Mary—sad
> busy street near the park
> white truck
> Dog runs away.

Revisit the text. Go back and read the notes together. Ask: **What would happen if I forgot to make notes about the characters, where the story happened, or something about what happened?** (*You need to include things about the character, setting, and plot in a book report and you might forget to include an important part.*)

- Guide children to combine details and organize them by placing what they remember about the characters together, the plot together, and the setting together. For example: Characters: Mary and her dog; Setting: a busy street by the park; Plot: A white truck was coming, and Mary's dog ran away.

On Your Own

Have children write notes about a story they have read. Ask them to make notes about the characters, setting, and plot.

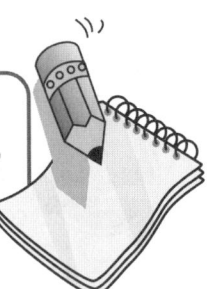

154 Lesson 15 • Intervention Teacher's Guide

AFTER
Spelling Lesson
page 42 II

Connect Spelling and Phonics

RETEACH **Long Vowel /ā/a-e.** Remind children that the /ā/ sound can be spelled with an *a* and an *e*. Tell children to number their papers 1–8. Dictate the following words, and have children write them. After each word is written, write it on the board so children can proofread their work. They should draw a line through a misspelled word and write the correct spelling below it.

| 1. shame* | 2. ate* | 3. hate | 4. cane |
| 5. cape | 6. rake* | 7. came* | 8. same |

* Word appears in "Miss Owl's Secret."

Dictate the following sentence and have children write it: *Molly came in from the sun with her rake.*

Build and Read Longer Words

Remind children that they have learned how to decode words with the vowel sound /ā/. Explain that now they will use what they have learned to help them read some longer words.

Write the word *pancake* on the board. Remind children that they can often figure out longer words by looking for smaller words in them. Cover the word *cake*, and have children read *pan*. Then cover *pan* and have them read *cake*. Model how to blend the two smaller words to read aloud the longer word *pancake*. Follow a similar procedure to have children blend smaller words to read these longer words: *handshake, baseball, nickname*.

INTERVENTION ASSESSMENT BOOK

FLUENCY BUILDER Have children choose a passage from "Miss Owl's Secret" to read aloud to a partner. You may have children choose passages that they found particularly interesting, or have them choose one of the following options:

- Read pages 119–120. (From *The leaves were small . . .* through *. . . the sun came up.* Total: 119 words.)
- Read pages 123–124. (From *You will win . . .* through *. . . She was SO right!* Total: 112 words.)

Children should read the selected passage aloud to their partners three times. Have the reader rate each reading on a scale from 1 to 4.

Pumpkin Fiesta/Miss Owl's Secret

BEFORE Weekly Assessments

Review Vocabulary

To revisit Vocabulary Words prior to the weekly assessment, use these sentence frames. Have volunteers take turns reading aloud the sentence clues and choices. Tell children to identify the correct choice and explain how they made their decision.

1. If you **boasted** about winning a contest, you
   a. bragged about it.　　b. sang a song.
2. If your cat **crept** into your room, you might not have
   a. heard it enter.　　b. eaten dinner yet.
3. A **crown** is worn by
   a. a long tailed-fox.　　b. a special person.
4. Living in a **village** is like living in
   a. a small town.　　b. school.
5. **Vines** are what
   a. pumpkins eat.　　b. watermelons grow on.

Correct responses: 1a, 2a, 3b, 4a, 5b.

You may want to display the Vocabulary Words and definitions on page 149 and have children copy them to use when they study for the vocabulary test.

(Focus Skill) Review Predict Outcomes

To review predicting outcomes before the weekly assessment, distribute *Intervention Practice Book* p. 62. Have volunteers read aloud the first direction line and the sentences. Guide children to look for clues to help them predict what will happen.

INTERVENTION PRACTICE BOOK page 62

Review Test Prep

Ask children to turn to page 425 of the *Pupil Edition*. Call attention to the tips for answering the test questions. Tell children that paying attention to these tips can help them answer not only the test questions on this page but also other test questions like these.

JUST FOR YOU page 425

Have children follow along as you read each test question and the tip that goes with it. Explain that clues are usually given to help you figure out what will happen. Remind children to look back at the text for clues to see if a choice makes sense.

INTERVENTION ASSESSMENT BOOK

AFTER Weekly Assessments

Self-Selected Reading

Have children select their own books to read independently. They might choose books from the classroom library shelf, or you may wish to offer a group of appropriate books from which children can choose.

- *Apple Picking Time* by Judy Nayer. (See page 425S of the *Teacher's Edition* for an Independent Reading Plan.)
- *Seven Little Rabbits* by John Becker. Scholastic, 1984.
- *Small Pig* by Arnold Lobel. HarperCollins, 1988.

After children have chosen their books, give each child a copy of My Reading Log, which can be found on page R35 in the back of the *Teacher's Edition*. Have children fill in the information at the top of the form. Then have them use the log to keep track of their reading and to record their responses to the literature.

Conduct student-teacher conferences. Arrange time for each child to confer with you individually about his or her self-selected reading. Have children bring their Reading Logs to share with you at the conference. Children might also like to choose a favorite passage to read aloud to you. Ask questions designed to stimulate discussion about the book. For example, you might ask children to locate details about the plot and ask if what happened in the story could happen in real life.

FLUENCY PERFORMANCE Have children read aloud to you the passage from "Miss Owl's Secret" that they selected and practiced with their partners. Keep track of the number of words the child reads correctly. Ask the child to rate his or her own performance on the 1–4 scale. If children are not happy with their oral reading, give them an opportunity to continue practicing and then to read the passage to you again.

See *Oral Reading Fluency Assessment* for monitoring progress.

Pumpkin Fiesta/Miss Owl's Secret

LESSON 16

BEFORE
Building Background and Vocabulary

Use with

"The Day Jimmy's Boa Ate the Wash"

Review Long Vowels: /ō/o-e; /yōō/u-e

Identify the sound. Have children repeat the following sentence three times: *I rode a mule that had a cute nose.* Ask them which words in the sentence have the /ō/ sound that they hear in *note*. (*rode, nose*) Then ask which words have the /yōō/ sound that they hear in *use*. (*mule, cute*)

Associate letters to sound. On the board, write: *I rode a mule that had a cute nose.* Circle the words *rode* and *nose*. Explain that both words have an *o* and an *e*, the same vowel sound, and a *CVCe* pattern. Underline the letters *o* and *e* in *rode* and *nose* and tell children that they stand for the /ō/ sound. Repeat the procedure for the words that have the /yōō/ sound.

Word blending. Model how to blend and read the word *hose*. Slide your hand under the letters as you slowly elongate the sounds: /hhōōzz/. Then read *hose* naturally. Follow a similar procedure for *rose, hope, fuse, stone,* and *cube*.

INTERVENTION PRACTICE BOOK
page 64

Apply the skill. *Vowel Substitution* Write the following words on the board, and have children read them aloud. Make the changes necessary to form the words in parentheses. Have children read each new word.

pot (pole)   **rod** (rode)   **hop** (hope)   **not** (note)
cub (cube) **mug** (mule)   **cut** (cute)   **fuss** (fuse)

Introduce Vocabulary

PRETEACH lesson vocabulary. Tell children that they are going to learn five new words that they will see again when they read a story called "The Day Jimmy's Boa Ate the Wash." Teach every Vocabulary Word using the strategies in the box below.

Use the following suggestions or similar ideas to give the meaning or context.

boring	Point out the *-ing* ending. Show an appropriate facial expression.
ducked	Point out the *-ed* ending. Relate by bending down suddenly as if to avoid being hit.
sense	Say something that makes *sense* and something that is *nonsense*.

> Write the word.
> Say the word.
> Track the word and have children repeat it.
> Give the meaning or context.

suppose	Suggest related words: *guess*, *think*, *imagine*. Explain that if you *suppose* something, you don't know it for certain.
tractor	Show a picture of a *tractor*. Discuss the uses of *tractors* on farms.

For vocabulary activities, see Vocabulary Games on pages 2–7.

> **Vocabulary Words**
> **boring** not interesting or exciting
> **ducked** bent down suddenly
> **sense** meaning (as in "make sense")
> **suppose** think or imagine
> **tractor** a farm machine

AFTER — Building Background and Vocabulary

Apply Vocabulary Strategies

RETEACH lesson vocabulary. Write the word *boring* on chart paper and help children define it. Tell children that they can sometimes figure out the meaning of a word if they know its *antonym*. An *antonym* is a word that means the opposite of another word.

MODEL The word *boring* means "dull," or "not exciting." If I take away the *not* in the phrase *not exciting*, I am left with *exciting*. *Exciting* is the opposite of *boring*. *Exciting* and *boring* are *antonyms*.

Guide children in using a similar strategy with the words *sense* and *ducked*.

Vocabulary Activity. Have children listen to each of the following sentences. Tell them to hold up the word card that completes each rhyme. Reread the sentence aloud with the correct answer. Then ask children how they made their choices.

1. On the farm, I am not an actor. When the farmer rides me, I am a __(tractor)__.
2. When my mom is snoring, it is definitely not __(boring)__.
3. When I talk, I am not tense, because I know that I make __(sense)__.
4. Is this flower a daisy or a rose? What do you __(suppose)__?
5. The big horse bucked, and I quickly __(ducked)__.

FLUENCY BUILDER Use *Intervention Practice Book* page 63. Read each word in the first column aloud and have children repeat it. Then have children work in pairs to read the words in the first column aloud to each other. Follow the same procedure with each of the remaining columns. After partners have practiced reading aloud the words in each column separately, have them practice the entire list. Save *Intervention Practice Book* page 63 to use on pages 161 and 163.

INTERVENTION PRACTICE BOOK
page 63

The Day Jimmy's Boa Ate the Wash/The Not-So-Boring Night

BEFORE

"The Day Jimmy's Boa Ate the Wash"
pages 16–31

USE SKILL CARD 16A

Focus Skill: Cause and Effect

PRETEACH the skill. Point out to children that there are reasons why things happen in a story. Why something happens is the *cause*. What happens is the *effect*. Explain that sometimes it is easy to see why things happen in a story, and other times, readers need to ask themselves why they think something happened.

Have children look at **side A of Skill Card 16: Cause and Effect**. Read the definition of *cause* and *effect*. Next read the story with children.

Now call attention to the chart and have volunteers take turns reading the information aloud. Ask:

- Why was the class trip fun? (*Possible response: because the horse started laughing*)

- Why are some sentences found on both sides of the chart? (*Possible response: Something causes an effect, and that effect causes something else to happen.*)

Prepare to Read: "The Day Jimmy's Boa Ate the Wash"

BANNER DAYS
pages 16–31

Preview. Tell children that they are going to read a selection entitled "The Day Jimmy's Boa Ate the Wash." Explain that this is a fantasy selection about a girl who describes things that probably did not really happen on her class trip. Then preview the selection.

- **Pages 16–17:** I see the title, "The Day Jimmy's Boa Ate the Wash," and the name of the author on pages 16–17. I see a picture of a big snake. I think this snake is Jimmy's boa.

- **Pages 18–19:** I see pictures of a girl coming home from school. The characters and setting look as if they could be real. The girl tells her mother that a cow cries when a haystack falls on her. I think that the girl is making things up about her class trip.

- **Pages 20–23:** I see pigs jumping on a school bus and throwing lunches. I know that pigs cannot really do this. And I see other fantastic things that supposedly happened on the class trip, too. I think the girl in the story is exaggerating what really happened.

Set purpose. Model setting a purpose for reading "The Day Jimmy's Boa Ate the Wash."

MODEL Judging from what I have seen in my preview, I think I will probably find out about a snake who ate some clothes on the class trip. I will read to be entertained by this funny story.

Lesson 16 • Intervention Teacher's Guide

AFTER

Reading "The Day Jimmy's Boa Ate the Wash"
pages 16–31

Reread and Summarize

Have children reread and summarize "The Day Jimmy's Boa Ate the Wash" in sections, as described below.

Pages 18–21

Let's reread pages 18–21 to recall what the girl said happened on her class trip.

Summary: The girl said a cow started crying because a haystack fell on her because a farmer crashed into it with his tractor because he was yelling at pigs to get off the school bus and stop eating the children's lunches.

Pages 22–23

Let's reread pages 22–23 to recall why the pigs were eating the children's lunches.

Summary: The children ran out of eggs and threw the pigs' corn, so the pigs didn't have anything to eat.

Pages 24–27

Let's reread pages 24–27 to recall what happened when Jimmy brought his boa constrictor to the farm.

Summary: The chickens didn't like the boa, and a hen laid an egg that fell on Jenny's head. Jenny thought Tommy threw the egg, so she threw one at him. Tommy ducked and the egg hit Marianne in the face, and she threw one at Jenny, but it hit Jimmy.

Pages 28–31

Let's reread pages 28–31 to remember what happened at the end of the story.

Summary: The boa constrictor ate the wash, and the children had to leave in a hurry. Jimmy had to leave his boa, but he found a pig on the bus and now he has a pet pig.

FLUENCY BUILDER Be sure children have copies of *Intervention Practice Book* page 63, which you used for yesterday's Fluency Builder activity. Call attention to the sentences on the bottom half of the page. The slashes break the sentences into phrases to allow you to work on natural phrasing. Tell children that their goal is to read each phrase or sentence smoothly. Model appropriate pace, expression, and phrasing as you read each sentence, and have children read it after you. Then have children practice by reading the sentences aloud three times to a partner.

INTERVENTION PRACTICE BOOK
page 63

BEFORE
Making Connections
pages 36–37

Directed Reading: "The Not-So-Boring Night," pp. 126–132

SOUNDS OF SUNSHINE pp. 126–132

Pages 126–127

Ask a volunteer to read aloud the title. Help children to see that Jerome is bored because he does not want to play a little kid's game. Read pages 126–127 while children listen to find out how Jerome feels about the night. Ask: **How does Jerome feel about the night?** (*Possible response: He feels bored.*) **NOTE DETAILS**

Ask: **Why does Jerome leave?** (*Possible response: Duke barks to go for a walk, and Jerome wants to go for a walk, too.*) **CAUSE AND EFFECT**

Pages 128–129

Have children read pages 128-129 to find out where Jerome and Duke go on their walk. Ask: **Where does this part of the story take place? What is it like there?** (*Possible response: Down at the cove; there are dunes and a lake.*) **SETTING**

Pages 130–131

Read aloud pages 130-131 to children. Model using the Make and Confirm Predictions strategy in order for children to predict why the fisherman is throwing all the fish back.

> **MODEL** As I read, I try to figure out what will happen next in a story. I don't understand why the farmer is fishing with a magnet. Then I read that the fish are red, with numbers on them. This sounds like the game that Rose is playing. I predict that the farmer is playing a game. As I continue reading, I find out that I was right. **MAKE AND CONFIRM PREDICTIONS**

Page 132

Have children read page 132 to find out what really happened to Jerome. Ask: **Did Jerome go down to the cove and see a farmer fishing? What really happened?** (*Possible response: No, Jerome was dozing and he dreamt about the farmer.*) **DRAW CONCLUSIONS**

Summarize the Selection. Ask children to think about why some people might think a game is boring and other people might think it is fun.

INTERVENTION PRACTICE BOOK page 65

162 Lesson 16 • Intervention Teacher's Guide

Answers to *Think About It* Questions

1. He gets bored, falls asleep, and has a strange dream about a farmer who is fishing with magnets. **SUMMARY**
2. His dream is not boring; he realizes that fishing with magnets can be fun. **INTERPRETATION**
3. Accept reasonable responses. **TASK**

AFTER
Skill Review
pages 371

USE SKILL CARD 16B

(Focus Skill) Review Cause and Effect

RETEACH the skill. Have children look at **side B of Skill Card 16: Cause and Effect**. Read the Skill Reminder with them, and have a volunteer read the story aloud.

Read aloud the directions. Explain that children will work with partners to create their own charts. Remind them to look for the things that happen and the reasons that these things happen.

After children have completed their cause and effect charts, have them display and explain their work. Point out that the selection "The Not-So-Boring Night" has causes and effects. Ask volunteers to name some of the things that happen and the reasons that they happen.

(Focus Skill) Review Phonics Skill from "The Day Jimmy's Boa Ate the Wash"

RETEACH Vowel Diphthongs: /ou/*ou, ow*. Read aloud the following sentence: *The cow made a loud sound*. Have children listen for the /ou/ sound. Then write the sentence on the board. Have children circle the letters that form the sound /ou/ in *cow*, *loud*, and *sound*. Now read this list aloud and have children raise their hands when they hear the /ou/ sound: *owl*, *towel*, *ground*, *noon*, *count*, *about*, and *crown*.

FLUENCY BUILDER Be sure that children have copies of *Intervention Practice Book* page 63. Explain that today children will practice the sentences on the bottom half of the page by recording them on tape. Assign new partners. Have children take turns reading the sentences aloud to each other and then recording them on tape.

INTERVENTION PRACTICE BOOK
page 63

The Day Jimmy's Boa Ate the Wash/The Not-So-Boring Night

BEFORE

Drafting a Good Beginning
page 39C

Writer's Craft: Writing a Good Beginning

Build on Prior Knowledge. Tell children that they are going to write a good beginning to a story. Explain that a good beginning may help readers understand what the story will be about, or it may tell about something surprising that will make the reader interested or curious about the story. Ask children to share beginnings of their favorite stories.

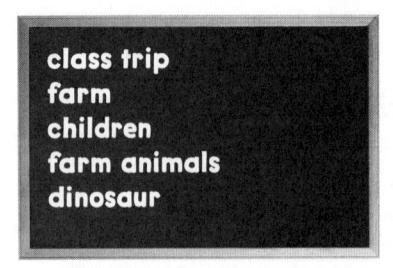

> class trip
> farm
> children
> farm animals
> dinosaur

Construct the Text. "Share the pen" with children. Write the list above on the board. Tell children that the list names things that are in a story. Help children to organize some or all of the items on the list into a good beginning. For example:

> Today I went on a class trip to a farm. I saw a lot of farm animals. I saw a dinosaur. The other children were afraid of the dinosaur.

Revisit the Text. Go back and read the story beginning together. Ask: **What does this beginning tell you about the story?** (*It will be about a class trip to a farm; there are farm animals and a scary dinosaur there.*)

- Guide children to make the story beginning more lively. Ask: **How can I change this beginning to make readers wonder what I saw on the farm besides farm animals?** (*Don't tell right away that there is a dinosaur on the farm.*) Make appropriate changes.

- Ask: **Can I have someone talking in the beginning of the story? What might he or she say about the class trip?** Make appropriate changes.

- Have children read the completed story beginning aloud and then copy it on their papers.

On Your Own

Have children write one sentence that could be a story beginning. Invite them to read their sentences aloud.

AFTER

Spelling Lesson
pages 331

Connect Spelling and Phonics

RETEACH Long Vowels: /ō/*o-e*; /yōō/*u-e*. Remind children that the /ō/ sound can be spelled *o-e* and that the /yōō/ sound can be spelled *u-e*. Tell children to number their papers 1–7. Dictate the following words, and have children write them. After each word is written, write it on the board so children can proofread their work. They should draw a line through a misspelled word and write the correct spelling below it.

1. note	2. cute	3. mule*	4. rope*
5. cube	6. nose*	7. poke*	

* Word appears in "The Not-So-Boring Night."

Dictate the following sentence and have children write it: *Rose thinks the mule has a cute nose.*

Build and Read Longer Words

Remind children that they have learned how to decode words with the /ō/ and /yōō/ sounds. Explain that now they will use what they have learned to help them read some longer words.

Write the word *notepad* on the board. Remind children that they can often figure out longer words by looking for parts they know. Cover *pad*, and point out the *CVCe* spelling pattern. Have children use the pattern to help them read the word part. Then cover *note*, and have children read *pad*. Point out the *CVC* pattern. Model how to blend the word parts to read aloud the longer word *notepad*. Do the same to have children blend word parts to read these longer words: *hopeless* and *rosebud*.

INTERVENTION ASSESSMENT BOOK

FLUENCY BUILDER Have children choose a passage from "The Not-So-Boring Night" to read aloud to a partner. You may have children choose passages that they found particularly interesting, or have them choose one of the following options:

- Read pages 126–127. (*From It was a hot . . . through . . . and I ran off.* Total: 119 words.)
- Read pages 128–129. (*From "Thanks, Duke! . . . through . . . lots of fish," I said.* Total: 122 words.)

Children should read the selected passage aloud to their partners three times. Have the child rate each reading on a scale from 1 to 4.

The Day Jimmy's Boa Ate the Wash/The Not-So-Boring Night

BEFORE Weekly Assessments

Review Vocabulary

To revisit Vocabulary Words prior to the weekly assessment, use these sentence frames. Have volunteers take turns reading aloud the sentence clues and choices. Tell children to identify the correct choice and explain how they made their decision.

1. When she **ducked**, she
   a. stood up tall.
   b. bent down fast.

2. The movie was **boring**, so I
   a. watched the whole thing.
   b. fell asleep.

3. If something makes **sense**, you can
   a. understand it.
   b. not figure it out.

4. If you **suppose** something, you
   a. think it.
   b. know it for sure.

5. A **tractor** is usually driven by a
   a. sailor.
   b. farmer.

Correct responses: 1b, 2b, 3a, 4a, 5b

You may want to display the Vocabulary Words and definitions on **page 159** and have children copy them to use when they study for the vocabulary test.

Review Cause and Effect

To review cause and effect before the weekly assessment, distribute *Intervention Practice Book* page 66. Have volunteers read aloud the first direction line and the sentences. Guide children to think about the reasons why things happen.

Review Test Prep

Ask children to turn to page 39 of the *Pupil Edition*. Call attention to the tips for answering the test questions. Tell children that paying attention to these tips can help them answer not only the test questions on this page, but other test questions like these, also.

BANNER DAYS page 39

Have children follow along as you read each test question and the tip that goes with it. Remind children that they can reread the story before they make their choices.

INTERVENTION PRACTICE BOOK page 66

INTERVENTION ASSESSMENT BOOK

Lesson 16 • Intervention Teacher's Guide

AFTER Self-Selected Reading

Weekly Assessments

Have children select books to read independently. They might choose books from the classroom library shelf, or you may wish to offer a group of appropriate books from which children can choose.

- *Never Bored on the Farm.* (See page 390 of the *Teacher's Edition* for an Independent Reading Plan.)
- *Zoo* by Gail Gibbons. HarperCollins, 1991.
- *A Dog Named Sam* by Janice Boland. Penguin Putnam, 1997.

After children have chosen their books, give each child a copy of My Reading Log, which can be found on page R35 in the back of the *Teacher's Edition*. Have children fill in the information at the top of the form. Then have them use the log to keep track of their reading and to record their responses to the literature.

Conduct student-teacher conferences. Arrange time for each child to confer with you individually about his or her self-selected reading. Have children bring their Reading Logs to share with you at the conference. Children might also like to choose a favorite passage to read aloud to you. Ask questions designed to stimulate discussion about the book. For example, you might ask children to describe a humorous event in the story and to tell what caused it to happen.

FLUENCY PERFORMANCE Have children read aloud to you the passages from "The Not-So-Boring Night" that they selected and practiced with their partners. Keep track of the number of words each child reads correctly. Ask the child to rate his or her own performance on the 1–4 scale. If children are not happy with their oral reading, give them an opportunity to continue practicing and then to read the passage to you again.

See *Oral Reading Fluency Assessment* for monitoring progress.

LESSON 17

BEFORE
Building Background and Vocabulary

Use with

"How I Spent My Summer Vacation"

Review Phonics: Long Vowel /ī/ *i-e, ie*

Identify the sound. Have children repeat the following sentence three times: *Mike flies a kite with a big stripe.* Ask them which words in the sentence have the /ī/ sound that they hear in *five.* (*Mike, flies, kite, stripe*)

Associate letters to sound. On the board, write: *Mike flies a kite with a big stripe.* Circle the words *Mike, kite,* and *stripe.* Explain that they all have an *i* and an *e,* the same vowel sound, and a *CVCe* pattern. Underline the letters *i-e* in *Mike* and *kite* and tell children that they stand for the /ī/ sound. Circle the word *flies,* underline the letters *ie,* and explain that they also stand for the /ī/ sound.

Word blending. Model how to blend and read the word *dime.* Slide your hand under the letters as you slowly elongate the sounds: /ddīīmm/. Then read *dime* naturally. Follow a similar procedure for *bike, pies, tries,* and *wipe.*

Apply the skill. *Vowel Substitution* Write the following words on the board, and have children read them aloud. Make the changes necessary to form the words in parentheses. Have children read each new word.

rid (ride) **hid** (hide) **to** (tie) **pins** (pies)
dim (dime) **pin** (pine) **lit** (lie) **flips** (flies)

Introduce Vocabulary

PRETEACH lesson vocabulary. Tell children that they are going to learn seven new words that they will see again when they read a story called "How I Spent My Summer Vacation." Teach each Vocabulary Word using the strategies in the box below.

Use the following suggestions or similar ideas to give the meaning or context.

captured	Point out the *-ed* ending. Relate by role-playing the *capture* of a stuffed toy.
imagination	Point out related words: *image, imagine.*
manners	Relate by role-playing good *manners.*
matador	Show a picture. Role-play a *matador* using a cape.

> Write the word.
> Say the word.
> Track the word and have children repeat it.
> Give the meaning or context.

INTERVENTION PRACTICE BOOK
page 68

168 Lesson 17 • Intervention Teacher's Guide

plains	Show a picture of plains. Point out the location of *plains* on a map of the U.S.
relax	Role-play how to *relax*.
vacation	Point out the dates of school *vacation* on a calendar.

For vocabulary activities, see Vocabulary Games on pages 2–7.

Vocabulary Words
- **captured** took control over
- **imagination** the ability to think of things that aren't real
- **manners** polite ways to behave
- **matador** bullfighter
- **plains** flat, open areas of land
- **relax** have fun doing very little
- **vacation** time off from work or school

AFTER
Building Background and Vocabulary

Apply Vocabulary Strategies

RETEACH lesson vocabulary. Write the word *matador* on chart paper and underline the letters *mat*. Tell children that they can sometimes figure out a word by looking for letter patterns that they know.

MODEL The letter combination *mat* is familiar to me. It forms the small word *mat*. The letter combination *ad* forms the small word *ad*. The letter combination *or* forms the small word *or*. When I blend together the letter patterns that I know, I read *matador*.

Guide children in using a similar procedure to decode the words *vacation* and *relax*.

Vocabulary Activity. Have children listen to each of the following riddles. Tell them to hold up the word card that answers each riddle. Reread the riddles aloud with the correct answer.

1. I don't do very much, but I have fun. (*relax*)
2. I am flat and open, and cows like to graze on me. (*plains*)
3. When a bull sees my red cape, it runs! (*matador*)
4. I am not in school, and I am not at work. (*vacation*)
5. I am not free. (*captured*)
6. I can make up all kinds of fantastic things. (*imagination*)
7. I always say "please" and "thank-you." (*manners*)

FLUENCY BUILDER Use *Intervention Practice Book* page 67. Read each word in the first column aloud and have children repeat it. Then have children work in pairs to read the words in the first column aloud to each other. Follow the same procedure with each of the remaining columns. After partners have practiced reading aloud the words in each column separately, have them practice the entire list.

Save *Intervention Practice Book* page 67 to use on pages 171 and 173.

INTERVENTION PRACTICE BOOK
page 67

How I Spent My Summer Vacation/The Matador and Me

BEFORE

"How I Spent My Summer Vacation"
pages 42–59

USE SKILL CARD 17A

(Focus Skill) Cause and Effect

PRETEACH the skill. Point out to children that there are reasons why things happen in a story. Why something happens is the *cause*. What happens is the *effect*. Explain that sometimes it is easy to see why things happen in a story, and other times, readers need to ask themselves why they think something happened.

Have children look at **side A of Skill Card 17: Cause and Effect**. Read the definition of *cause* and *effect*. Next, read the story with children.

Now call attention to the chart and have volunteers take turns reading the information aloud. Ask:

- **Why was the matador sad?** (*because she lost her cape.*)

- **What happens because the matador wants to remember where her cape might be?** (*Possible response: She wrote a list of all the places she had been that morning.*)

Prepare to Read "How I Spent My Summer Vacation"

Preview. Tell children that they are going to read a selection entitled "How I Spent My Summer Vacation." Explain that this is a fantasy selection. Tell children that "How I Spent My Summer Vacation" is about a boy who describes a vacation that he imagines happened to him. Then preview the selection.

BANNER DAYS
pages 42–59

- **Pages 42–43:** I see the title, "How I Spent My Summer Vacation," and the name of the author on pages 42–43. I see a picture of a cowboy capturing a little boy. I can tell from this picture that what happened to the boy is made up.

- **Pages 44–45:** On pages 44–45, I see a picture of a boy reading a report. I can read that the report is about the boy's summer vacation. I see a train on the board. I think this train is in the boy's imagination.

- **Pages 46–49:** On these pages, I see cowboys running off with the boy and then asking the boy to help them. The boy writes a postcard to his aunt. I don't think he would really write that he had been captured by cowboys. I think the boy has a very good imagination.

Set Purpose. Model setting a purpose for reading "How I Spent My Summer Vacation."

MODEL Judging from what I have seen in my preview, I think I will probably find out about the boy's make-believe vacation. I will read to be entertained by this funny story.

AFTER

"How I Spent My Summer Vacation"
pages 42–59

Reread and Summarize

Have children reread and summarize "How I Spent My Summer Vacation" in sections, as described below.

Pages 44–49

Let's reread pages 44–49 to recall what the boy was supposed to do on his summer vacation and what he said happened instead.

Summary: The boy's parents sent him to visit his Aunt Fern, but he was captured by cowboys instead.

Pages 50–51

Let's reread pages 50-51 to recall three new cowboy tricks Wallace learned.

Summary: The cowboys taught Wallace to rope, ride, and make fires with sticks.

Pages 52–53

Let's reread pages 52–53 to recall what happened when the roundup was through.

Summary: Aunt Fern invited the boy and the cowboys to a barbecue. They cleaned up, rode to Aunt Fern's, and had a great time.

Pages 54–57

Let's reread pages 54–57 to remember what happened at the end of the story.

Summary: The cattle stampeded toward the party, but the boy used a tablecloth, like a matador's cape, and frightened them away.

FLUENCY BUILDER Be sure children have copies of *Intervention Practice Book* page 67, which you used for yesterday's Fluency Builder activity. Call attention to the sentences on the bottom half of the page. The slashes break the sentences into phrases to allow you to work on natural phrasing. Tell children that their goal is to read each phrase or sentence smoothly. Model appropriate pace, expression, and phrasing as you read each sentence, and have children read it after you. Then have children practice by reading the sentences aloud three times to a partner.

INTERVENTION PRACTICE BOOK
page 67

BEFORE
Making Connections
pages 62–63

Directed Reading: "The Matador and Me," pp. 134–139

Ask a volunteer to read aloud the title. Ask what a *matador* is. (*a bullfighter*) Have children read page 134. Ask: **Where does the girl go for vacation?** (*Possible response: to visit her Aunt Clementine*) **NOTE DETAILS**

SOUNDS OF SUNSHINE
pp. 134–139

Page 134

Ask: **What does it mean to "work one's imagination overtime"?** (*Possible response: to make things up a lot*) **SPECULATE**

Page 135

Have children read page 135 to find out about Aunt Clementine. Ask: **Why doesn't Aunt Clementine care much about manners and rules?** (*Possible response: Aunt Clementine thinks rules are for parents and school.*) *(Focus Skill)* **CAUSE AND EFFECT**

Ask: **What is the only thing missing when the girl visits her aunt?** (*Possible responses: someone to play games with; someone her age*) **UNDERSTAND AUTHOR'S USE OF LANGUAGE**

What do you think the surprise will be? (*Possible response: a playmate*) **MAKE PREDICTIONS**

Page 136

Have children read page 136. Ask: **What is the surprise?** (*Possible response: a big kid dressed like a matador*) **CONFIRM PREDICTIONS**

Pages 137–138

Read aloud pages 137–138 to children. Model using the Make Inferences strategy to infer whether the big kid in the story is really a matador.

MODEL As I read, I think about what is happening. I think about what I know about bulls. Then I read what the author tells me and I study the illustrations to infer that the big kid is not really a matador, though he might like to be one when he grows up.
(Focus Strategy) **MAKE INFERENCES**

Page 139

Have children read page 139. Ask: **How does the girl help the boy?** (*Possible response: She names other things he can do.*) **SUMMARIZE**

What does the boy decide to do? (*He decides to be a farmer.*) **INTERPRET STORY EVENTS**

Do you think the girl's story is true? (*Accept reasonable responses.*) **EXPRESS OPINIONS**

Summarize the Selection. Ask children to think about why people use their imaginations to tell about experiences they have not really had.

INTERVENTION PRACTICE BOOK
page 69

172 Lesson 17 • Intervention Teacher's Guide

Page 140

Answers to *Think About It* Questions

1. The girl goes to visit her aunt. She meets a new pal and helps him decide not to be a matador. **SUMMARY**
2. No, he has not, because he is not very good at being a matador. He is also very young to be a matador. **INTERPRETATION**
3. Accept reasonable responses. **TASK**

AFTER

Skill Review
pages 65C

USE SKILL CARD 17B

(Focus Skill) Review Cause and Effect

RETEACH the skill. Have children look at **side B of Skill Card 17: Cause and Effect.** Read the Skill Reminder with them, and have a volunteer read the story aloud.

Read aloud the directions. Explain that children will work with partners to create their own charts. Remind them to look for the things that happen and the reasons that these things happen.

After children have completed their cause and effect charts, have them display and explain their work. Point out that the selection "The Matador and Me" has causes and effects. Ask volunteers to name some of the things that happen and the reasons that they happen.

(Focus Skill) Review Phonics Skill from "How I Spent My Summer Vacation"

RETEACH Vowel Diphthongs: /oi/*oi,oy*. Read aloud the following sentence: *The snake coiled up when he heard the cowboy's voice.* Have children listen for the /oi/ sound. Then read this list aloud and have children raise their hands when they hear the /oi/ sound: *coin, boy, horse, poison, hoof, joyful, toy.*

FLUENCY BUILDER Be sure that children have copies of *Intervention Practice Book* page 67. Explain that today children will practice the sentences on the bottom half of the page by reading them aloud on tape. Assign new partners. Have children take turns reading the sentences aloud to each other and then reading them on tape.

INTERVENTION PRACTICE BOOK
page 67

How I Spent My Summer Vacation/The Matador and Me **173**

BEFORE
Drafting a Friendly Letter
page 65G

Writer's Craft: Audience and Purpose

Build on Prior Knowledge. Tell children that they are going to write a letter. Explain that writers write to different people and have many different reasons for writing. Ask children to discuss letters they have written or received. Discuss and list reasons why writers write friendly letters.

> to tell about a vacation
> to give directions
> to invite someone
> to thank someone

Construct the Text. "Share the pen" with children. Tell them that the list names purposes for writing a friendly letter. Help children to choose a purpose from the list and think of an audience for whom this purpose would be appropriate. Then help them construct a friendly letter. For example:

Dear Aunt Fern,

   I am on vacation with my friends, the cowboys.
I am having a lot of fun on my vacation.
I learned how to ride a horse on my vacation.

Your nephew,

Sean

Revisit the Text. Go back and read the friendly letter together. Ask: **What is the purpose of this letter?** (*to tell about a vacation*)

- Guide children to make the letter read more smoothly. Ask: **What words can I take out of the second and third sentences to make the letter read more smoothly?** (*on my vacation*) Make appropriate changes.

- Ask: **What other audiences might this letter be written to?** (*parents, grandparents, friends, teachers*)

- Have children read the completed friendly letter aloud and then have them copy it on their papers.

On Your Own

Have children list two purposes and two audiences for friendly letters they would like to write.

Lesson 17 • Intervention Teacher's Guide

AFTER

Spelling Lesson page 59I

Connect Spelling and Phonics

RETEACH Long Vowel /ī/ *i-e, ie.* Tell children to number their papers 1–8. Write the word *time* on the board, and tell children that in the words you say, the /ī/ sound will be spelled *i-e*. Dictate the following words, and have children write them. After each word is written, write it on the board so children can proofread their work. They should draw a line through a misspelled word and write the correct spelling below it.

1. ride*	2. nine	3. wide*	4. kite
5. pride	6. mine*	7. size*	8. pile

*** Word appears in "The Matador and Me."**

Dictate the following sentence and have children write it: *He tries to get the pie.*

Build and Read Longer Words

Remind children that they have learned how to decode words with the /ī/ sound. Explain that now they will use what they have learned to help them read some longer words.

Write the word *sunshine* on the board. Remind children that they can often figure out longer words by looking for smaller words in them. Cover *shine*, and have children read the smaller word *sun*. Follow a similar procedure to have them read the smaller word *shine*. Model how to blend the two smaller words to read aloud the longer word *sunshine*. Do the same to have children blend word parts to read these longer words: *pinstripe* and *butterflies*.

INTERVENTION ASSESSMENT BOOK

FLUENCY BUILDER Have children choose a passage from "The Matador and Me" to read aloud to a partner. You may have children choose passages that they found particularly interesting, or have them choose one of the following options:

- Read pages 136–137. (From *When I saddled . . .* through *. . . I ran after that.* Total: 115 words.)
- Read pages 138–139. (From *I plowed into him . . .* through *. . . do you?* Total: 129 words.)

Children should read the selected passage aloud to their partners three times. Have children rate each reading on a scale from 1 to 4.

How I Spent My Summer Vacation/The Matador and Me

BEFORE Weekly Assessments

Review Vocabulary

To revisit Vocabulary Words prior to the weekly assignments, use these sentence frames. Have volunteers take turns reading aloud the sentence stems and choices. Children should identify the correct choice and explain why that choice makes sense in the sentence.

1. When you go on **vacation**, you
   a. rest and relax.
   b. study and take tests.

2. On the **plains**, you can
   a. go skiing.
   b. round up cattle.

3. When you **relax**, you
   a. take it easy.
   b. work very hard.

4. If you are a **matador**, you will
   a. use a cape to make a bull turn.
   b. use a fishing rod.

5. If you have good **manners**, you are
   a. rude.
   b. polite.

6. When the bull was **captured**, it was
   a. put in a pen.
   b. let free.

7. He has a good **imagination**, so he
   a. never makes things up.
   b. plays make-believe.

Correct responses: 1a, 2b, 3a, 4a, 5b, 6a, 7b

You may want to display the Vocabulary Words and definitions on page 169 and have children copy them to use when they study for the vocabulary test.

(Focus Skill) Review Cause and Effect

To review cause and effect before the weekly assessment, distribute *Intervention Practice Book* page 70. Have volunteers read aloud the first direction line and the sentences. Guide children to think about the reasons why things happen.

Review Test Prep

Ask children to turn to page 65 of the *Pupil Edition*. Call attention to the tips for answering the test questions. Tell children that paying attention to these tips can help them answer not only the test questions on this page but also other test questions.

BANNER DAYS page 65

Have children follow along as you read each test question and the tip that goes with it. Remind children that they can say each word softly to themselves before making their choice.

INTERVENTION PRACTICE BOOK page 70

INTERVENTION ASSESSMENT BOOK

Lesson 17 • Intervention Teacher's Guide

AFTER Self-Selected Reading
Weekly Assessments

Have children select their own books to read independently. They might choose books from the classroom library shelf, or you may wish to offer a group of appropriate books from which children can choose.

- *Around the Campfire* by Dottie Makem. See page 65S of the *Teacher's Edition* for an Independent Reading Plan.
- *Paul Bunyan and His Blue Ox* by Patsy Jensen. American Frontier, 1994.
- *Way Out West Lives a Coyote Named Frank* by Jillian Lund. Dutton, 1993.

After children have chosen their books, give each child a copy of My Reading Log, which can be found on page R35 in the back of the *Teacher's Edition*. Have children fill in the information at the top of the form. Then have them use the log to keep track of their reading and to record their responses to the literature.

Conduct student-teacher conferences. Arrange time for each child to confer with you individually about his or her self-selected reading. Have children bring their Reading Logs to share with you at the conference. Children might also like to choose a favorite passage to read aloud to you. Ask questions to stimulate discussion about the book. For example, you might ask what children like to do when they are alone and how their activities might differ if they are with friends.

FLUENCY PERFORMANCE Have children read aloud to you the passages from "The Matador and Me" that they selected and practiced with their partners. Keep track of the number of words each child reads correctly. Ask the child to rate his or her own performance on the 1–4 scale. If children are not happy with their oral reading, give them an opportunity to continue practicing and then to read the passage to you again.

See *Oral Reading Fluency Assessment* for monitoring progress.

LESSON 18

BEFORE
Building Background and Vocabulary

Use with

"Dear Mr. Blueberry"

Review Phonics: Long Vowel: /ē/ ee, ea

Identify the sound. Have children repeat the following sentence three times: *Ben feeds beans and beets to Jean and Ted.* Ask them which words in the sentence have the /ē/ sound that they hear in *speak*. (*feeds, beans, beets, Jean*)

Associate letters to sound. On the board, write: *Ben feeds beans and beets to Jean and Ted.* Circle the words *feeds* and *beets*. Underline the letters *ee* in *feeds* and *beets* and tell children that they stand for the long /ē/ sound. Explain that when two vowels come together in a word, they often stand for the long vowel sound of the first vowel. Then follow a similar procedure with the letters *ea* in *beans* and *Jean*.

Word blending. Model how to blend and read the word *green*. Write the word *green* on the board. Then slide your hand under the letters as you slowly elongate the sounds /ggrrēēnn/. Now read *green* naturally. Follow a similar procedure for *tree*, *read*, and *beak*.

Apply the skill. *Vowel Substitution* Write the following words on the board, and have children read them aloud. Make the changes necessary to form the words in parentheses. Have children read each new word.

fed (feed)   **met** (meet)   **bed** (bead)   **set** (seat)
step (steep)   **sped** (speed)   **net** (neat)   **bet** (beat)

INTERVENTION PRACTICE BOOK
page 72

Introduce Vocabulary

PRETEACH lesson vocabulary. Tell children that they are going to learn six new words that they will see again when they read a story called "Dear Mr. Blueberry." Teach each Vocabulary Word using the following process.

Use the following suggestions or similar ideas to give the meaning or context.

details	Show a map. Use your hand to frame the whole map, then point out individual *details*.
disappoint	Role-play a scene in which a gift is promised but not delivered.
forcibly	Use your hands to show how flippers can *forcibly* swim.
information	Point out and define the small word *inform*.

> Write the word.
> Say the word.
> Track the word and have children repeat it.
> Give the meaning or context.

178 Lesson 18 • Intervention Teacher's Guide

oceans	Point out and discuss *oceans* on a world map or globe.
stroke	Use a stuffed animal to role-play how to *stroke* a pet.

For vocabulary activities, see Vocabulary Games on pages 2–7.

AFTER
Building Background and Vocabulary

Apply Vocabulary Strategies

Use synonyms. Write the word *forcibly* on chart paper, and help children define it. Tell children that if they know the meaning of a word, they can find synonyms for it. A synonym is a word that has nearly the same meaning as another word.

> **MODEL** If I want to understand what the word *forcibly* means, I can find synonyms, or other familiar words that have the same meaning. *Forcibly* and *strongly* are synonyms. I am familiar with the word *strongly*. Now I know that the word *forcibly* means nearly the same as the word *strongly*.

Guide children in using a similar procedure to define the words *information* and *oceans*.

RETEACH lesson vocabulary. Have children listen to each of the following sentences. Tell them to hold up the word card that tells the opposite of what is being described. Then reread the sentences aloud with the correct answer. Discuss how children made their choices.

1. We are small bodies of fresh water. (*oceans*)
2. We are the main ideas of a story. (*details*)
3. I am very happy because I get whatever I expect. (*disappoint*)
4. I move very softly and weakly. (*forcibly*)
5. I slap and punch in a rough way. (*stroke*)
6. I am a bunch of nonsense. (*information*)

Vocabulary Words
- **details** small bits of information
- **disappoint** to make someone sad because something expected did not happen
- **forcibly** strongly; by force
- **information** facts about a person, place, or thing
- **oceans** large bodies of salt water where whales and other animals live
- **stroke** to rub something gently

FLUENCY BUILDER Use *Intervention Practice Book* page 71. Read each word in the first column aloud, and have children repeat it. Then have children work in pairs to read the words in the first column aloud to each other. Follow the same procedure with each of the remaining columns. After partners have practiced reading aloud the words in each column separately, have them practice the entire list. Save *Intervention Practice Book* page 71 to use with pages 181 and 183.

INTERVENTION PRACTICE BOOK
page 71

Dear Mr. Blueberry/Mr. Whiskers

BEFORE

"Dear Mr. Blueberry"
pages 68–88

USE SKILL CARD 18A

⭐ Focus Skill Make Inferences

PRETEACH the skill. Point out to children that readers use clues in what they read and what they already know to understand what happens in a story. Explain that sometimes readers need to use their personal experience as well as story clues to figure out why something happens. Discuss how children use what they know from real life to make sense of things that happen in a story.

Have children look at **side A of Skill Card 18: Make Inferences**. Read the definition of Make Inferences. Next read the story aloud while children read along with you.

Now call attention to the chart and have volunteers take turns reading the information aloud. Ask:

- **What does the story tell you about polar bears?** (*Possible response: They live near the North Pole.*)

- **How do people learn about polar bears?** (*Possible response: They read books about them.*)

Prepare to Read: "Dear Mr. Blueberry"

Preview. Tell children that they are going to read a selection entitled "Dear Mr. Blueberry." Explain that this is an informational story. Tell children that "Dear Mr. Blueberry" tells about a girl who learns about whales from her teacher. Then preview the selection.

BANNER DAYS
pages 68–88

- **Pages 68–69:** I see the title, "Dear Mr. Blueberry," and the name of the author on pages 68–69. I see pictures of a girl writing letters. I think that the girl is writing letters to Mr. Blueberry.

- **Pages 70–71:** On page 70, I see a letter from a girl named Emily to someone called Mr. Blueberry. On page 71, I see a big whale in a small pond. I think that Emily is imagining this.

- **Pages 72–73:** On these pages, I see the letter that Mr. Blueberry has written back to Emily. I see a picture of Emily reading his letter. I think that they will continue to write to each other throughout the story.

- **Pages 74–75:** On these pages, I see another letter from Emily to Mr. Blueberry and his letter back to her. I can tell who is writing the letter by looking at the signature.

Set Purpose. Model setting a purpose for reading "Dear Mr. Blueberry."

MODEL From my preview, I think I will read more letters about whales. I will read to find out information about whales and also to be entertained by Emily's imagination.

Lesson 18 • Intervention Teacher's Guide

AFTER

"Dear Mr. Blueberry"
pages 68–88

Reread and Summarize

Have children reread and summarize "Dear Mr. Blueberry" in sections, as described below.

Pages 70–73

Let's reread pages 70–73 to recall who Emily is, why she is writing to Mr. Blueberry, and who Mr. Blueberry is.

Summary: Emily is a little girl. She is writing to her teacher, Mr. Blueberry, because she thinks she sees a whale in her pond.

Pages 74–78

Let's reread pages 74–78 to recall what else Mr. Blueberry teaches Emily about whales.

Summary: Whales don't get lost and they always know where they are in the oceans. Blue whales are blue and they eat tiny shrimplike creatures that live in the sea. Blue whales are too big to live in ponds.

Pages 79–81

Let's reread pages 79–81 to recall what Emily does next.

Summary: Emily reads Mr. Blueberry's letter to the whale. After that, she strokes his head. Then she secretly feeds him some crunched-up cornflakes and bread crumbs. She names the whale Arthur.

Pages 82–88

Let's reread pages 82–88 to remember what else Mr. Blueberry teaches Emily about whales and what happens at the end of the story.

Summary: Mr. Blueberry teaches Emily that whales are migratory and travel great distances each day. Arthur leaves the pond to be migratory again. Then Emily goes to the beach and she sees Arthur in the ocean. She tells Arthur that she loves him and that Mr. Blueberry does, too.

FLUENCY BUILDER Be sure children have copies of *Intervention Practice Book* page 71. Call attention to the sentences on the bottom half of the page. Tell children that their goal is to read each phrase or sentence smoothly. Model appropriate pace, expression and phrasing as you read each sentence and have children read it after you. Then have children practice by reading the sentences aloud three times to a partner.

INTERVENTION PRACTICE BOOK
page 71

BEFORE
Making Connections pages 92–93

Directed Reading: "Mr. Whiskers," pp. 142–148

SOUNDS OF SUNSHINE pages 142–148

Ask a volunteer to read aloud the title. Ask children who they think Mr. Whiskers is. Have children read page 142 to find out. Ask: **Who is Mr. Whiskers? Where does Mr. Whiskers live?** (*Possible response: Mr. Whiskers is a seal. He lives in the sea.*) **NOTE DETAILS** Ask: **What does Neal learn from Mr. Whiskers?** (*Possible response: He learns about other animals that live in the ocean.*) **INTERPRET STORY EVENTS**

Page 143

Have children read page 143 to find out if Mr. Whiskers really teaches Neal. Ask: **Do you think Mr. Whiskers talks to Neal when he teaches him? Why or why not?** (*Possible response: No, because seals cannot talk to humans.*) *Focus Skill* **MAKE INFERENCES**

Page 144

Have children read page 144 to find out more about seals. Ask: **What are three things you read about seals?** (*Possible response: Seals are good swimmers; they use their flippers to help them swim fast; they swim long distances.*) **SUMMARIZE**

Page 145

Read aloud page 145 to children. Model using the Read Ahead strategy in order for children to understand the swimming contest.

> **MODEL** As I read, I may not understand what is happening in the story. Reading ahead a bit may help me. If I don't know what happens during the swimming contest, I can find out quickly by reading ahead. *Focus Strategy* **READ AHEAD**

Pages 146–147

Have children read pages 146–147 to find out more about Mr. Whiskers and Neal. Ask: **How did Mr. Whiskers get his name?** (*Possible response: He has long whiskers.*) **DRAW CONCLUSIONS** Ask: **How do whiskers help seals?** (*Possible response: They help seals feel around in the water and find fish to eat.*) **NOTE DETAILS** Ask: **Do seals make good pets? Why?** (*Possible response: No, because they don't walk well on land; they are wild animals.*) **DRAW CONCLUSIONS** Ask: **Do you think Neal really wants to be a seal?** (*Possible response: Answers will vary.*) **SPECULATE**

Page 148

Have children read page 148 to find out what Neal's parents think about Mr. Whiskers. Ask: **Have Neal's parents ever seen Mr. Whiskers?** (*Possible response: No.*) **NOTE DETAILS** Ask: **What do Neal's parents think about Mr. Whiskers?** (*Possible response: They think he is not real.*) **DRAW CONCLUSIONS** Ask: **Do you think Mr. Whiskers is real?** (*Possible response: Answers will vary.*) **EXPRESS PERSONAL OPINIONS**

Summarize the selection. Ask children to think about why it is important to learn facts about animals.

INTERVENTION PRACTICE BOOK
page 73

AFTER

Skill Review
pages 93I

USE SKILL CARD 18B

Answers to *Think About It* Questions

1. Seals have whiskers that they use to help them feel for food in the water. Seals swim fast and far. **SUMMARY**
2. They do not believe that a seal would come to the beach each weekend and speak to their son. **INTERPRETATION**
3. Accept reasonable pictures. **TASK**

(Focus Skill) Make Inferences

RETEACH the skill. Have children look at **side B of Skill Card 18: Make Inferences**. Read the skill reminder with them, and have a volunteer read the story aloud.

Read aloud the set of directions. Explain that children will work with partners to create their own charts. Remind them to look for word clues as they listen to the story being read aloud.

After children have completed their inference charts, have them display and explain their work. Point out that inferences can also be made about the selection "Mr. Whiskers." Ask volunteers to make an inference about Neal.

(Focus Skill) Review Phonics Skill from "Dear Mr. Blueberry"

RETEACH varient vowel: /o͞o/*oo, ue*. Write the following sentence on the board: *At school Sue used glue to hold the blue yarn she looped around her zoo picture.*

Have children copy the sentence. Then have them circle the words with *oo* and underline the words with *ue*. Ask children to tell you which words they circled, and which words they underlined.

FLUENCY BUILDER Be sure that children have copies of *Intervention Practice Book* page 71. Explain that today children will practice the sentences on the bottom half of the page by reading them aloud on tape. Assign new partners. Have children take turns reading the sentences aloud to each other and then reading them on tape.

INTERVENTION PRACTICE BOOK
page 71

Dear Mr. Blueberry/Mr. Whiskers

BEFORE
Drafting a Letter of Invitation
page 93A

Writing Process: Letter of Invitation

Build on prior knowledge. Tell children that they are going to talk about and write letters of invitation. Explain that people write letters of invitation to invite people to something. Talk about the reasons why people write letters of invitation and the people they write these letters to. Ask children to discuss letters of invitation they have written or received.

> A Party
> time
> place
> date

Construct the text. "Share the pen" with children. Tell them that the list names a purpose for writing a letter of invitation and some of the things to be included in the letter. Then help them construct a letter of invitation. For example:

> Dear Peggy,
>
> I am having a party. The party is at my house. The party will be on Sunday, May 27. The party is at 4:00 in the afternoon.
>
> Your friend,
>
> Kiko

Revisit the text. Go back and read the letter of invitation together. Ask: **What is the purpose of this letter?** (*to invite a friend to a party*)

- Guide children to make the letter read more smoothly. Ask: **How can I combine sentences to make the letter read more smoothly?** (*For example: I am having a party at my house. The party will be on Sunday, May 27, at 4:00 in the afternoon.*) Make appropriate changes.

- Ask: **What other information could you include in the letter?** (*why the party is being held, for whom the party will be given, directions to the party*)

- Have children read the completed letter of invitation aloud and then copy it on their papers.

On Your Own

Have children list four things to include in a different letter of invitation. Then have them use their list to write a letter of invitation.

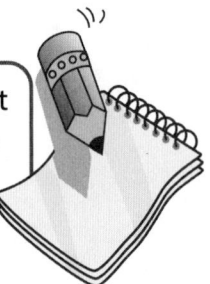

AFTER
Spelling Lesson
page 89I

Connect Spelling and Phonics

RETEACH long vowel: /ē/ ee, ea. Tell children to number their papers 1–8. Write the word *beet* on the board, and tell children that in the words you say, the /ē/ sound will be spelled *ee* as in *beet*. Dictate the following words, and have children write them. After each word is written, write it on the board so children can proofread their work. They should draw a line through a misspelled word and write the correct spelling below it.

1. need*	2. deep*	3. sleep	4. street
5. meet*	6. sheet	7. see*	8. cheeks*

* Word appears in "Mr. Whiskers."

Tell children that in the following sentence, the long /ē/ sound will be spelled *ea*. Dictate the sentence, and have children write it: *I dream that seals in the sea swim to the beach.*

Build and Read Longer Words

Remind children that they have learned how to decode words with the /ē/ sound. Explain that now they will use what they have learned to help them read some longer words.

Write the word *beanbag* on the board. Remind children that they can often figure out longer words by looking for smaller words in them. Cover *bag*, and have children read the smaller word *bean*. Then cover *bean* and have them read the smaller word *bag*. Model how to blend the two smaller words to read aloud the longer word *beanbag*. Follow a similar procedure to have children read these longer words: *dreamland*, *teatime*, and *teammate*.

INTERVENTION ASSESSMENT BOOK

FLUENCY BUILDER Have children choose a passage from "Mr. Whiskers" to read aloud to a partner. You may have children choose passages that they found particularly interesting, or have them choose one of the following options:

- Read pages 142–143. (*From Mr. Whiskers and I meet... through... friends to greet!* Total: 70 words.)
- Read page 147. (*From Mr. Whiskers keeps... through... be a real treat.* Total: 66 words.)

Children should read the selected passage aloud to their partners three times. Have the child rate his or her own readings on a scale from 1 to 4.

Dear Mr. Blueberry/Mr. Whiskers

BEFORE
Weekly Assessments

Review Vocabulary

To revisit Vocabulary Words prior to the weekly assignments, use these sentence frames. Have volunteers take turns reading aloud the sentence stems and choices. Children should identify the correct choice and explain why that choice makes sense in the sentence.

1. When you visit the **ocean**, you can see
   a. lions and tigers.
   b. whales and other sea creatures.
2. If I give you **information**, you will
   a. not have the facts.
   b. have the facts.
3. He spoke **forcibly**, because he
   a. wanted to make a point.
   b. didn't care if anyone listened.
4. If you know the **details**, you know
   a. the most important fact.
   b. small bits of information.
5. I **stroke** my cat because she likes to be
   a. hit hard.
   b. rubbed gently.
6. I don't want to **disappoint** you because you will be
   a. sad.
   b. very happy.

Correct responses: 1. b, 2. b, 3. a, 4. b, 5. b, 6. a

You may want to display the vocabulary words and definitions on page 179 and have children copy them to use when they study for the vocabulary test.

INTERVENTION PRACTICE BOOK
page 74

★ Focus Skill — Review Make Inferences

To review making inferences before the weekly assessment, distribute *Intervention Practice Book* page 74. Have volunteers read aloud the direction line and the story. Remind children to use their personal experience when making inferences.

Review Test Prep

INTERVENTION ASSESSMENT BOOK

Ask children to turn to page 95 of the *Pupil Edition*. Call attention to the tips for answering the test questions. Tell children that paying attention to these tips can help them answer not only the test questions on this page but also other test questions like these.

BANNER DAYS
page 95

Have children follow along as you read each test question and the tip that goes with it. Remind children to reread each choice before making their final decision.

186 Lesson 18 • Intervention Teacher's Guide

AFTER
Weekly Assessments

Self-Selected Reading

Have children select their own books to read independently. They might choose books from the classroom library shelf, or you may wish to offer a group of appropriate books from which children can choose.

- *The World Under the Water* by Ted Jamison. (See page 950 of the *Teacher's Edition* for an Independent Reading Plan.)
- *What's Under the Ocean* by Janet Craig. Troll, 1989.
- *What Is a Reptile?* by Susan Kuchalla. Troll, 1982.

After children have chosen their books, give each child a copy of "My Reading Log," which can be found on page R35 in the back of the *Teacher's Edition*. Have children fill in the information at the top of the form. Then have them use the log to keep track of their reading and to record their responses to the literature.

Conduct student-teacher conferences. Arrange time for each child to meet with you individually to discuss his or her self-selected reading. Have children bring their Reading Logs to share with you at the conference. Children might also like to choose a favorite passage to read aloud to you. Ask questions designed to stimulate discussion of the book. For example, you might ask what sea animals live in the ocean.

FLUENCY PERFORMANCE Have children read aloud to you the passage from "Mr. Whiskers" that they selected and practiced with their partners. Keep track of the number of words each child reads correctly. Ask the child to rate his or her own performance on the 1–4 scale. If children are not happy with their oral reading, give them an opportunity to continue practicing and then to reread the passage again to you.

See *Oral Reading Fluency Assessment* for monitoring progress.

Dear Mr. Blueberry/Mr. Whiskers

LESSON 19

BEFORE
Building Background and Vocabulary

Use with

"Cool Ali"

Review Phonics: Vowel Variants: /o͞o/ *u-e, ue, ui*

Identify the sound. Have children repeat the following sentence three times: *Sue eats fruit in June.* Ask them which words in the sentence have the /o͞o/ sound. (*Sue, fruit, June*)

Associate letters to sound. On the board, write: *Sue eats fruit in June.* Circle the words *Sue, fruit,* and *June.* Ask children to tell how the words are alike. (*All have the /o͞o/ sound.*) Then underline the letters *ue* in *Sue, ui* in *fruit,* and *u-e* in *June.* Tell children that the letters *ue, ui,* and *u-e* can all stand for the /o͞o/ sound they hear in *Sue, fruit,* and *June.* Have children repeat each word and listen for the /o͞o/ sound.

Word blending. Model how to blend and read the word *blue.* Write *blue* on the board. Slide your hand under the letters as you slowly elongate the sounds /bblloo/. Then read *blue* naturally. Follow a similar procedure for *true, flute* and *suit.*

Apply the skill. *Vowel Substitution* Write the following words on the board, and have children read them aloud. Make the changes necessary to form the words in parentheses. Have children read each new word.

| **so** (Sue) | **sit** (suit) | **role** (rule) | **Jane** (June) |
| **clay** (clue) | **fret** (fruit) | **dud** (dude) | **tub** (tube) |

INTERVENTION PRACTICE BOOK
page 76

Introduce Vocabulary

PRETEACH lesson Vocabulary. Tell children that they will learn six new words that they will see again when they read a story called "Cool Ali." Teach each Vocabulary Word using the following process.

Use the following suggestions or similar ideas to give the meaning or context.

> Write the word.
> Say the word.
> Track the word and have children repeat it.
> Give the meaning or context.

admired — Point out the *-ed* ending. Role-play *admiration* of classroom objects or displays of children's work.

fussed — Point out the *-ed* ending. Talk about how babies may *fuss* when they are hungry or uncomfortable.

haze — Draw a simple outdoor scene on the board. Hold a piece of chalk sideways and lightly create a *haze* over the scene.

mimicked — Point out the *-ed* ending. Have a volunteer pantomime a classroom chore. *Mimick* the volunteer's actions.

188 Lesson 19 • Intervention Teacher's Guide

notice   Display an interesting object, and talk about the details children *notice*.

pale   Show different colored crayons, some *pale* and some dark.

For vocabulary activities, see Vocabulary Games on page 2–7.

> **Vocabulary Words**
> **admired** noticed something and liked it
> **fussed** showed unhappiness; complained
> **haze** misty, smoky, or dusty air
> **mimicked** copied
> **notice** be aware of
> **pale** light in color

AFTER
Building Background and Vocabulary

Apply Vocabulary Strategies

Use familiar patterns. Write the word *fussed* on chart paper and underline the letters *ed*. Tell children that they can sometimes figure out the meaning of a new word by looking for letter patterns that they know.

> **MODEL** The letter combination *ed* is familiar to me because I have seen it in words like *walked*. I know that this ending means that the word tells about something that happened in the past. The letter combination *us* forms the small word *us*. When I blend the letter patterns that I know all together with the initial consonant *f*, I read *fussed*.

Guide children in using a similar procedure to decode the other Vocabulary Words.

Vocabulary Activity

RETEACH lesson Vocabulary. Have children write each Vocabulary Word on a word card and then listen to each of the following groups of words. Tell them to hold up the word that matches each group of words. Discuss how children made their choices.

1. light / color (*pale*)
2. enjoyed / liked (*admired*)
3. see / pay attention (*notice*)
4. copied / same actions (*mimicked*)
5. unhappy / fidgeted (*fussed*)
6. mist / dust (*haze*)

FLUENCY BUILDER Use *Intervention Practice Book* page 75. Read each word in the first column aloud and have children repeat it. Then have partners read the words in the first column aloud to each other. Tell children to follow the same procedure with each of the remaining columns. After partners have practiced reading aloud the words in each column, have them practice the entire list. (Save *Intervention Practice Book* page 75 to use on pages 191 and 193.)

INTERVENTION PRACTICE BOOK
page 75

BEFORE
"Cool Ali"
pages 98–112

USE SKILL CARD 19A

(Focus Skill) Antonyms

PRETEACH the skill. Point out to children that *antonyms* are words that have opposite meanings. Help children see that good readers use clues in what they read to help them find the meanings of *antonyms*. Discuss how children feel on a hot day, and how they feel on a very cold day. Guide children to notice *antonyms* in their discussion.

Have children look at **side A of Skill Card 19: Antonyms**. Read the definition of *antonyms*. Next read the story, and then have children read it with you. Have volunteers take turns reading the information in the chart aloud. Ask:

- **What word tells the opposite of the word terrible?** (Possible response: *wonderful*)

- **What word tells the opposite of the word ugly?** (Possible response: *beautiful*)

Prepare to Read: "Cool Ali"

Preview. Tell children that they are going to read a selection entitled "Cool Ali." Explain that this is a realistic fiction story about a girl who uses her creativity to solve a problem. Then preview the selection.

BANNER DAYS
pages 98–112

Pages 98–99: I see the title, "Cool Ali," and the name of the author. I see a picture of a girl drawing on a sidewalk. I think that the girl in the picture is Ali.

Pages 100–101: I see pictures and read about people who live in the same building. I read about a girl named Ali who loves to draw. I think that I will read more about what the people in the building think about Ali's drawings.

Pages 102–103: I see pictures and read about the things Ali draws. I think that Ali is trying to help her neighbors imagine cool things so that they forget how hot they are.

Set purpose. Model setting a purpose for reading "Cool Ali."

> **MODEL** From what I have seen and read so far, I think I will read more about Ali's drawings and how they help her neighbors feel cool in the heat. I will read to find out what happens to Ali and her drawings.

Lesson 19 • Intervention Teacher's Guide

AFTER

"Cool Ali"
pages 98–112

Reread and Summarize

Have children reread and summarize "Cool Ali" in sections.

Pages 98–101

Let's reread pages 98–101 to recall who Ali is and what is happening outside her building.

Summary: Ali is a girl who loves to draw. She is drawing on the sidewalk while her neighbors complain and fuss because it is so hot.

Pages 102–105

Let's reread pages 102–105 to recall the things that Ali drew and why she drew them.

Summary: Ali drew a lake, a beach umbrella, the North Wind, and a polar bear. She drew these things because they make people think of things that are cool. She hopes they will help her neighbors forget the heat.

Pages 106–107

Let's reread pages 106–107 to recall Ali's coolest idea of all and how her neighbors felt about it.

Summary: Ali drew snow dots and polar bear prints and icicles to make it seem like winter. Her neighbors were very happy and felt cooler.

Pages 108–112

Let's reread pages 108–112 to remember what happened to Ali's drawings and how she felt about it.

Summary: A rain storm surprised everyone. The rain washed Ali's drawings away. At first she was upset, but then she was happy when her neighbors cheered for her because she had helped them beat the heat.

FLUENCY BUILDER Use *Intervention Practice Book* page 75. Call attention to the sentences on the bottom half of the page. The slashes break the sentences into phrases to allow you to work on natural phrasing. Tell children that their goal is to read each phrase or sentence smoothly. Model appropriate pace, expression, and phrasing as you read each sentence, and have children read it after you. Then have children practice by reading the sentences aloud three times to a partner.

INTERVENTION PRACTICE BOOK
page 75

Cool Ali/Sounds All Around **191**

BEFORE
Making Connections
pages 118–119

Directed Reading: "Sounds All Around," pp. 150–156

Ask a volunteer to read aloud the title. Ask children what sounds they might hear all around. Have children read page 150 to see if Jules, the boy in the story, hears some sounds. Ask: **Does Jules hear sounds as he walks home?** (*Possible response: Not yet.*) **INTERPRET STORY EVENTS**

SOUNDS OF SUNSHINE pp. 150–156

Why is Jules sad? (*Possible response: He misses Mrs. Lee.*) **INDENTIFY CHARACTERS' FEELINGS**

What word on this page is an antonym for *happy*? (*Possible response: sad*) **ANTONYMS**

Page 151

Have children read to find out what sounds Jules hears. Ask: **What does Jules hear as he walks?** (*Possible response: He hears Mr. Jones's chalk on the sidewalk; children playing; Mrs. Peck selling fruit; Sue's tune on her flute; a dump truck; rain.*) **What do you think Jules's plan is?** (*Possible response: He will draw a picture for Mrs. Lee. Accept reasonable responses.*) **MAKE PREDICTIONS**

Page 152

Have children read page 152 to find out what Jules does the next day. Ask: **What does Jules do the next morning?** (*Possible response: He visits Mrs. Lee in the hospital.*) **NOTE DETAILS**

What do you think is in the bag? (*Possible response: It is a surprise for Mrs. Lee. Accept reasonable responses.*) **MAKE PREDICTIONS**

Page 153

Have children read page 153 to find out what is in Jules's bag. Ask: **What is in Jules's bag?** (*Possible response: fruit from Mrs. Peck, drawings from the children, and chalk from Mr. Jones*) **NOTE DETAILS**

What do you think the coolest present of all will be? (*Possible response: It is something that makes a nice sound. Accept reasonable responses, but encourage children to think about the title before they answer.*) **MAKE PREDICTIONS**

Pages 154–155

Read aloud pages 154–155 to children. Model using the Create Mental Images strategy in order for children to understand why the tape of sounds helped Mrs. Lee feel as if she were right there in the crowd.

> **MODEL** I picture the story in my mind to help me understand what I am reading. I use the details about characters, setting, and events to picture the scene the author is describing. I think Mrs. Lee was creating pictures in her mind based on the sounds she heard and what she remembers about her neighborhood. That's why she felt like she was right there in the crowd. **CREATE MENTAL IMAGES**

Page 156

Read aloud the first sentence on page 156. Then have children read the page to find out about the last sound on the tape. Ask: **What is the last sound on the tape?** (*Possible response: the sound of rain*) **NOTE DETAILS** **Why do you think Mrs. Lee draws a rainbow?** (*Possible response: because*

192 Lesson 19 • Intervention Teacher's Guide

it is pretty and cheerful; because it can appear after a rainstorm. Accept reasonable responses.) **SPECULATE**

Does Jules's plan work? *(Possible response: Yes; he plans to cheer up Mrs. Lee, and he does.)* **DRAW CONCLUSIONS**

Summarize the selection. Ask children to tell how the sounds of Jules's neighborhood tell what the place is like. Then have them complete *Intervention Practice Book* page 77.

Answers to *Think About It* Questions

1. Jules brings her gifts from everyone in the neighborhood. He also brings a tape of all the neighborhood sounds. **SUMMARIZE**
2. He asks them to help. They all like Mrs. Lee, so they are happy to help. **DRAW CONCLUSIONS**
3. Accept reasonable responses. Encourage children to picture Jules's neighborhood in their minds to help them decide what to draw. **GENERALIZE**

(Focus Skill) Antonyms

RETEACH the skill. Have children look at **side B of Skill Card 19: Antonyms**. Read the skill reminder with them, and have a volunteer read the story aloud.

Read aloud the set of directions. Explain that partners will create their own charts. Remind them to look for words that have opposite meanings as they read the story. After children have completed their antonym charts, have them explain their work. Ask volunteers to name some words and their antonyms from the "Sounds All Around."

Review Phonics Skill from "Cool Ali."

RETEACH Inflections: -es (f to v). Read aloud the following sentence: *Books about leaves, wolves, and elves are on the shelves.* Have children identify words with inflection *-es* in which *f* was changed to *v*. *(leaves, wolves, elves, shelves)* Write the words on the board and read them with children.

FLUENCY BUILDER Use *Intervention Practice Book* page 75. Explain that children will practice the sentences on the bottom half of the page by reading them aloud on tape. Assign new partners. Have children take turns reading the sentences aloud to each other and then reading them on tape. Have children listen to the tape and tell how they think their reading has improved. Then have them record the sentences one more time.

Cool Ali/Sounds All Around

BEFORE

Drafting a Personal Story Beginning
page 119A

Writing Process: Personal Story

Build on prior knowledge. Tell children that they are going to talk about and write personal stories. Explain that sometimes people write personal stories to tell about events that have happened to them. Tell children that it is important to have a good beginning in a personal story, so that readers can understand what the story will be about, or to tell about something surprising that will make the reader interested or curious about the story. Have children share ideas for a good beginning of a personal story they might write if they lived in the neighborhood in "Cool Ali."

> city neighborhood
> hot weather
> lots of nice neighbors
> chalk pictures

Construct the text. "Share the pen" with children. Help children to organize some or all of the items on the list into a good beginning for a personal story. For example:

It was a very hot day in my neighborhood. All my neighbors in my neighborhood were complaining about the hot weather. I drew chalk pictures of the ocean to keep my neighbors cool.

Revisit the text. Read the personal story beginning together. Ask: **What is this personal story about?** (*It is about someone who drew chalk pictures to help their neighbors forget about the heat.*)

- Guide children to make the beginning read more smoothly. Ask: **What words can I take out of the second sentence to make the beginning read more smoothly?** (*in my neighborhood*) Make appropriate changes.

- Ask: **What else can we add to continue this personal story?** (*Possible response: details about the chalk pictures and how the neighbors reacted to them*) Make appropriate changes.

- Have children read the completed personal story beginning aloud and then copy it onto their papers.

On Your Own

Have children write three sentences that could be the beginning of their own personal story about something they did. Invite them to read their story beginnings aloud.

Lesson 19 • Intervention Teacher's Guide

AFTER

Spelling Lesson pages 119G

Connect Spelling and Phonics

RETEACH vowel variant: /o͞o/ *u-e, ue, ui.* Tell children to number their papers 1–8. Write the letters *u-e* on the board, and tell children that in the words you say, the /o͞o/ sound will be spelled *u-e*. Dictate the following words, and have children write them. After children write each word, write it on the board so that they can proofread their work. They should draw a line through a misspelled word and write the correct spelling beside it.

1. duke	2. plume	3. Jules*	4. dune
5. June	6. tune*	7. rule	8. flute*

* Word appears in "Sounds All Around."

Tell children that in the following sentence, the /o͞o/ sound will be spelled *ue* or *ui*. Dictate the sentence and have children write it: *It is true that Sue has a blue fruit.*

Build and Read Longer Words

Remind children that they have learned how to decode words with the /o͞o/ sound. Explain that now they will use what they have learned to help them read some longer words.

Write the word *fruitcake* on the board. Remind children that they can often figure out longer words by looking for smaller words in them. Cover *cake*, and have children read the remaining word. Follow a similar procedure to have them read the smaller word *cake*. Model how to blend the two smaller words to read aloud the longer word *fruitcake*. Do the same to have children blend word parts to read these longer words: *suitcase* and *bluebird*.

INTERVENTION ASSESSMENT BOOK

FLUENCY BUILDER Have children choose a passage from "Sounds All Around" to read aloud to a partner. You may have children choose passages that they found particularly interesting, or have them choose one of the following options:

- Read pages 150–151. (From *Jules was one*... through... *went rushing by.* Total: 107 words.)

- Read pages 154–155. (From *He pressed*... through... *"That's a truck," she said.* Total: 90 words.)

Children should read the selected passage aloud to their partners three times. Have children rate each of their own readings on a scale of 1 to 4.

SCALE
1 Not so good
2 Pretty good
3 Good
4 Great!

Cool Ali/Sounds All Around

BEFORE Weekly Assessments

Review Vocabulary

To review the Vocabulary Words prior to the weekly assessment, use these sentences. Read aloud the sentence stems and answer choices. Children identify the correct answer and explain why it makes sense.

1. If you are in a **haze**, it will
    a. be hard to see things clearly.
    b. be clear.
2. The chalk was **pale**, so it was a
    a. dark color.
    b. light color.
3. If you **notice** things, you are
    a. aware of them.
    b. not seeing them.
4. If you **mimicked** a dog, you would want to
    a. sound just like the dog.
    b. sound just like a cat.
5. I **admired** her bracelet because I
    a. did not like it.
    b. liked it a lot.
6. The baby **fussed** because it was
    a. uncomfortable.
    b. very happy.

Correct responses: 1.a, 2.b, 3.a, 4.a, 5.b, 6.a

You may want to display the Vocabulary Words and definitions from page 189, and have children copy them to use when they study.

(Focus Skill) Review Antonyms

To review antonyms before the weekly assessment, distribute *Intervention Practice Book* page 78. Have volunteers read aloud the direction line and the story. Guide children to remember to write words that mean the opposite of the words in the story.

Review Test Prep

Ask children to turn to page 121 of the *Pupil Edition*. Call attention to the Tips for answering the test items. Tell children that paying attention to these tips can help them answer not only the items on this page but also other items like them.

BANNER DAYS page 121

Have children follow along as you read each test item and the Tips. Tell children to choose the antonym and then reread the item with the answer to check whether it is correct.

INTERVENTION PRACTICE BOOK page 78

INTERVENTION ASSESSMENT BOOK

Lesson 19 • Intervention Teacher's Guide

AFTER Self-Selected Reading

Weekly Assessments

Have children select their own books to read independently. They might choose books from the classroom library shelf, or you may wish to offer a group of appropriate books from which children can choose.

- *Rainy Day Pictures* by Dana Catherine. Harcourt. BOOKS FOR ALL LEARNERS
- *D. W. All Wet* by Marc Brown. Little, Brown, 1991.
- *At the Beach* by Huy Voun Lee. Holt, 1998.

After children have chosen their books, give them a copy of My Reading Log, which can be found on page R35 in the back of the *Teacher's Edition*. Have children fill in the information at the top of the form. Then have them use the log to keep track of their reading and to record their responses to the literature.

Conduct student-teacher conferences. Arrange time for each child to confer with you individually about his or her self-selected reading. Have children bring their Reading Logs to share with you at the conference. Children might also like to choose a favorite passage to read aloud to you. Ask questions designed to stimulate discussion about the book. For example, ask why children chose the book, whether they would like to do any of the activities they read about, or what was the funniest/saddest/most interesting part.

FLUENCY PERFORMANCE Have children read aloud to you the passage from "Sounds All Around" that they practiced. Observe the children's pronunciation, intonation, phrasing, and the amount of words, in general, that they read correctly. Ask each child to rate his or her own performance on the 1–4 scale. If children are not happy with their oral reading, give them an opportunity to continue practicing and then to reread the passage to you.

See the *Oral Reading Fluency Assessment* for monitoring progress.

LESSON 20

BEFORE Building Background and Vocabulary

"The Emperor's Egg"

Review Phonics: Long Vowel: /ā/ai, ay

Identify the sound. Have children repeat the following sentence three times: *Gail plays with pails in the rain all day.* Ask them which words in the sentence have the long *a* vowel sound that they hear in *may*. (*Gail, plays, pails, rain, day*)

Associate letters to sound. On the board, write: *Gail plays with pails in the rain all day*. Circle the words *Gail*, *plays*, *pails*, *rain*, and *day*. Ask children to tell how the words are alike. (*All have the /ā/ sound*) Then underline the letters *ai* in *Gail*, *pails*, and *rain*, and the letters *ay* in *plays*, and *day*. Tell children that the letters *ai* and *ay* can stand for the /ā/ sound they hear in *Gail*, *plays*, *pails*, *rain*, and *day*.

Word blending. Model how to blend and read the word *train*, having children repeat each step after you. Write *train* on the board. Slide your hand under the letters as you slowly elongate the sounds /trrāānn/. Then read *train* naturally. Follow a similar procedure for *sail* and *clay*. Then write these words on the board: *chain*, *hay*. Have children blend the sounds and read them aloud.

Apply the skill. *Vowel Substitution* Write the following words on the board, and have children read them aloud. Make the changes necessary to form the words in parentheses. Have children read each new word aloud.

see (say)   **we** (way)   **ran** (rain)   **pal** (pail)

bee (bay)   **tree** (tray)   **bat** (bait)   **chin** (chain)

INTERVENTION PRACTICE BOOK page 80

Introduce Vocabulary

PRETEACH lesson vocabulary. Tell children that they will learn six new words that they will see again when they read a story called "The Emperor's Egg." Teach each Vocabulary Word using the following process.

Use the following suggestions or similar ideas to give the meaning or context.

flippers	Point out the -s ending. Show pictures of penguin or fish flippers and use your hands to show how they move.
hatch	Discuss how chicks break out of eggs.
miserable	Share related words: *misery, sad, unhappy*. Role-play the facial expression of a person who feels miserable.

> Write the word.
> Say the word.
> Track the word and have children repeat it.
> Give the meaning or context.

198 Lesson 20 • Intervention Teacher's Guide

slippery	Point out the base word *slip*. Role-play a person walking on a floor that is slippery.
waddled	Have children role-play waddling like ducks.
horizon	Draw a picture of a simple landscape with the sun setting or rising on the horizon.

For vocabulary activities, see Vocabulary Games on pages 2–7.

> **Vocabulary Words**
> **flippers** small fins used like hands or feet
> **hatch** to break out of an egg
> **miserable** very unhappy
> **slippery** not sticky, causing sliding
> **waddled** moved in a funny way, like a duck
> **horizon** where the sky seems to meet the earth

AFTER
Building Background and Vocabulary

Apply Vocabulary Strategies

Use familiar patterns. Write the word *flippers* on chart paper and underline the letters *fl*. Tell children that they can sometimes figure out a new word by looking for letter patterns that they know.

MODEL The letter combination *fl* is familiar to me because I have seen it in words like *flat*. I have seen the letter combination *ip* in the word *trip*. I have seen the *-s* ending in words like *cats*. When I blend the letter patterns that I know, I read *flippers*.

Guide children in using a similar procedure to decode the other Vocabulary Words.

RETEACH lesson vocabulary. Have children write each Vocabulary Word on a word card and then listen to each of the following cloze sentences. Tell them to hold up the word card that completes each sentence. Reread the sentences aloud with the correct answers. Then discuss how children made their choices.

1. The floor was __(slippery)__, so it was hard to walk.
2. The duck __(waddled)__ around the lake.
3. I saw the sun rise over the __(horizon)__.
4. The fish used its __(flippers)__ to help it swim.
5. The chick will __(hatch)__ any day now.
6. The girl felt so __(miserable)__, she cried.

FLUENCY BUILDER Use *Intervention Practice* Book page 79. Read each word in the first column aloud and have children repeat it. Then have partners read the words in the first column aloud to each other. Tell children to follow the same procedure with each of the remaining columns. After partners have practiced reading aloud the words in each column, have them practice the entire list. (Save *Intervention Practice Book* page 79 to use on page 201 and 203.)

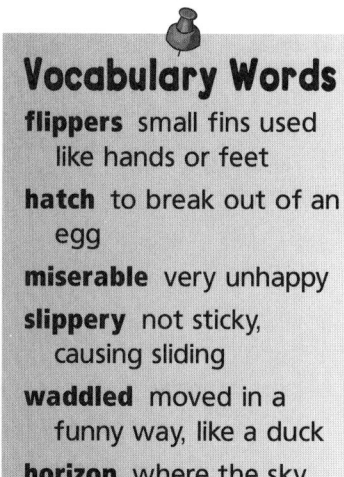

INTERVENTION PRACTICE BOOK
page 79

The Emperor's Egg/Little Blue Penguins

BEFORE
Reading "The Emperor's Egg"
pages 124–144

USE SKILL CARD 20A

(Focus Skill) Fact and Fiction

PRETEACH the skill. Point out to children that a fact is information that is real and can be proved and that fiction is information that is made up and did not happen in real life. Discuss the difference between real and make-believe things. Guide children to see that facts can be proved by methods such as observation, looking them up in books, or by asking experts.

Have children look at **side A of Skill Card 20: Fact and Fiction.** Read the definitions of *fact* and *fiction*. Next read the story, and then have children reread it with you. Then have volunteers take turns reading the information in the chart aloud. Ask:

- **How can you prove that cats like to eat goldfish?**
  (*Possible response: I can look it up in a book.*)

- **Why is the detail** "*I have a plan," said Gert* **fiction?**
  (*Possible response: Goldfish cannot talk.*)

Prepare to Read: "The Emperor's Egg"

Preview. Tell children that they are going to read an informational story called "The Emperor's Egg." Tell children that "The Emperor's Egg" gives information about a certain kind of penguin called the Emperor penguin. Then preview the selection.

BANNER DAYS
pages 124–144

- **Pages 124–125:** I see the title, "The Emperor's Egg," and the name of the author, and the illustrator. I see a picture of some big penguins and a baby penguin. I think that the story will tell about the baby penguin.

- **Pages 126–127:** On these pages, I see pictures and read about a place called Antarctica. I think that the shape in the picture is a penguin.

- **Pages 128–129:** On these pages, I see pictures and read about an Emperor penguin, his mate, and their egg. I think I will read more facts about the Emperor penguin and his egg.

Set purpose. Model setting a purpose for reading "The Emperor's Egg."

MODEL From what I have seen and read so far, I think I will read more about the life of the Emperor penguin while he is waiting for his egg to hatch. I will read to find out how the Emperor penguin takes care of his egg and the chick once it hatches.

AFTER

Reading "The Emperor's Egg"
pages 124–144

Reread and Summarize

Have children reread and summarize "The Emperor's Egg" in sections, as described below.

> Pages 124–129
> **Let's reread pages 124–129 to recall what Antarctica is like and who lives there.**
>
> Summary: Antarctica is the coldest and windiest place on Earth. Emperor penguins live there.
>
> Pages 130–137
> **Let's reread pages 130–137 to recall what the female and male Emperor penguins do after the female lays an egg.**
>
> Summary: For two months, the female swims and eats as much as she can. The male penguin stands on the ice with the egg tucked between his feet and his tummy to keep it warm so it will hatch.
>
> The father penguin has thick feathers and lots of fat to keep him warm. All the father penguins snuggle together and move around slowly on the ice.
>
> Pages 138–140
> **Let's reread pages 138–140 to remember what happens when the egg hatches.**
>
> Summary: A penguin chick pops out of the egg. The father penguin keeps it warm and feeds it with something like milk that he makes in a pouch in his throat.
>
> Pages 141–144
> **Let's reread pages 141–144 to recall what happens when the father runs out of the milky stuff.**
>
> Summary: The mother penguin comes back. Then the mother penguin feeds the chick. Now it is her turn to take care of it while the father goes away to eat.

FLUENCY BUILDER Use *Intervention Practice Book* page 79. Call attention to the sentences on the bottom half of the page. The slashes break the sentences into phrases to allow you to work on natural phrasing. Tell children that their goal is to read each phrase or sentence smoothly. Model appropriate pace, expression and phrasing as you read each sentence, and have children read it after you. Then have children practice by reading the sentences aloud three times to a partner.

INTERVENTION PRACTICE BOOK

page 79

The Emperor's Egg/Little Blue Penguins

BEFORE
Making Connections
pages 146–147

Directed Reading: "Little Blue Penguins," pp. 158–163

Ask a volunteer to read aloud the title. Ask children what they might find out about little blue penguins. Have children read pages 158–159 to find out if the story tells facts or fiction about little blue penguins. Ask: **Are the penguins in this story real? How can you tell?** (*Possible response: Yes. I read facts about them that I can check in a book.*) **Focus Skill FACT AND FICTION**

SOUNDS of SUNSHINE
pp. 158–163

Reread page 159 aloud. Model using the Look at Word Bits and Parts strategy to help for children understand how to read and figure out the meanings of long or unfamiliar words.

> **MODEL** As I read, I don't always know every word. If I have trouble reading a long word, I look at the bits and parts that I know. I see *flip* in the word *flippers,* so now I can read *flippers,* too.

Focus strategy LOOK AT WORD BITS AND PARTS

Page 160

Have children read page 160 to compare and contrast little blue penguins and emperor penguins. Ask: **How are little blue penguins and emperor penguins alike? How are they different?** (*Possible responses: They are both penguins; the little blue penguin is the smallest kind of penguin and the emperor is the largest kind of penguin.*) **COMPARE AND CONTRAST**

Page 161

Have children read page 161 to find out why the little blue penguin would be miserable in Antarctica. Ask: **Why would little blue penguins be miserable in Antarctica?** (*Possible response: Antarctica is always cold, and little blue penguins like the warmer seas and beaches of Australia and New Zealand.*) **CAUSE AND EFFECT**

Page 162

Have children read page 162 to find out what happens after the little blue penguins lay their eggs. Ask: **What happens after the little blue penguin has laid two eggs? What happens next?** (*Possible response: The parents take turns on the nest; one stays on the eggs while the other goes for food; next, the eggs hatch, and a month after that, the chicks come up out of their nests.*) **SEQUENCE OF EVENTS**

Page 163

Have children read page 163 to find out what happens to the chicks. You may need to explain that in this story, *down* means "the soft feathers of very young birds." Ask: **How do the chicks change after they are born?** (*Possible response: At first, they are covered with plain, dark down, but then they turn blue just like their parents.*) **NOTE DETAILS**

INTERVENTION PRACTICE BOOK
page 81

Summarize the selection. Ask children to summarize the selection by telling about the stages in a little blue penguin's life, beginning with the egg. Then have them complete *Intervention Practice Book* page 81.

Page 164

Answers to *Think About It* Questions

1. Little blue penguins live in underground nests in the sand dunes of Australia and New Zealand. They eat little sea animals called *krill* and small fish. **SUMMARIZE**

2. Possible response: Yes, because we have sandy beaches and warm ocean water. Accept reasonable responses. Encourage children to support their answers. **DRAW CONCLUSIONS/INTERPRETATION**

3. Accept reasonable responses. Encourage children to add details to the picture and the words on their posters. **IMPORTANT DETAILS**

AFTER
Skill Review
pages 149C–149D

USE SKILL CARD 20B

(Focus Skill) Fact and Fiction

RETEACH the skill. Have children look at **side B of Skill Card 20: Fact and Fiction**. Read the skill reminder with them, and have a volunteer read the story aloud.

Read aloud the set of directions. Explain that children will work with partners to create their own charts. Remind them to think about what is real or facts, and what is make-believe or fiction, as they read the story.

After children have completed their fact and fiction charts, have them display and explain their work. Point out that there are many facts in the selection "Little Blue Penguins." Ask volunteers to name some facts that they have learned about little blue penguins.

Review Phonics from "The Emperor's Egg"

RETEACH suffixes *-ing, -ly*. Read aloud the following sentences, and have children repeat each one three times: *The wind blew strongly. It was raining as we went sailing on the lake.* Have children identify words with suffixes *-ing* or *-ly*. Write them on the board and have children read them. Then have volunteers think of more words with these suffixes.

FLUENCY BUILDER Use *Intervention Practice Book* page 79. Explain that children will practice the sentences on the bottom half of the page by reading them aloud on tape. Assign new partners. Have children take turns reading the sentences aloud to each other and then reading them on tape. Have children listen to the tape and tell how they think their reading has improved. Then have them record the sentences one more time.

INTERVENTION PRACTICE BOOK
page 79

The Emperor's Egg/Little Blue Penguins

BEFORE
Drafting a Fantasy Story Beginning
page 147A

Daily Writing: Fantasy Story Beginning

Build on prior knowledge. Tell children that they are going to talk about and write the beginning of a fantasy story. Explain that fantasy stories tell about things that are make-believe. Tell children that fantasy stories can take place in made-up places or settings. Have children share ideas for characters and settings for a fantasy story.

> tiny red penguin
> pink sky
> purple clouds
> snow

Construct the text. "Share the pen" with children. Tell them that the list names things that are in a fantasy story. Help children organize the items on the list into the beginning of a fantasy story. Guide them to focus on the setting of their story. For example:

> Once upon a time, there lived a tiny red penguin. The tiny red penguin lived in a wonderful place. He could see a pink sky and purple clouds. There was snow all around.

Revisit the text. Reread the fantasy story beginning together. Ask: **What is the setting of this story?** (*a wonderful place with a pink sky, purple clouds, and snow*) **Who is the character in this story?**
(*a tiny red penguin*)

- Guide children to add details to the story. Ask: **What does the snow look like?** (*Possible response: It is orange and sparkly.*) Make appropriate changes.

- Ask: **How else can I tell about the setting?** (*Tell when the story takes place.*) Make appropriate changes.

- Have children read aloud the completed fantasy story beginning and then copy it onto their papers.

On Your Own
Have children draw a picture and then write a list of details that tell about the setting of a fantasy story they would like to write.

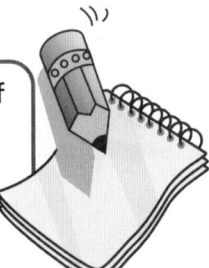

AFTER

Spelling Lesson
page 149A

Connect Spelling and Phonics

RETEACH long vowel: /ā/*ai, ay.* Tell children to number their papers 1–8. Write *say* on the board, and tell children that in the words you will say, the /ā/ sound will be spelled *ay* as in *say*. Dictate the following words, and have children write them. After children write each word, write it on the board so that they can proofread their work. They should draw a line through a misspelled word and write the correct spelling beside it.

| 1. bay* | 2. away* | 3. days* | 4. way* |
| 5. play* | 6. gray* | 7. lay* | 8. stays* |

* Word appears in "Little Blue Penguins."

Tell children that in the following sentence, the long vowel *a* sound will be spelled *ai*. Dictate the sentence and have children write it: *Gail sails next to the train on the plain.*

Build and Read Longer Words

Remind children that they have learned how to decode words with the /ā/ sound. Explain that now they will use what they have learned to help them read some longer words.

Write the word *crayon* on the board. Remind children that they can often figure out longer words by looking for smaller parts in them. Cover the letters *on*, and have children read the word part that is left. Then cover *cray* and have them read the word part *on*. Model how to blend the word parts to read aloud the longer word *crayon*. Follow a similar procedure to have children blend word parts to read these longer words: *raining, daytime,* and *haystack*.

INTERVENTION ASSESSMENT BOOK

FLUENCY BUILDER Have children choose a passage from "Little Blue Penguins" to read aloud to a partner. You may have children choose passages that they found particularly interesting, or have them choose one of the following options:

- Read pages 158–159. (From the title . . . through . . . *under the ground*. Total: 94 words.)
- Read pages 162–163. (From *In summer* . . . through . . . *like their parents*. Total: 95 words.)

Children should read the selected passage aloud to their partners three times. Have children rate each of their own readings on a scale from 1 to 4.

The Emperor's Egg/Little Blue Penguins

BEFORE Weekly Assessments

Review Vocabulary

To review the Vocabulary Words prior to the weekly assessments, use these sentences. Read aloud the sentence stems and answer choices. Children identify the correct answer and explain why it makes sense.

1. At the **horizon**, the sun seems to
   - a. touch the ground.
   - b. be many miles from the earth.
2. In the play, the girl **waddled** like a
   - a. cat.
   - b. duck.
3. The boy was **miserable**, and so he
   - a. laughed.
   - b. cried.
4. If the floor is **slippery**, it will be
   - a. easy to slide on.
   - b. sticky.
5. When the chicks **hatch**, the egg shells
   - a. will not break.
   - b. will break.
6. The penguin uses its **flippers** to help it
   - a. chew food.
   - b. swim.

Correct responses: 1.a, 2.b, 3.b, 4.a, 5.b, 6.b.

You may want to display the Vocabulary Words and definitions on page 199, and have children copy them to use when they study for the vocabulary test.

Focus Skill ★ Review Fact and Fiction

To review Fact and Fiction before the weekly assessment, distribute *Intervention Practice Book* page 82. Have volunteers read aloud the direction line and the story. Remind children to think about which details are make-believe, or fiction, and which are real, or facts.

Review Test Prep

Ask children to turn to page 149 of the *Pupil Edition*. Call attention to the Tips for answering the test questions. Tell children that paying attention to these tips can help them answer not only the items on this page but also other test items like them.

Have children follow along as you read each test item and the Tips. Tell children to take their time as they think about the answer choices for each item.

INTERVENTION PRACTICE BOOK
page 82

INTERVENTION ASSESSMENT BOOK

BANNER DAYS
page 149

Lesson 20 • Intervention Teacher's Guide

AFTER
Weekly Assessments

Self-Selected Reading

Have children select their own books to read independently. They might choose books from the classroom library, or you may wish to offer appropriate books from which children can choose, such as these:

- *Staying Warm* by Jane Manners. Harcourt. INDEPENDENT READER
- *Frogs* by Gail Gibbons. Holiday House, 1993.
- *Owl Babies* by Martin Waddel. Candelwick, 1995.

After children have chosen their books, give them a copy of My Reading Log, which can be found on page R35 in the back of the *Teacher's Edition*. Have children fill in the information at the top of the form. Then have them use the log to keep track of their reading and to record their responses to the literature.

Conduct student-teacher conferences. Arrange time for each child to confer with you individually about his or her self-selected reading. Have children bring their Reading Logs to share with you at the conference. Children might also like to choose a favorite passage to read aloud to you. Ask questions designed to stimulate discussion about the book. For example, ask what children find especially interesting, whether or not they would read another book about that topic, or why they chose the book.

FLUENCY PERFORMANCE Have children read aloud to you the passage from "Little Blue Penguins" that they practiced. Observe children's pronunciation, intonation, phrasing, and the amount of words, in general, that they read correctly. Ask each child to rate his or her own performance on the 1–4 scale. If children are not happy with their oral reading, give them an opportunity to continue practicing and then to reread the passage to you.

See *Oral Reading Fluency Assessment* for **monitoring progress.**

LESSON 21

BEFORE
Building Background and Vocabulary

Use with

"The Pine Park Mystery"

Review Phonics: Long Vowels /ē/e, /ī/ i, /ō/o

Identify the sound. Ask children to repeat the following sentence three times: *She told me to find this kind, old man.* Ask children to name the words in the sentence that have the /ē/, /ī/, or /ō/ sound. (*she, me, find, kind, told, old*)

Associate letters to sound. On the board, write the sentence: *She told me to find this kind old man.* Circle the words *she* and *me*, and ask how these two words are alike. (*same vowel sound, /ē/; letter e*) Tell children that in words like *she* and *me*, the e often stands for the /ē/ sound. Follow a similar procedure with the vowel sounds /ī/ in *find* and *kind* and /ō/ in *told* and *old*.

Word blending. Model how to blend and read the word *fold*. Slide your hand under the word as you elongate the sounds: /ffōōlld/. Then say the word naturally—*fold*. Follow a similar procedure for the words *we, child, mind* and *bold*.

Apply the skill. *Letter Substitution* Write the following words on the board, and have children read each aloud. Make the changes necessary to form the words in parentheses. Have a volunteer read aloud each new word.

mend (mind)	**hay** (he)	**tail** (toll)	**blend** (blind)
say (so)	**grand** (grind)	**may** (me)	**must** (most)

Introduce Vocabulary

PRETEACH **lesson vocabulary.** Tell children that they are going to learn seven new words that they will see again when they read "The Pine Park Mystery." Teach each Vocabulary Word using the following process.

Use the following suggestions or similar ideas to give the meaning or context.

> Write the word.
> Say the word.
> Track the word and have children repeat it.
> Give the meaning or context.

caused — Knock some papers off your desk. Ask what caused the papers to end up on the floor. Have children come up with other cause-and-effect pairs.

clasp — Children might be familiar with clasping hands. Explain that this *clasp* means "a hook." Have children show clasps they might have on clothing or jewelry.

confused — Have children share a time they were confused, perhaps when they did not know in which direction to walk.

INTERVENTION PRACTICE BOOK
page 84

cornered	Have children look at the corner of the room. Have them think of a cat cornering a mouse there.
objects	Place several things in front of you, such as a stapler, book, and so on. Explain that these things are objects. Things you can touch are objects.
removes	Point out the word *move*. Have a child take objects from a pile one at a time. Explain that he or she is removing the objects.
typical	Have a child describe what usually happens during a school day. Explain that this is a typical day.

Vocabulary Words
caused made something happen
clasp a small hook that holds parts together
confused to be uncertain or unclear about something
cornered to get a person or an animal into a situation or position that is a trap
objects things that you can see and touch but are not alive
removes takes away
typical normal or usual for a kind of thing

For vocabulary activities, see Vocabulary Games on pages 2–7.

AFTER
Building Background and Vocabulary

Apply Vocabulary Strategies

Use familiar word parts. Write the word *cornered* on chart paper and underline the *-ed* ending. Tell children that they can sometimes figure out the meaning of a word by looking for letter patterns that they know.

> **MODEL** I know the word part *-ed* because I have seen it in action words. If I leave it off, I know the base word *corner*.

RETEACH lesson vocabulary. Have children listen to each of the following sentences. Tell them to hold up the word card that completes each one.

1. On a __(typical)__ day, I eat cereal for breakfast.
2. We will count the __(objects)__ before we put them in the box.
3. The rain __(caused)__ the flowers to grow.
4. The directions were not clear, so I was __(confused)__.
5. My brother is too little, so my mom __(removes)__ his boots for him.
6. I lost my necklace when the __(clasp)__ broke.
7. I __(cornered)__ Dad and made him promise to take me to the park.

FLUENCY BUILDER Using *Intervention Practice Book* page 83, read each word in the first column aloud and have children repeat it. Then have children work in pairs to read the words in the first column aloud to each other. Follow the same procedure with each of the remaining columns. (Save *Intervention Practice Book* page 83 to use on pages 211 and 213.)

INTERVENTION PRACTICE BOOK
page 83

The Pine Park Mystery/A Secret Place

BEFORE
Reading "The Pine Park Mystery"
pages 154–169

USE SKILL CARD 21A

Focus Skill: Narrative Elements

PRETEACH the skill. Point out to children that characters in a story have a problem that they must solve. Keeping track of how the characters solve the problem will help children understand the plot of the story.

Have children look at **side A of Skill Card 21: Narrative Elements.** Read the definition of narrative elements. Next, have children read through the story. Have them identify the problem that Jo is trying to solve. Then call attention to the chart. Ask:

1. **What is Jo's problem?** (*Possible response: She has a secret she wants to tell.*)

2. **How does she go about trying to find someone to tell?** (*Possible response: She goes to Mark's, Matt's, and Jill's homes, and then she goes to the park. She finds her friends there.*)

3. **What happens at the end of the story?** (*Possible response: Jo tells her friends she got a new mitt.*)

Explain that all of these are events in the plot.

Prepare to Read: "The Pine Park Mystery"

Preview. Tell children that they are going to read a selection entitled "The Pine Park Mystery." Explain that this is a play written for seven characters. The play is about how a mystery is solved. Then preview the selection.

BANNER DAYS
pages 154–169

- **Page 154:** On page 154, under the heading "Time," I see when the story takes place. It says *The present,* which means it could be happening right now. The setting is where the action takes place. It says *Pine Park,* which is a typical town park. There is also a list of the characters.

- **Page 155:** I see the title, "The Pine Park Mystery," and the names of the author and illustrator on page 155. Just under that, I see Scene One. Scenes are a way of dividing up the action in a play. Usually, there is an important event in each scene.

- **Pages 156–157:** I see four people—a man running, a woman sitting on a bench, and a girl and a boy playing catch.

- **Pages 158–159:** On these pages, I see a picture of a police officer looking for something. This part must be about what he is looking for.

- **Pages 160–161:** I see people looking at a sign. It lists things that are missing. That must be part of the mystery.

Set purpose. Model setting a purpose for reading "The Pine Park Mystery."

MODEL From my preview, I can see that I will probably be reading about a mystery involving some missing objects. I will read to find out what happened to them.

AFTER

Reading "The Pine Park Mystery"
pages 154–169

Reread and Summarize

Have children reread and summarize "The Pine Park Mystery" in sections, as described below.

Pages 154–155

Let's reread pages 154–155 to recall where and when the play takes place.

Summary: The play takes place in Pine Park on a beautiful, sunny afternoon.

Pages 156–161

Let's reread pages 156–161 to recall what objects people are missing.

Summary: Mayor Pitt lost the silver pin off her jacket. Lan is missing her charm bracelet. Chief Wilson is missing his badge, and Coach Lee is missing his whistle. Miss Rosa is looking for something, too, but we do not know what.

Pages 162–163

Let's reread pages 162–163 to see how Lan and Jeff try to solve the mystery.

Summary: Lan and Jeff put a bicycle lock key out to see if they can use it to catch the thief, who seems to like small, shiny objects.

Pages 164–168

Let's reread pages 164–168 to see who the thief is.

Summary: Jeff and Lan discover that Miss Rosa's mynah bird, Dynah, is taking the objects and keeping them in a tree in the park.

FLUENCY BUILDER Be sure children have copies of *Intervention Practice Book* page 83, which you used for the previous Fluency Builder activity. Call attention to the sentences on the bottom half of the page. The slashes break the sentences into phrases to allow children to work on natural phrasing. Tell children that their goal is to read each phrase or sentence smoothly. Model appropriate pace, expression, and phrasing as you read each sentence and have children read it after you. Then have children practice by reading the sentences aloud three times to a partner.

INTERVENTION PRACTICE BOOK
page 83

The Pine Park Mystery/A Secret Place

BEFORE
Making Connections
pages 172–173

Directed Reading: "A Secret Place" pp. 166–173

Read aloud the title of the play. Then have children read aloud the characters' names. Ask what a narrator is. Tell children to read page 166 to find out why it is not a typical day. Ask: **Why isn't it a typical day?** (*Possible response: It is a snow day, so there is no school.*) **CAUSE-EFFECT**

SOUNDS OF SUNSHINE
pp. 166–173

Ask: **What problem does Jo have when she comes in for lunch?** (*Possible response: The blocks have been knocked over.*) **NARRATIVE ELEMENTS**

Page 167

Have children read page 167 to find out who Jo and Lee think took their things. Ask: **Who does Lee think took the car?** (*Jo*) **Who does Jo think took the blocks?** (*Lee*) **DRAW CONCLUSIONS**

Ask: **Who do the children call?** (*Mom*) **Why?** (*Possible response: They think she can help solve the problem.*) **SPECULATE**

Page 168

Ask a volunteer to read aloud the "Mom" part on page 168 while children listen to find out the meaning of *objects*. Model the Use Context to Confirm Meaning strategy:

> **MODEL** When I listened to this section, I listened to the sentences after the one that mentioned the word *objects*. It mentioned blocks and a small, shiny car. Those things must be objects. Objects must be items that you can touch, like toys. **USE CONTEXT TO CONFIRM MEANING**

Ask: **What does Mom tell the children to do?** (*Possible response: Look for clues.*) **SUMMARIZE**

Ask: **What do the children think of Mom's idea?** (*Possible response: They think it's a good idea.*) **DRAW CONCLUSIONS**

Ask: **Who is Wags?** (*a dog*) **DRAW CONCLUSIONS/NOTE PICTURE CLUES**

Page 169

Have children read page 169 to find out why Mom comes back. Ask: **Why does Mom come back?** (*Possible responses: She is confused; she is missing her car key.*) **DRAW CONCLUSIONS**

Ask: **Where do you think all the missing objects are?** (*Possible responses: in a secret hiding place; lost*) **MAKE PREDICTIONS**

Pages 170–171

Have children read pages 170–171 to find out whether the children find the toys. Ask: **Do Lee and Jo find the missing objects?** (*no*) **What do they do?** (*They start to clean up.*) **NOTE DETAILS**

Ask: **What do you think the lumps in Wags's bed might be?** (*Possible responses: bones; the missing objects*) **MAKE PREDICTIONS**

212 Lesson 21 • Intervention Teacher's Guide

Page 172

Have children read page 172 to confirm their predictions. Ask: **What are the lumps in Wags's bed?** (*the missing objects*) **CONFIRM PREDICTIONS**

Ask: **Why does Jo say, "Now we know Wags has a secret hiding place of his own"?** (*Possible response: because Wags hid the toys in his bed*) **SUMMARIZE**

Summarize the selection. Ask children to think about what Jo and Lee lost and how they found the objects.

INTERVENTION PRACTICE BOOK *page 85*

Answers to *Think About It* Questions

1. They do not know that the missing things are hidden in Wags's bed. **SUMMARIZE**
2. They are surprised and happy to find the missing things. They say that they don't mind and that they will know where to look next time. **INTERPRET STORY EVENTS**
3. Accept reasonable responses. **WRITE A STORY**

AFTER
Skill Review *page 173I*

USE SKILL CARD 21B

(Focus Skill) Narrative Elements

RETEACH the skill. Have children look at **side B of Skill Card 21: Narrative Elements**. Read the skill reminder with them, and have a volunteer read the paragraph aloud. Then read aloud the next set of directions. Explain that children will work with partners to create their story maps. Remind them to identify the characters and the setting and then name the problem, the events, and the solution to the problem.

After children have completed their story maps, have them display and explain their work. Point out that in the problem, the steps the characters take to solve it, and the solution are all parts of the plot.

Review Phonics Skill: from "The Pine Park Mystery"

RETEACH prefixes *re-*, *pre-*. Write the words *reset*, *remake*, and *replay* on the board. For each word, ask a volunteer to circle the prefix *re-* and underline the base word. Then discuss the meaning of *re-* and how it changes the meaning of the words. Follow a similar procedure with the words *preset*, *prepay*, and *preview*.

FLUENCY BUILDER Be sure that children have copies of *Intervention Practice Book* page 83. Explain that today children will practice the sentences on the bottom half of the page by reading them aloud on tape. Assign new partners. Have children take turns reading the sentences aloud to each other and then reading them on tape.

INTERVENTION PRACTICE BOOK *page 83*

The Pine Park Mystery/A Secret Place

BEFORE
Drafting a Descriptive Paragraph
page 175C

Word Choice: Descriptive Paragraph

Build on prior knowledge. Tell children that they are going to talk and write about popcorn. Display the following information.

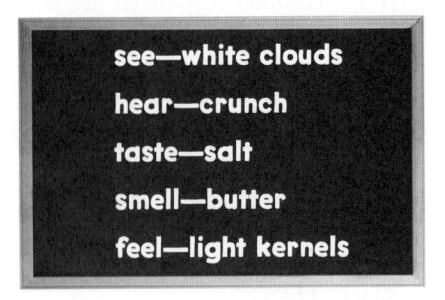

> see—white clouds
> hear—crunch
> taste—salt
> smell—butter
> feel—light kernels

Construct the text. "Share the pen" with children. Guide them in using the words above to write descriptive sentences. For example:

- I see the white clouds of popcorn.
- I hear a crunch when I bite it.
- I taste the salt.
- I smell the butter.
- I feel the light kernels.

Revisit the text. Go back and read the sentences together. Ask: **What sentences seem to go together?** (*see* and *feel*; *smell* and *taste*)

- Guide children to combine sentences, using conjunctions.
- Ask: **What sequence words, like *then* and *next*, can we add to connect the sentences?** Make the appropriate changes.
- Have children read the completed paragraph aloud and then copy it on their papers.

On Your Own

Have children write a short descriptive paragraph about their favorite food. Suggest that they try to include all five senses in their descriptions.

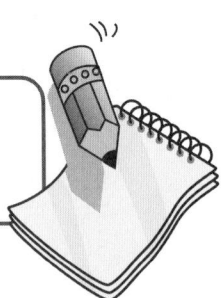

AFTER
Spelling Lesson
page 169H

Connect Spelling and Phonics

RETEACH long vowels /ē/e, /ī/ i, /ō/o. Write the word *we* on the board. Explain that you will say three more words which have the /ē/ sound. Have volunteers write each word on the board. Then write the word *kind* on the board, explain that you will say three more words which have the /ī/ sound, and repeat the process. Finally, write the word *old* on the board, explain that you will say three more words which have the /ō/ sound, and repeat the process.

| 1. be* | 2. he* | 3. me* | 4. find* | 5. mind* |
| 6. wild* | 7. no* | 8. hold* | 9. gold* | |

* Word appears in "A Secret Place."

Dictate the following sentence, and have children write it: *Mo told me that she will not mind the cold.*

Build and Read Longer Words

Explain to children that they will now use what they have learned about the vowel sounds to help them read some longer words. Write the word *moment* on the board. Tell children that they can sometimes figure out an /ē/, /ī/, and /ō/ long word by looking for word parts within it. Cover *ment* and have a volunteer read *mo*. Then cover *mo* and have a volunteer read *ment*. Point out that *mo* has the /ō/ sound. Have children blend the word parts to read the longer word *moment*. Follow a similar procedure with these words: *silent, program, prevent, become,* and *spider.* Encourage children to build other long words with long vowel sounds. Suggest that they use a dictionary to look up words they are not sure about.

INTERVENTION ASSESSMENT BOOK

FLUENCY BUILDER Have children choose a passage from "A Secret Place" to read aloud to a partner. You may have children choose passages that they found particularly interesting, or have them choose one of the following options:

- Read pages 166–167. (From *Narrator: Today is . . .* through *. . . Mom!!!* Total: 107 words)

- Read pages 169–171. (From *Narrator: Mom comes back in . . .* through *. . . the lumps for you.* Total: 107 words)

Children should read the selected passage aloud to their partners three times. Have the child rate each reading on a scale of 1 to 4.

The Pine Park Mystery/A Secret Place

BEFORE Weekly Assessments

Review Vocabulary

To revisit Vocabulary Words prior to the weekly assessment, use these sentences. Have volunteers take turns reading aloud the sentence stems and the possible choices. Children should identify the correct choice and explain why that choice makes sense in the sentence.

1. When a boy **removes** his cap, he
   a. takes it off.　　　　　　b. hides it.
2. A **typical** summer day is a
   a. school day.　　　　　　b. day off.
3. The **clasp** on a necklace is what
   a. keeps it around your neck.　　b. cleans it.
4. The girl was **confused** because she
   a. took a wrong turn.　　　b. knew her way home.
5. A **cornered** animal feels
   a. safe.　　　　　　　　　b. trapped.
6. A good example of an **object** is a
   a. person.　　　　　　　　b. rock.
7. What probably caused the **flood** was too much
   a. sun.　　　　　　　　　b. rain.

Correct responses: 1a, 2b, 3a, 4a, 5b, 6b, 7b.

You may want to display the Vocabulary Words and definitions on page 209 and have children copy them to use when they study for the vocabulary test.

Focus Skill — Review Narrative Elements

To review narrative elements before the weekly assessment, distribute *Intervention Practice Book* page 86. Have volunteers read aloud the first direction line and the sentences. Guide children by having them read the first sentence together. Discuss whether this is the character's problem. Have children underline the problem.

Review Test Prep

Ask children to turn to page 175 of the *Pupil Edition*. Call attention to the tips for answering the test questions. Tell children that paying attention to these tips can help them answer not only the test questions on this page but also other test questions like these.

Have children follow along as you read each test question and the tip that goes with it. Discuss why the beginning of the story is most important to reread. (*The problem is usually found at the beginning.*) Discuss why it is important to read each answer choice carefully before choosing an answer to question 2. (*Some answers are very similar.*)

AFTER Weekly Assessments

Self-Selected Reading

Have children select their own books to read independently. They might choose books from the classroom library shelf, or you may wish to offer a group of appropriate books from which children can choose. Titles might include the following:

- *Minnie, the Talking Bird*. (See page 1750 of the *Teacher's Edition* for a Lesson Plan.)
- *Pigsty* by Mark Teague. Scholastic, 1994.
- *A Dog Named Sam* by Janice Boland. Dial, 1998.

You may also wish to choose additional books that are of the same genre or by the same author or that have the same kind of text structure as the selection.

After children have chosen their books, give each child a copy of My Reading Log, which can be found on page R35 in the back of the *Teacher's Edition*. Have children fill in the information at the top of the form. Then have them use the log to keep track of their reading and to record their responses to the literature.

Conduct student-teacher conferences. Arrange time for each child to confer with you individually about his or her self-selected reading. Have children bring their Reading Logs to share with you at the conference. Children might also like to share a favorite passage to read aloud to you. Ask questions designed to stimulate discussion about the book. For example, you might want to ask what the problem and the solution were in a fiction text or how the child figured out a new vocabulary word in a nonfiction text.

FLUENCY PERFORMANCE Have children read aloud to you the passage from "A Secret Place" that they selected and practiced with their partners. Keep track of the number of words each child reads correctly. Ask the child to rate his or her own performance on the 1–4 scale. If children are not happy with their oral reading, give them an opportunity to continue practicing and then to reread the passage to you.

See *Oral Reading Fluency Assessment* for monitoring progress.

The Pine Park Mystery/A Secret Place

LESSON 22

BEFORE Building Background and Vocabulary

Use with

"Good-bye, Curtis"

Review Phonics: Long Vowel: /ī/y

Identify the sound. Ask children to repeat the following sentence three times: *Ty will try to fly five kites in the sky.* Ask children to name the words in the sentence that have the /ī/ sound. (*Ty, try, fly, five, kites, sky*)

Associate letters to sound. On the board, write the sentence *Ty will try to fly five kites in the sky.* Circle the words *five* and *kites,* and explain that these words have the same vowel sound: long *i* spelled *i—e.* Then circle the words *Ty, try, fly,* and *sky,* and underline the *y* in each. Tell children that the letter *y* can sometimes stand for the /ī/ sound. Have children repeat the words and listen for the /ī/ sound.

Word blending. Model blending the sounds to read the word *spy.* Slide your hand under the word as you slowly elongate the sounds /sspīī/. Then read the word naturally—*spy.* Follow a similar process with *why, by,* and *shy.*

Apply the skill. *Vowel Substitution* Write the first word in each pair below on the board, and have children read it aloud. Make the changes necessary to form the words in parentheses. Have children read each new word.

free (fry)   **tree** (try)   **be** (by)   **stay** (sty)
she (shy)   **flow** (fly)   **crow** (cry)   **me** (my)

INTERVENTION PRACTICE BOOK page 88

Introduce Vocabulary

PRETEACH **lesson vocabulary.** Tell children that they are going to learn six new words that they will see again when they read a story called "Good-bye, Curtis." Teach each Vocabulary Word using the following process.

Use the following suggestions or similar ideas to give the meaning or context.

> Write the word.
> Say the word.
> Track the word and have children repeat it.
> Give the meaning or context.

addresses   Point out the word part *dress.* Have several children state their addresses.

clerk   Explain some of the jobs that clerks do in a store. Have children give examples of stores where they find clerks.

grown   Relate to being an adult. Have children share what they want to do when they are grown.

honor   Have children discuss honors that they have received or that they have heard of others receiving.

pour	Children should be familiar with pouring water. Explain that the same word can be applied to a lot of something moving from one place to another. For example, *A lot of fan mail poured in after the new song was released.*
route	Explain that mail carriers, paper carriers, and other delivery people all have regular routes.

For vocabulary activities, see Vocabulary Games on pages 2–3.

Vocabulary Words
addresses the street names, street numbers, cities, and states where businesses or homes can be found
clerk a salesperson in a store
grown to be an adult
honor show of respect and love
pour to move somewhere quickly and in large numbers
route a series of places or customers visited regularly by person who delivers or sells something

AFTER
Building Background and Vocabulary

Apply Vocabulary Strategies

Use familiar word parts. Write the word *addresses* on chart paper and underline the letters *d-r-e-s-s*. Tell children that they can sometimes figure out a word by looking for letter patterns or word parts that they already know.

MODEL The letters *d-r-e-s-s* are familiar to me. I know they spell *dress*. When I blend that familiar word with *ad*, which I know from words like *mad* and *sad*, I get *address*.

Guide children to use a similar process to decode the word *grown*.

RETEACH lesson vocabulary. Have children give examples of each.
1. Directions that include an address
2. A job a clerk would do
3. A person who is not grown
4. Something that is an honor
5. Something that can pour
6. A job that involves a regular route

FLUENCY BUILDER Using *Intervention Practice Book* page 87, read each word in the first column aloud, and have children repeat it. Then have children work in pairs to read the words in the first column aloud to each other. Follow the same procedure with each of the remaining columns. After partners have practiced reading aloud the words in each column separately, have them practice the entire list.

INTERVENTION PRACTICE BOOK
page 87

Good-bye, Curtis/Hello from Here

BEFORE
Reading "Good-bye, Curtis"
pages 178–193

USE SKILL CARD 22A

Focus Skill: Compare and Contrast

PRETEACH the skill. Point out to children that figuring out how characters, settings, and plots are the same and different can help them remember more about the characters and events in a story.

Have children look at **side A of Skill Card 22: Compare and Contrast**. Read the definition of compare and contrast. Next, have children read the two stories and compare and contrast them.

Now call attention to the Venn diagram. Ask:

- What character is in only the first story? (*the girl*)
- What character is in only the second story? (*the owl*)
- What character is in both stories? (*a mouse*)

Follow the same procedure for the setting and plot. Explain that by comparing and contrasting these elements, the children can recognize important elements more easily.

Prepare to Read: "Good-bye, Curtis"

Preview. Tell children that they are going to read a selection entitled "Good-bye, Curtis." Explain that this is a story about a letter carrier. It is his last day on the job after forty-two years. Then preview the selection.

BANNER DAYS pages 178–193

- **Pages 178–179:** On pages 178–179, I see a man wearing a uniform. I also see a postmark and some stamps. The man must be a letter carrier. I see the title, "Good-bye, Curtis," and the names of the author and illustrator on these pages.

- **Pages 180–181:** I see four pictures. These must be people Curtis sees when he delivers the mail. I see an old woman on a porch, another woman with a baby, a butcher, and a crossing guard.

- **Pages 182–183:** I see all sorts of things that look like presents. I see a man with his arm around Curtis. People must like him a lot to be so nice to him. Is it his birthday?

- **Pages 184–185:** These look like the same people we saw on pages 180 and 181. They look like they are giving Curtis hugs. They must like him, too.

Set purpose. Model setting a purpose for reading "Good-bye, Curtis."

MODEL From my preview, I can see that people really seem to like Curtis. One purpose for reading is to understand the characters. I will read to find out why everyone likes Curtis so much.

AFTER
Reading "Good-bye, Curtis"
pages 178–193

Reread and Summarize

Have children reread and summarize "Good-bye, Curtis" in sections, as described below.

> Pages 180–181
>
> **Let's reread pages 180–181 to recall what is important about this day.**
>
> Summary: This is Curtis's last day as a letter carrier after forty-two years.
>
> Pages 182–183
>
> **Let's reread pages 182–183 to recall what Curtis finds in the mailboxes along his route.**
>
> Summary: Curtis finds all kinds of surprises in the mailboxes all along his route.
>
> Pages 184–185
>
> **Let's reread pages 184–185 to see what people say to Curtis.**
>
> Summary: The old woman, the baby, the clerk, and the crossing guard all say that they will miss Curtis.
>
> Pages 186–187
>
> **Let's reread pages 186–187 to see what changes have occurred during the forty-two years Curtis has had this route.**
>
> Summary: Children have grown up and had children and grandchildren of their own. Pets have had babies, too. Trees have grown. Houses have been torn down and built. People have moved.
>
> Pages 188–192
>
> **Let's reread pages 188–192 to see what happens to Curtis.**
>
> Summary: Everyone meets at Curtis's home to have a party for him. Curtis writes thank-you notes.

FLUENCY BUILDER Use *Intervention Practice Book* page 87, which you used for the previous Fluency Builder activity. Call attention to the sentences on the bottom half of the page. The slashes break the sentences into phrases to allow children to work on natural phrasing. Tell children that their goal is to read each phrase or sentence smoothly. Model appropriate pace, expression, and phrasing as you read each sentence, and have children read each sentence after you. Then have children practice by reading the sentences aloud three times to a partner.

INTERVENTION PRACTICE BOOK
page 87

Good-bye, Curtis/Hello from Here

BEFORE
Making Connections
pages 196–197

Directed Reading: "Hello from Here," pp. 174–180

SOUNDS OF SUNSHINE pages 174–180

Read aloud the title of the story. Ask children where they think someone is saying hello from. Then have children read page 174 to find out about Myles's street. Ask: **What is Myles's street like?** (*Possible response: like most streets*) **Why?** (*Possible responses: The houses sit side by side; kids play in the yards.*) **MAKE COMPARISONS**

Is your street like Myles's street? (*Possible responses: Our houses are like that; we live in apartments.*) **COMPARE/CONTRAST**

Who lives on Myles's street? (*Possible responses: Myles, Ms. Pryor, Mr. Clyde*) **DRAW CONCLUSIONS**

Page 175

Read aloud the first sentence on page 175, and ask what children think the surprise might be. Have them read to find out. Ask: **What is the surprise?** (*Possible response: The children on the boy's street started getting lots of mail.*) **DRAW CONCLUSIONS**

Who is the postcard from? (*Possible response: It does not say.*) **UNDERSTAND AUTHOR'S PURPOSE**

What is the person writing the postcard doing? (*Possible response: sky diving*) **DRAW CONCLUSIONS**

Page 176

Have children read page 176 to find out where the second postcard is from. Ask: **Where is this postcard from?** (*Possible response: the desert*) **DRAW CONCLUSIONS**

How would you answer the two questions on page 176? (*Possible responses: They like us; someone who lives near us.*) **SPECULATE**

Page 177

Have children read page 177 to find out what Myles does to find responses to his questions. Ask: **What does Myles do?** (*Possible response: He tries to think like a spy and look for clues.*) **NOTE DETAILS**

What clues does Myles find? (*Possible response: The postcards have no stamps.*) **How does the clue help Myles?** (*Possible response: He knows that they are not coming through the mail.*) **SYNTHESIZE**

Whom do you think Myles catches? (*Possible responses: Ms. Pryor, Mr. Clyde*) **MAKE PREDICTIONS**

Page 178

Have children read page 178 to find out whom Myles catches at the mailbox. Ask: **Whom does Myles catch?** (*Possible response: Mr. Clyde*) **NOTE DETAILS**

Why is Mr. Clyde sending the cards? (*Possible response: He is doing it for fun.*) **CAUSE AND EFFECT**

Page 179

Ask children to read page 179 to find out about this postcard. Ask: **Who writes this postcard?** (*Possible response: Myles*) **NOTE DETAILS**

Why do you think Myles is having a party for Mr. Clyde? (*Possible response: Myles wants to do something nice for Mr. Clyde.*) **INTERPRET CHARACTERS' MOTIVATIONS**

Lesson 22 • Intervention Teacher's Guide

Ask a volunteer to restate briefly the events of the story by looking at the pictures and describing what is happening in each.

> **MODEL** As I listened to the story being retold, I tried to make sure I understood the story. I need the story to make sense to me.
>
> (Focus Strategy) SEQUENCE EVENTS/SUMMARIZE

Discuss whether children agree with your thinking.

Summarize the selection. Ask children to think about Myles's mystery, his clues, and his solution. Then help them summarize the story.

Answers to *Think About It* Questions

1. Mr. Clyde likes the children. He feels as though they are his grandchildren. He sends them postcards. **SUMMARIZE**
2. Myles likes Mr. Clyde but thinks Mr. Clyde is lonely. Myles decides to have a birthday party for him. **INTERPRET STORY DETAILS**
3. Accept reasonable responses. **EXPRESS OPINIONS**

(Focus Skill) Compare and Contrast

RETEACH the skill. Have children look at **side B of Skill Card 22: Compare and Contrast**. Read the skill reminder and directions with them, and have a volunteer read the paragraphs aloud.

Explain that children will work with partners to create their own Venn diagrams. Remind them to include characters, setting, and plot. After children have completed their Venn diagrams, have them display and explain their work.

Review Phonics Skill from "Good-bye, Curtis"

RETEACH contractions *'ll, n't, 's.* Write the following contractions and phrases on the board. Have children read the contractions and match them to the correct phrases. Children should tell what letters in each contraction have been replaced by an apostrophe.

let's	they will
can't	we will
we'll	cannot
they'll	let us

FLUENCY BUILDER Use *Intervention Practice Book* page 87. Explain that today children will practice the sentences on the bottom half of the page by reading them aloud on tape. Assign new partners. Have children take turns reading the sentences aloud to each other and then reading them on tape.

Good-bye, Curtis/Hello from Here

BEFORE
Drafting a Poem
Page 199G

Using Rhythm and Rhyme: Poems

Build on prior knowledge. Tell children that they are going to talk and write about things they like using words that rhyme. On a chart, create rhyming pairs of words representing things they like, for example, *bikes/hikes; cats/hats.*

Construct the text. "Share the pen" with children. Guide them in using the words generated above to fill in only the second blank of the following couplets. Add as many "I like" lines as needed.

I like _____, and I like _____.

I like _____, and I like _____.

I like _____, and I like _____.

But most of all I like _____.

Revisit the text. Go back and read the sentences together. Ask: **What words can we write in the first blanks to make the lines rhyme?**

- Guide children to put words in similar categories in the first blank of each couplet.

- Ask: **Do we need to change the order of any of the couplets to make the poem flow more smoothly?** Make the appropriate changes.

- Have children read the completed poem aloud and then copy it onto their papers.

On Your Own

Have children write a similar poem using the frame "I don't like." Suggest that they use a rhyming dictionary to help them find words or brainstorm a list of rhyming words to use in their poems.

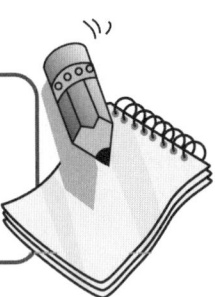

AFTER

Spelling Lesson
page 195I

Connect Spelling and Phonics

RETEACH phonics: long vowel /ī/y. Write the word *July* on the board. Explain that you will say more words which have the /ī/ sound spelled *y*. Have volunteers write each word on the board.

| 1. by* | 2. my* | 3. sky* | 4. dry* |
| 5. spy* | 6. fry* | 7. why* | 8. flying* |

* Word appears in "Hello from Here."

Dictate the following sentence, and have children write it: *Why do birds fly by in the sky?*

Build and Read Longer Words

Write on the board the sentence *I try to ride,* and have children read it with you. Then write this sentence below it: *Jack tries to ride.* Read it aloud. Remind them that they can figure out a new word like *tries* by first looking for word parts they know within it. Point out the ending *-es*. Then model changing the *y* in *try* to *i* before adding *-es*. Explain that in many words that end in *y*, children should change the *y* to *i* before adding *-es* or *-ed*. Follow a similar procedure with these words: *fried, skies, dragonflies*. Encourage children to build other long words like these. Suggest that they use a dictionary to look up words they are not sure about.

FLUENCY BUILDER Have children choose a passage from "Hello from Here" to read aloud to a partner. You may have children choose passages that they found particularly interesting, or have them choose one of the following options:

- Read pages 174–175. (From *My street . . .* through *. . . pour into our mailboxes.* Total: 78 words)

- Read pages 177–178. (From *I had to find out . . .* through *. . . my secret.* Total: 137 words)

Children should read the selected passage aloud to their partners three times. Have the child rate each reading on a scale of 1 to 4.

Good-bye, Curtis/Hello from Here

BEFORE Weekly Assessments

Review Vocabulary

To revisit Vocabulary Words prior to the weekly assessment, use these sentence frames. Children identify the correct choice and explain why that choice makes sense in the sentence.

1. You would write **addresses** on
    a. children.
    b. letters.
2. A **clerk** would help you
    a. buy a book.
    b. paint a picture.
3. A person who is **grown** goes to
    a. work.
    b. a babysitter.
4. It would be an **honor** to
    a. take out the trash.
    b. win a prize.
5. Kids might **pour** out of a
    a. bag.
    b. bus.
6. A person who follows a **route** is
    a. a paperboy.
    b. a doctor.

Correct responses: 1b, 2a, 3a, 4b, 5b, 6a

You may want to display the Vocabulary Words and definitions on page 219 and have children copy them to use when they study for the vocabulary test.

Focus Skill Compare/Contrast

To review compare/contrast before the weekly assessment, distribute *Intervention Practice Book* page 90. Have volunteers read aloud the first direction line and the paragraphs. Guide children by having them identify the main characters in the stories. Discuss whether these characters are the same or different in each story. Have them put them in the appropriate places on the Venn diagram.

INTERVENTION PRACTICE BOOK page 90

Review Test Prep

Ask children to turn to page 199 of the *Pupil Edition*. Call attention to the tips for answering the test questions. Tell children that paying attention to these tips can help them answer not only the test questions but also other test questions like these.

BANNER DAYS page 199

Have children follow along as you read each test question and the tip that goes with it. Discuss why it is important to disregard answers that you know are not correct. (*Possible response: It helps you focus on the correct answer.*) Review that the apostrophe replaces some letters.

INTERVENTION ASSESSMENT BOOK

Lesson 22 • Intervention Teacher's Guide

AFTER Self-Selected Reading

Weekly Assessments

Have children select their own books to read independently. They might choose books from the classroom library shelf, or you may wish to offer a group of appropriate books from which children can choose.

- *In Eight More Years* by Julie Verne. (See page 199S of the *Teacher's Edition* for an Independent Reading Plan.)
- *Frog and Toad Are Friends* by Arnold Lobel. HarperCollins, 1970.
- *My Friends* by Taro Gomi. Chronicle, 1990.

You may also wish to choose additional books that are the same genre or by the same author, or that have the same kind of text structure as the selection.

After children have chosen their books, give each child a copy of My Reading Log, which can be found on page R35 in the back of the *Teacher's Edition*. Have children fill in the information at the top of the form. Then have them use the log to keep track of their reading and to record their responses to the literature.

Conduct student-teacher conferences. Arrange time for each child to confer with you individually about his or her self-selected reading. Have children bring their Reading Logs to share with you at the conference. Children might also like to share a favorite passage to read aloud to you. Ask questions about the book to stimulate discussion. For example, you might want to ask what the problem and the solution were in a fiction text or how the meaning of a new vocabulary word was determined in a nonfiction text.

FLUENCY PERFORMANCE Have children read aloud to you the passage from "Hello from Here" that they selected and practiced with their partners. Keep track of the number of words each child reads correctly. Ask the child to rate his or her own performance on the 1–4 scale. If children are not happy with their oral reading, give them an opportunity to continue practicing and then to reread the passage to you.

See *Oral Reading Fluency Assessment* for monitoring progress.

Good-bye, Curtis/Hello from Here

LESSON 23

BEFORE Building Background and Vocabulary

Use with

"Max Found Two Sticks"

Review Phonics: Long Vowel /ī/ *igh*

Identify the sound. Ask children to listen as you repeat the following sentence three times: *Mike likes to see bright lights in the sky at night.* Ask children to identify the words that have the /ī/ sound. (*Mike, likes, bright, lights, sky, night*)

Associate letters to sound. On the board, write the sentence: *Mike likes to see bright lights in the sky at night.* Circle the words *Mike, likes,* and *sky,* and ask how they are alike. (*same vowel sound; long* i *sound*) Remind children that the letters *i-e* (CVCe) and *y* often stand for the long *i* sound. Then circle the words *bright, lights,* and *night,* and ask how these words are alike. (*All have the same vowel sound spelled* igh.) Tell children that when the letter *i* is followed by *gh*, the *igh* usually stands for the /ī/ sound they hear in *bright, lights,* and *night.* Have children repeat the words and listen for the /ī/ sound.

Word blending. Write *might* on the board. Model blending the sounds to read *might:* Slide your hand under the word as you slowly elongate the sounds /mmīītt/. Then read the word naturally—*might*. Have children practice blending sounds to read aloud these words: *tright, sigh, tight.*

Apply the skill. *Letter Substitution* On the board, write the first word in each pair below, and have children read them aloud. Make the changes necessary to form the words in parentheses. Have volunteers read aloud each new word.

INTERVENTION PRACTICE BOOK page 92

| **mat** (might) | **rat** (right) | **flat** (flight) | **lit** (light) |
| **say** (sigh) | **sit** (sight) | **he** (high) | **neat** (night) |

Introduce Vocabulary

PRETEACH lesson vocabulary. Tell children that they are going to learn six words that they will see when they read "Max Found Two Sticks." Teach the Vocabulary Words using the following process.

Use these suggestions or similar ideas to provide the meaning or context.

appeared	Something that *appeared* became visible. For example, the cat appeared from behind the chair.
conductor	Relate to the two kinds of *conductors*—the one who makes things run smoothly on a train and the one who leads a band or orchestra.
created	Explain that *created* means something was made that did not exist before.

> Write the word.
> Say the word.
> Track the word and have students repeat it.
> Give the meaning or context.

228 Lesson 23 • Intervention Teacher's Guide

imitated — Perform an action and have children repeat the action. Tell them that they have just imitated you.

rhythm — Turn on some music. Have children clap their hands to the beat. Say that they are following the *rhythm.*

startled — Explain that being *startled* is like being surprised. Have volunteers act out being startled.

For vocabulary activities, see Vocabulary Games on pages 2–7.

Vocabulary Words

appeared came into view

conductor someone who is in charge of a train

created made or designed something

imitated copied something or someone

rhythm regular beat in music, poetry, or dance

startled surprised someone and made the person jump

AFTER
Building Background and Vocabulary

Apply Vocabulary Strategies

Use familiar word parts. Write the word *appeared* on chart paper and underline the letters *ed*. Tell children that they can sometimes figure out a word by looking for letter patterns that they know.

> **MODEL** I know that *ed* at the end of a word often means it is a past tense verb. The letters *ear* help me to pronounce the vowel sound. This helps me read the whole word—***appeared.***

Guide children in using a similar procedure to decode the words *conductor* and *startled.*

RETEACH lesson vocabulary. Have children listen to each of the following sentences. Tell them to hold up the word card that completes each rhyme. Reread the sentence aloud with the correct word choice. Then discuss how the meaning of the vocabulary word fits the sentence.

1. The loud, sudden noise _____ me. (startled)
2. The _____ of the song made me feel sleepy. (rhythm)
3. The _____ walked through the train. (conductor)
4. The boy _____ a castle from sand. (created)
5. The parrot _____ the sound of my voice. (imitated)
6. A cat suddenly _____ on the window ledge. (appeared)

FLUENCY BUILDER Using *Intervention Practice Book* page 91, read each word in the first column aloud and have children repeat it. Then have partners read the words in the first column aloud to each other. Follow the same procedure with the remaining columns. After partners have practiced reading aloud the words in each column separately, have them read the entire list.

INTERVENTION PRACTICE BOOK
page 91

(Save *Intervention Practice Book* page 91 to use on pages 231 and 233.)

Max Found Two Sticks/The Music Maker

BEFORE

Reading "Max Found Two Sticks"
pages 202–220

USE SKILL CARD 23A

Multiple-Meaning Words

PRETEACH **the skill.** Point out to children that some words, such as *back*, have more than one meaning. Paying attention to the words around a word with multiple meanings can help readers decide which meaning to use.

Have children look at **side A of Skill Card 23: Multiple-Meaning Words.** Read the definition of multiple-meaning words. Next, have children read through the sentences. Explain that each boldface word has at least two different meanings. Now call attention to the sentences. Ask:

- Read the two definitions for *pick*. **Which definition makes the most sense in the sentence? Why?**
- Read the two definitions for *bug*. **Which definition makes the most sense in the sentence? Why?**
- Read the two definitions for *school*. **Which definition makes the most sense in the sentence? Why?**
- Read the two definitions for *can*. **Which definition makes the most sense in the sentence? Why?**

Review how children used context to decide which meaning of the word made sense in the sentence.

Prepare to Read: "Max Found Two Sticks"

Preview. Tell children that they are going to read a story called "Max Found Two Sticks." Tell them that this story is about a boy who likes to play music. Then preview the selection.

BANNER DAYS
pages 202–220

- **Pages 202–203:** On pages 202–203, I see the title, "Max Found Two Sticks," and a picture of a boy. Brian Pinkney wrote and illustrated the story.

- **Pages 204–207:** I see a boy sitting outside. He must be Max. I see two sticks and a lot of leaves blowing around. I see a man washing windows, a woman, and children running.

- **Pages 208–211:** The story is all happening on the same street. I see Max drumming. I also see two drummers in a marching band.

Set Purpose. Model setting a purpose for reading "Max Found Two Sticks."

MODEL From what I have seen in my preview, I am curious. I wonder who the people are. I will read to find out what Max does with the two sticks.

AFTER

Reading "Max Found Two Sticks"
pages 202–220

Reread and Summarize

Have children reread and summarize "Max Found Two Sticks" in sections, as described below.

> Pages 202–205
> **Let's reread pages 202–205 to recall whom the story is about and when it takes place.**
>
> Summary: The story takes place on a day Max did not feel like talking to anyone. It was cloudy and windy.
>
> Pages 206–209
> **Let's reread pages 206–209 to recall the things on which Max tapped his sticks.**
>
> Summary: Max tapped the sticks on his thighs to imitate the sound of pigeons in flight. He tapped them on Grandpa's bucket like rain falling against the windows.
>
> Pages 210–215
> **Let's reread pages 210–215 to see what else Max played and what it sounded like.**
>
> Summary: Max played hatboxes like tom-toms. He played soda bottles like church bells. He played garbage cans that sounded like train wheels.
>
> Pages 216–217
> **Let's reread pages 216–217 to see what Max heard.**
>
> Summary: Max heard a marching band coming around the corner.
>
> Pages 218–220
> **Let's reread pages 218–220 to see what happened when the marching band went by.**
>
> Summary: The last drummer in the marching band tossed Max his spare set of sticks.

FLUENCY BUILDER Use *Intervention Practice Book* page 91. Point out the sentences at the bottom of the page. Remind children to pay attention to the slashes and to read each phrase or unit smoothly. Model appropriate pace, expression, and phrasing as you read each sentence. Have children read it after you. Then have children practice reading the sentences aloud to a partner three times.

INTERVENTION PRACTICE BOOK
page 91

BEFORE
Making Connections
pages 224–225

Directed Reading: "The Music Maker" pp. 182–188

Read aloud the title of the story. Ask children who they think the music maker is and what music he might make. Then have them read page 182 to find out.

SOUNDS OF SUNSHINE pp. 182–188

Page 182

Direct children's attention to the second sentence in the second paragraph. Model using the self-correct strategy:

> **MODEL** The first time I read this story, I read *w-o-u-n-d* as /wo͞ond/—an injury. It did not make sense for Dwight to hurt rubber bands, so I went back and read the sentence again. I realized the word must be /wound/—meaning Dwight wrapped the rubber bands around the sticks. Then the sentence made sense. **SELF-CORRECT**

Pages 183–184

Ask: **What is Dwight doing?** UNDERSTAND CHARACTERS' ACTIONS

What is Dwight trying to do? (*Possible response: He is trying to create a specific sound.*) DETERMINE CHARACTERS' MOTIVATIONS

Why are the children covering their ears? (*Possible response: The noise from the garbage can lid is too loud.*) CAUSE AND EFFECT

Page 185

Ask: **Why is Dwight drumming on the garbage can lid?** (*Possible response: He is practicing for playing at the baseball game.*) NOTE DETAILS

Ask a volunteer to read aloud the last sentence on the page. Draw attention to the words *play* and *notes* in the sentence. Ask: **What does the word *play* mean in this sentence? How do you know?** (*Possible response: It means to play music; I know because they're talking about a song.*) Repeat for the word *notes*.
MULTIPLE-MEANING WORDS

Does Linda think he will be able to play the notes on a drum? (*no*) **Do you?** (*Accept reasonable responses.*) SPECULATE

Page 186

Ask: **Why does Jon think Dwight can't play real music on a drum?** (*because he thinks drums can't play notes*) NOTE DETAILS

What do you think Dwight will show Jon and Linda? (*Possible response: a special kind of drum*) MAKE PREDICTIONS

Pages 187–188

Ask: **What does Dwight show his friends?** (*Possible response: He shows them how to make a steel drum.*) INTERPRET STORY EVENTS

Lesson 23 • Intervention Teacher's Guide

What did Jon and Linda learn? (*They learned that some drums can play musical notes.*) **IMPORTANT DETAILS**

How do you think Dwight feels after he plays his steel drum for the fans? (*Possible responses: He feels proud because he has played well and entertained the crowd; he feels happy because he likes playing music.*) **IDENTIFY WITH CHARACTERS**

Summarize the selection. Ask children to think about what happens first, next, and last in the story. Then help them summarize the story in a few sentences.

Answers to *Think About It* Questions

1. Dwight can play a tune on his drum. He can play musical notes. **SUMMARIZE**
2. Dwight feels proud of his dad's drums. He shows them to his friends, and he plays one at the baseball game. **INTERPRET EVENTS**
3. Accept reasonable responses. **TASK**

(Focus Skill) Multiple-Meaning Words

RETEACH the skill. Have children look at **side B of Skill Card 23: Multiple-Meaning Words**. Read the skill reminder with them, and have a volunteer read the sentences aloud.

Read aloud the next set of directions. Tell children that they will work with partners to choose the correct definition for each boldface word. Remind them to use context to help them choose the appropriate meaning. After children have completed their work, have them share why they made the choices they did.

Review Phonics from "Max Found Two Sticks"

RETEACH vowel digraphs /o͞o/ew, ui. Create sets of word cards for the following words: *new, flew, fruit, stew, suit, juice, grew,* and *chew*. Have children work with a partner to sort the words into two groups according to how the sound /o͞o/ is spelled.

FLUENCY BUILDER Be sure that children have copies of *Intervention Practice Book* page 91. Explain that today they will read the sentences at the bottom of the page on tape. Assign new partners. Have children take turns reading the sentences aloud and then recording them.

Max Found Two Sticks/The Music Maker

BEFORE
Drafting a Poem
page 225A

Writing Process: Poem

Build on prior knowledge. Tell children that they are going to talk and write a poem about the Fourth of July. Have children brainstorm words they associate with the Fourth of July. For example, *fireworks*, *marching bands*, *boom*, *corn on the cob*, and *red*, *white*, and *blue*.

Construct the text. "Share the pen" with children. Write the title "The Fourth of July." Guide them in using the words generated above to create descriptive images. For example:

> The Fourth of July
>
> People wear red, white, and blue.
>
> The marching band plays its way down the street.
>
> Fireworks boom and light up the sky.
>
> We go home, sleepy and happy in the dark.

Revisit the text. Read the poem together. Ask: **How can we make our writing more poetic?** (*Possible response: add more descriptive language*)

- Guide children to add descriptive language.

- Ask: **How can we rearrange the parts of the sentences to make them sound more like poetry? What details can we add to bring readers into the poem's events?** Make the appropriate changes.

- Have children read the completed poem aloud. They may copy it on their papers if they like.

On Your Own

Have children write a title and a three line poem about something they feel strongly about. Have them try to include descriptive language.

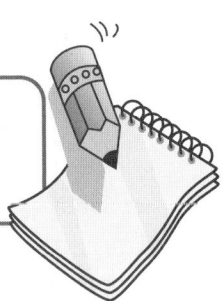

Lesson 23 • Intervention Teacher's Guide

AFTER

Spelling Lesson
page 221H

Connect Spelling and Phonics

RETEACH **long vowel /ī/ *igh*.** Write the word *sight* on the board. Explain that you will say more words which have the sound /ī/ spelled *igh*. Have volunteers write each word on the board.

1. high*	2. night*	3. right*	4. tight*
5. fright*	6. mighty*	7. sighed*	8. delighted*

*Word appears in "The Music Maker."

Dictate the following sentence and have children write it: *The bright light gave me a fright last night.*

Build and Read Longer Words

Write the word *nighttime* on the board. Tell children that they can often figure out longer words by looking for smaller words in them. Cover the word *time*, and have children read aloud the word *night*. Follow a similar procedure to have children read the word *time*. Then blend the two smaller words and read aloud the word *nighttime*. Follow the same procedure with the words *flashlight*, *highway*, and *tightrope*. Encourage children to build other long words with long *i* spelled *igh*.

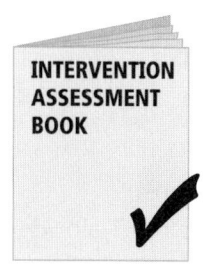

INTERVENTION ASSESSMENT BOOK

FLUENCY BUILDER Have children choose a passage from *"The Music Maker"* to read aloud to a partner. You may have children choose passages that they found particularly interesting, or have them choose one of the following options:

- Read pages 182–183. (From *Wherever Dwight went . . . through . . . on something else.* Total: 116 words)

- Read pages 186–188 (From *MY drum CAN make . . . through . . . on his steel drum.* Total: 130 words)

Children should read the selected passage aloud to a partner three times. Have the child rate each reading on a scale from 1 to 4.

BEFORE Weekly Assessments

Review Vocabulary

Write the Vocabulary Words on the board. Separate the group into two teams. Read the sentences below one at a time. The member at the front of each team's line tries to be the first to point to the word on the board that belongs in the blank.

1. She was so _____ that she dropped her books. (startled)
2. The artwork I _____ is on our refrigerator. (created)
3. The _____ yelled, "All aboard!" (conductor)
4. To dance well, you must feel the _____ of the music. (rhythm)
5. My little sister _____ everything that I did. (imitated)
6. The car suddenly _____ out of nowhere. (appeared)

You may want to display the Vocabulary Words and definitions on page 229 and have children copy them to use to study for the vocabulary test.

Review Multiple-Meaning Words

To review multiple-meaning words before the weekly assessment, distribute *Intervention Practice Book* page 94. Have volunteers read aloud the first direction line and the sentences. Guide children through the first exercise together. Discuss which definition of the boldface word makes the most sense in the sentence.

Review Test Prep

Ask children to turn to page 227 of the *Pupil Edition*. Call attention to the Tips for answering the test questions. Tell children that these tips can help them answer not only the questions on the page, but also other test questions like them.

Have children follow along as you read each question and the tip that goes with it. Discuss why choosing the correct meaning of the word is so important.

AFTER Self-Selected Reading

Weekly Assessments

Have children select their own books to read independently. They might choose books from the classroom library shelf, or you may wish to offer a group of appropriate books from which children can choose.

- *Neighborhood Band.* See page 227O of the *Teacher's Edition* for an Independent Reading Plan.
- *Listen to Rain* by Bill Martin, Jr., and John Archambault. Henry Holt, 1988.
- *Night Noises* by Mem Fox. Harcourt Brace, 1985.

You may also wish to choose additional books that are the same genre or by the same author, or that have the same kind of text structure as the selection

After children have chosen their books, give each child a copy of My Reading Log, which can be found on page R35 in the back of the *Teacher's Edition*. Have children fill in the information at the top of the form. Then have them use the log to keep track of their reading and to record their responses to the literature.

Conduct student-teacher conferences. Arrange time for each child to confer with you individually about his or her self-selected reading. Have children bring their Reading Logs to share with you at the conference. Children might also like to choose a favorite passage to read aloud to you. Ask questions about the book designed to stimulate discussion. For example, ask how a favorite character in the book compares or contrasts with a character in "Max Found Two Sticks."

FLUENCY PERFORMANCE Have children read aloud to you the passage from "The Music Maker" that they selected and practiced with a partner. Keep track of the number of words the child reads correctly. Ask the child to rate his or her own performance on the 1–4 scale. If children are not happy with their oral reading, give them an opportunity to practice more and then to read the passage to you again.

See *Oral Reading Fluency Assessment* **for monitoring progress.**

LESSON 24

BEFORE
Building Background and Vocabulary

Use with

"Anthony Reynoso: Born to Rope"

Review Phonics: Long Vowels /ē/ y, ie

Identify the sound. Ask children to repeat the following sentence three times: *The happy chief sees thirty puppies.* Ask children to name the words in the sentence that have the /ē/ sound. (*happy, chief, sees, thirty, puppies*)

Associate letters to sound. On the board, write this sentence: *The happy chief sees thirty puppies.* Circle the word *sees*, and ask children to read it aloud. Remind them that the letters *ee* usually stand for the /ē/ sound. Then circle the words *happy* and *thirty*, and ask how these two words are alike. (*Both have the same vowel sound at the end; both end in y; both have the long e sound.*) Remind children that *y* can also stand for the long *e* vowel sound. Then follow a similar procedure with the letters *ie* and the words *chief* and *puppies*.

Word blending. Write *bunnies* on the board. Model blending the sounds to read *bunnies*. Slide your hand under the word as you slowly elongate the sounds /buunnēēzz/ Then read the word naturally—*bunnies*. Have children practice blending sounds to read aloud these words: *thief*, *pennies*, *fluffy*.

Apply the skill. *Vowel Substitution* Write the first word in each pair of words on the board, and have children read it aloud. Make the changes necessary to form the word in parentheses. Have a volunteer read aloud the new word.

INTERVENTION PRACTICE BOOK
page 96

| **parts** (parties) | **tide** (tidy) | **shine** (shiny) |
| **happen** (happy) | **stores** (stories) | **tin** (tiny) |

Introduce Vocabulary

PRETEACH lesson vocabulary. Tell children that they will learn five new words that they will see again when they read a story called "Anthony Reynoso: Born to Rope." Teach each Vocabulary Word using the following process.

Use the following suggestions or similar ideas to give the meaning or context.

> Write the word.
> Say the word.
> Track the word and have children repeat it.
> Give the meaning or context.

dappled — Display a picture of an Appaloosa horse from an encyclopedia. Explain that this horse is *dappled*. Relate this to the dappled pattern of sunlight through trees.

exhibition — Children may be familiar with the word *exhibit*. Explain that an *exhibition* can be of artwork or skill. Ask what sorts of

	things might be seen at a school *exhibition*.
landscape business	Ask children if they know what *landscaping* is around a home. Explain that people who put in the plants, trees, and grass work in the *landscape business*.
ranch	Explain that a *ranch* is a large farm for raising animals such as horses or cattle. Have children describe what a ranch might look like.
thousands	Write the numbers 1,000, 2,000, and 3,000 on the board and explain *thousands*.

For vocabulary activities, see Vocabulary Games on pages 2–7.

Vocabulary Words
dappled marked with spots or patches of light and dark

exhibition show for the public

landscape business a company that makes money by designing, shaping, and planting gardens for customers

ranch a large farm for raising horses, beef cattle, or sheep

thousands whole numbers written 1,000, 2,000, 3,000, and so on

AFTER
Building Background and Vocabulary

Apply Vocabulary Strategies

Use familiar word parts. Write the word *ranch* on chart paper and underline *ran*. Tell children that they can sometimes figure out a new word by looking for letter patterns that they know.

> **MODEL** The word part *ran* is familiar to me because I have seen it as a word by itself. When I blend the familiar word part with the letter combination *ch*, I read *ranch*.

Guide children in using a similar procedure to decode the words *landscape* and *thousands*.

RETEACH lesson vocabulary. Have children write each Vocabulary Word on a word card. Have volunteers use each word in a sentence. The rest of the group repeats the Vocabulary Word that was used and holds up the correct word card.

FLUENCY BUILDER Use *Intervention Practice Book* page 95. Read each word in the first column aloud and have children repeat it. Then have partners read the words in the first column aloud to each other. Tell children to follow the same procedure with each of the remaining columns. After partners have practiced reading aloud the words in each column, have them practice the entire list.

(Save *Intervention Practice Book* page 95 to use on pages 241 and 243.)

INTERVENTION PRACTICE BOOK
page 95

Anthony Reynoso: Born to Rope/Rodeo!

BEFORE

Reading "Anthony Reynoso: Born to Rope"
pages 230–244

USE SKILL CARD 24A

Focus Skill: Summarize/Restate

PRETEACH the skill. Tell children that it is not important to remember every single detail of a story. The most important events are the ones they should be sure to recall. Keeping track of these most important events will help them remember the plot of the story.

Have children look at **side A of Skill Card 24: Summarize/Restate**. Read the definition of summarize/restate. Next, have children read the paragraph. Have them identify the most important events. Then discuss the web. Ask:

- What is the paragraph mainly about? (*the world's oldest rodeo*)
- Where does it take place? (*Prescott, Arizona*)
- When did it start? (*1888*) When is it held? (*the Fourth of July*)
- What is special about it? (*People come from all over.*)

Explain that these important details can help them write what mainly happens in a story in a short way, which is called a **summary**. Read aloud the summary. Help children notice how the details have been restated in the summary.

Prepare to Read: "Anthony Reynoso: Born to Rope"

Preview. Tell children that they are going to read "Anthony Reynoso: Born to Rope," a nonfiction story about a boy their age. Preview the selection.

BANNER DAYS
pages 230–244

- **Page 230:** I see the title, "Anthony Reynoso: Born to Rope," and the names of the authors. I see a boy wearing a sombrero, which is a kind of hat some people in Mexico and the Southwest wear.

- **Page 231:** I see the same boy with two men. The boy is holding a rope. I read that he is Anthony Reynoso, and he's with his father and grandfather.

- **Pages 232–235:** I see pictures of Anthony. I see Anthony doing something difficult with a rope. I read about Anthony learning to rope when he was very little and about his family and where he lives. I think this story will tell more about Anthony's life.

Set purpose. Model setting a purpose for reading the selection.

MODEL From my preview, I think roping is important to Anthony. It also looks very difficult. I will read to find out about Anthony's life and why he likes to rope.

240 Lesson 24 • Intervention Teacher's Guide

AFTER
Reading "Anthony Reynoso: Born to Rope"
pages 230–244

Reread and Summarize

Have children reread and summarize "Anthony Reynoso: Born to Rope" in sections, as described below.

> Pages 230–233
> **Let's reread pages 230–233 to recall whom the story is mainly about and what he is learning to do.**
>
> Summary: The story is about Anthony Reynoso, who lives with his family in Guadalupe, Arizona. He is learning to rope.
>
> Pages 234–237
> **Let's reread pages 234–237 to recall what things Anthony likes.**
>
> Summary: Anthony knows where there are petroglyphs, or rock paintings. He goes to church on Sunday. His grandparents own a restaurant. He likes to get together with his family. The best thing Anthony likes is to practice roping tricks on horseback.
>
> Pages 238–240
> **Let's reread pages 238–240 to find out about Anthony's daily life.**
>
> Summary: Anthony's parents work. He goes to school. He and his dad practice roping and play basketball. Anthony collects basketball cards.
>
> Pages 241–244
> **Let's reread pages 241–244 to find out about the day of the exhibition in Sedona.**
>
> Summary: Anthony and his dad do a good job performing their rope tricks. Anthony's mom watches. After the show, they go to Slide Rock.

FLUENCY BUILDER Use *Intervention Practice Book* page 95. Call attention to the sentences on the bottom half of the page. The slashes break the sentences into phrases to allow you to work on natural phrasing. Tell children that their goal is to read each phrase or sentence smoothly. Model appropriate pace, expression, and phrasing as you read each sentence, and have children read it after you. Then have children practice by reading the sentences aloud three times to a partner.

INTERVENTION PRACTICE BOOK
page 95

Anthony Reynoso: Born to Rope/Rodeo!

BEFORE
Making Connections
pages 246–247

Page 190

Directed Reading: "Rodeo!" pp. 190–196

Read aloud the title of the story. Ask volunteers to share their knowledge of rodeos. Explain that children will learn more about rodeos as they read. Have children look at the first sentence on page 190. Model using the Use Decoding/Phonics *strategy*:

SOUNDS OF SUNSHINE
pp. 190–196

> **MODEL** The two words in this sentence are new to me. In the first word I see the word *how* which I know. I add the /d/ sound and an /ē/ sound, which I know *y* can make at the end of a word. The word is *howdy*. In the second word, I see *part*. Then I see an /n/ sound and an /ər/ sound. Now I can read "Howdy, partner!"
> **USE DECODING/PHONICS**

Then have children read page 190 to find out about a rodeo. **What do you think people in a rodeo wear, use, and ride?** (*Possible response: They wear ten-gallon hats, they use ropes, and they ride dappled ponies.*)
DRAW CONCLUSIONS

Page 191

Have children read to find out some things cowboys do in rodeos. **What is one thing rodeo cowboys do?** (*Possible response: try to ride a bucking horse for eight seconds*) **DRAW CONCLUSIONS**

Why can eight seconds be a "very long time?" (*Possible response: When it is very difficult to do something, eight seconds seems like a long time.*) **UNDERSTAND FIGURATIVE LANGUAGE**

Page 192

Have children read to find out about another rodeo event. **What is the rodeo event on this page called?** (*roping*) **INTERPRET STORY EVENTS**

What is roping? (*throwing a rope to catch an animal, like a calf*) **DRAW CONCLUSIONS**

How does the pony help? (*Possible response: It backs up to keep the rope tight.*) **NOTE DETAILS**

Have children repeat the three answers above to create a summary for page 192. **SUMMARIZE/RESTATE**

Page 193

Have children read to find out what event this person is doing. **What event did you read about on this page?** (*riding a bull*) **MAIN IDEA**

Page 194

Ask children why a clown might be at a rodeo. Have them read to find out. **What do clowns do at a rodeo?** (*They keep horses and bulls away from riders who have fallen.*) **SUMMARIZE**

Lesson 24 • Intervention Teacher's Guide

Page 195

INTERVENTION PRACTICE BOOK
page 97

Have children read to find out about the rodeo's birthday. **When is the rodeo's birthday?** (*July 4*) **What else has a birthday on July 4?** (*the United States*) **NOTE DETAILS**

How might someone wish the rodeo a happy birthday? (*Possible response: go to a rodeo. Accept reasonable responses.*) **SPECULATE**

Summarize the selection. Ask children to tell the important things they learned about rodeos. Then help them summarize the selection by restating the main idea and only the most important details. Then have them complete *Intervention Practice Book* page 97.

Page 196

Answers to *Think About It* Questions

1. They do bronco riding, roping, and bull riding. **SUMMARIZE**
2. The riders probably like the clowns and are glad they are there because they help keep the riders safe. **DRAW CONCLUSIONS**
3. Accept reasonable responses. **MAIN IDEA**

AFTER
Skill Review
pages 249C–249D

USE SKILL CARD 24B

Focus Skill Summarize/Restate

RETEACH **the skill.** Have children look at **side B of Skill Card 24: Summarize/Restate.** Read the skill reminder with them, and have a volunteer read the paragraph aloud. After children have completed their webs and summaries, have them display and explain their work.

Review Phonics from "Anthony Reynoso: Born to Rope"

RETEACH **consonant digraphs /f/ *gh*, *ph*.** Read aloud the following sentence, and have children repeat it three times. *The photo of the rough, tough cowboy clown made me laugh.* Have children identify words with the /f/ sound. Write them on the board and have children read them. (*photo, rough, tough, laugh*) Help volunteers underline the letters that stand for the /f/ sound in each. Then have volunteers think of more words with the digraphs *gh* and *ph*.

FLUENCY BUILDER Use *Intervention Practice Book* page 95. Explain that children will practice the sentences on the bottom half of the page by reading them aloud on tape. Assign new partners. Have children take turns reading the sentences aloud to each other and then reading them on tape.

INTERVENTION PRACTICE BOOK
page 95

Anthony Reynoso: Born to Rope/Rodeo!

BEFORE

Drafting a Description of an Event
page 247A

Writing Process: Description

Build on prior knowledge. Tell children that they are going to talk and write about something interesting that has happened at school. Brainstorm a list of events with children and choose one. Then display information like the following, and have volunteers suggest describing words to add to the lists.

Event: Field Day				
Looks	**Tastes**	**Smells**	**Sounds**	**Feelings**
crowded	ice	fresh	cheering	happy
sunny	juice	cut grass	clapping	excited
			whistles blowing	fun
			hooray	

Construct the text. "Share the pen" with children. Guide them to use the words to write a description of the school event, such as the following:

> Our class had fun at Field Day. The day was nice, with the smell of fresh-cut grass in the air. After a few games, it was time for the big tug of war against the other class. The whistle blew and we tugged with all our might. We pulled and pulled. Then we pulled extra hard and won! Everyone was so happy that we jumped and clapped and cheered.

Revisit the text. Go back and read the sentences together.

- Ask: **Which words make pictures in your mind?** Underline those words.

- Ask: **Are there any sentences that do not have words that make pictures in your mind?** Make the appropriate changes.

- Guide children to add more descriptive words to each sentence, such as changing *nice* to *sunny*.

- Have children read the writing aloud and then copy it into their papers.

On Your Own

Have children draw a picture of something interesting they have done and then write about it. Include describing words that tell how things looked, sounded, tasted, and so on, and also how they felt about what happened.

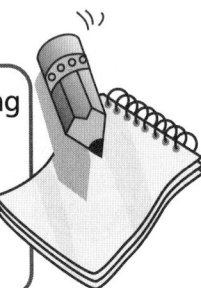

244 Lesson 24 • Intervention Teacher's Guide

AFTER
Spelling Lesson
page 245H

Connect Spelling and Phonics

RETEACH **long vowel /ē/y, ie.** Have children number their papers 1–8. Write *study* on the board and tell children that in the words you say, the long e vowel sound is spelled *y* as in *study*. Dictate the words and have children write them. After they write each word, write it on the board so children can proofread their work. Have them draw a line through a misspelled word and write the correct spelling beside it.

1. risky*
2. pony*
3. muddy*
4. dusty*
5. handy*
6. tricky*
7. funny*
8. safety*

* Word appears in "Rodeo!"

Tell children that in the following sentence, the /ē/ sound is spelled *ie*. Dictate the sentence and have children write it: *The thief met briefly with the chief.*

Build and Read Longer Words

Write the word *sunny* on the board. Tell children that they can often figure out longer words by looking for word parts they know. Ask children what smaller word they see in *sunny*. (*sun*) Then blend the word *sun* with the word part *ny* to read aloud the word *sunny*. Remind children that a longer word with double consonants, such as *sunny*, can be divided into syllables between those consonants. Follow the same procedure to have children blend word parts to read these longer words: *pennies*, *bubbly*, *frilly*. Encourage children to build other long words with /ē/ spelled *ie* or *y* like these. Suggest that they use a dictionary to look up words they are not sure about.

INTERVENTION ASSESSMENT BOOK

FLUENCY BUILDER Have children choose a passage from "Rodeo!" to read aloud to a partner. You may have children choose passages that they found particularly interesting, or have them choose one of the following options:

- Read pages 190–191. (From the title . . . through. . . *very long time!* Total: 83 words)
- Read pages 193–194. (From *Riding a bull* . . . through . . . *has to do it*. Total: 64 words)

Children should read the selected passage aloud to their partners three times. Have children rate each of their own readings on a scale from 1 to 4.

Anthony Reynoso: Born to Rope/Rodeo!

BEFORE Weekly Assessments

Review Vocabulary

To review Vocabulary Words prior to the weekly assessment, use these sentences. Read aloud the sentences and the answer choices. Children identify the better answer and explain why it makes sense in the sentence.

1. A **dappled** pony has
   a. a saddle.   b. spots.
2. An **exhibition** has
   a. many things to look at.   b. two feet.
3. **Thousands** of pennies would make up
   a. a tall pile.   b. a short pile.
4. In the **landscape business**, you work
   a. underwater.   b. outdoors.
5. On the **ranch** you will probably see
   a. a horse.   b. an elephant.

Correct responses: 1.b, 2.a, 3.a, 4.b, 5.a.

You may want to display the Vocabulary Words and definitions from **page 239** and have children copy them to use when they study for the vocabulary test.

(Focus Skill) Review Summarize/Restate

To review *summarize/restate* before the weekly assessment, distribute *Intervention Practice Book* page 98. Have volunteers read aloud the first direction line and the paragraph. Guide children by having them discuss what the main idea of the paragraph is.

Review Test Prep

Ask children to turn to page 249 in the *Pupil Edition*. Call attention to the Tip for answering the test items. Tell children that paying attention to the tip can help them answer not only the items on this page but also other items like them.

Have children follow along as you read the directions, each test item, and the Tip. Discuss with children why it is important to understand the directions. Discuss how to make sure the response answers the item. (*Possible response: Go back and reread the word by the number and then your answer to see if they have the same letter-sound.*)

AFTER Weekly Assessments

Self-Selected Reading

Have children select their own books to read independently. They might choose books from the classroom library, or you may wish to offer appropriate books from which children can choose such as these:

- *Pepe Finds His Home* by Maria Bates. (See page 249Q of the *Teacher's Edition* for an Independent Reading Plan.)
- *Potluck* by Anne Shelby. Orchard, 1994.
- *Shoes from Grandpa* by Mem Fox. Orchard, 1992.

You may also wish to choose additional books that are the same genre or are by the same author.

After children have chosen their books, give each child a copy of My Reading Log, which can be found on page R35 in the back of the *Teacher's Edition*. Have children fill in the information at the top of the form. Then have them use the log to keep track of their reading and to record their responses to the literature.

Conduct student-teacher conferences. Arrange time for each child to confer with you about his or her self-selected reading. Have children bring their Reading Logs to share with you at the conference. Children might also like to choose a favorite passage to read aloud to you. Ask questions designed to stimulate discussion about the book. For example, you might ask what the problem and the solution were in a fiction book or how the child figured out a new vocabulary word in a nonfiction book.

FLUENCY PERFORMANCE Have children read aloud to you the passage from "Rodeo!" that they practiced. Observe children's pronunciation, intonation, phrasing, and the amount of words, in general, that they read correctly. Ask each child to rate his or her own performance on a 1–4 scale. If children are not happy with their oral reading, give them an opportunity to continue practicing and then to reread the passage to you.

See *Oral Reading Fluency Assessment* **for monitoring progress.**

Anthony Reynoso: Born to Rope/Rodeo!

LESSON 25

BEFORE Building Background and Vocabulary

Use with

"Chinatown"

Review Phonics: Long Vowel: /ō/ ow, oa

Identify the sound. Ask children to repeat the following sentence three times: *Tom and Joan row the boat to tow the float home.* Ask children to name the words in the sentence that have the /ō/ sound. (*Joan, row, boat, tow, float, home*)

Associate letters to sound. On the board, write the sentence: *Tom and Joan row the boat to tow the float home.* Circle the word *Tom* and point out the CVC pattern. Remind children that the *o* stands for the short *o* vowel sound. Then circle the word *home* and point out the CVCe pattern. The *o-e* in *home* makes the long *o* vowel sound. Circle *Joan, boat,* and *float,* and ask how these three words are alike. (*They have the letters oa.*) Then ask how *Joan, boat,* and *float* are like *home.* (*All have the long o vowel sound.*) Then tell children that the letters *oa* often stand for the /ō/ sound they hear in *Joan, boat,* and *float.* Follow a similar procedure with the letters *ow* in *row* and *tow.*

Word blending. Write *goat* on the board. Model blending sounds to read *goat.* Slide your hand under the word as you slowly elongate the sounds /gōōt/. Then read the word naturally—*goat.* Have children blend sounds to read aloud these words: *soap, bowl, grow.*

Apply the skill. *Letter Substitution* Write the first word in each pair below on the board, and have children read it aloud. Make the changes necessary to form the words in parentheses. Have children read aloud each new word.

may (mow)   **cot** (coat)   **she** (show)   **gray** (grow)
tea (tow)   **got** (goat)   **rod** (road)   **flat** (float)

Introduce Vocabulary

PRETEACH lesson vocabulary. Tell children that they are going to learn six new words that they will see again when they read a story called "Chinatown." Teach every Vocabulary Word using the following process.

Use the following suggestions or similar ideas to give the meaning or context.

celebrations	Explain that celebrations can be for big things like birthdays or for little things like a good grade on a paper.
develop	Relate to improving something. When you develop an idea, you tell more about it. When you develop your muscles, you

> Write the word.
> Say the word.
> Track the word and have children repeat it.
> Give the meaning or context.

INTERVENTION PRACTICE BOOK page 100

Lesson 25 • Intervention Teacher's Guide

	make them stronger.
furious	Relate to being very angry. Ask children what makes them very angry.
graceful	Demonstrate by walking gracefully around the room.
grocery store	Display local grocery ads. Point out things you can get at a grocery store.
students	Explain that the children are all students.

For vocabulary activities, see Vocabulary Games on pages 2–7 *(Intervention Teacher's Guide)*.

> **Vocabulary Words**
> **celebrations** joyous gatherings, usually to mark important events
> **develop** to make something better; improve
> **furious** very angry
> **graceful** lovely way of moving
> **grocery store** a shop that sells food and household goods
> **students** people who go to school

AFTER
Building Background and Vocabulary

Apply Vocabulary Strategies

Use suffixes. Write the word *graceful* on chart paper and underline the letters *ful*. Tell children that they can sometimes figure out the meaning of a word by looking for suffixes that they know.

MODEL The base word *grace* is familiar to me. When I blend the base word *grace* with the suffix *-ful*, I read *graceful*.

Ask children what other words they know that end in *-ful*.

RETEACH lesson vocabulary. Have children give examples of each:
- a celebration they enjoy
- a way they have developed
- something that makes them furious
- someone or something that is graceful
- a grocery store where their family shops
- someone who is a student

FLUENCY BUILDER Using *Intervention Practice Book* page 99, read each word aloud in the first column and have children repeat it. Then have children work in pairs to read the words in the first column aloud to each other. Follow the same procedure with each of the remaining columns. After partners have practiced reading aloud the words in each separate column, have them read aloud the entire list.

INTERVENTION PRACTICE BOOK
page 99

(Save *Intervention Practice Book* page 99 to use on pages 251 and 253.)

Chinatown/Happy New Year!

BEFORE
Reading "Chinatown"
pages 252–270

USE SKILL CARD 25A

(Focus Skill) Details

PRETEACH the skill. Point out to children that the details in a story give extra information about the main idea. Details help to make stories more interesting. Keeping track of the details can help them understand the plot of the story.

Have children look at **side A of Skill Card 25: Details**. Read the definition of *details*. Next, have children read through the paragraph. Have them identify the important details.

Now call attention to the web. Ask:

- **Who makes up the lion?** (*Possible response: two men*)
- **To what sound does the lion move?** (*Possible response: loud music*)
- **What does the lion dance bring?** (*Possible response: good luck*)

Explain that all of these details help the reader understand the main idea better.

Prepare to Read: "Chinatown"

Preview. Tell children that they are going to read a selection entitled "Chinatown." Explain that this is a story about a special section of New York City. Then preview the selection.

BANNER DAYS
pages 252–270

- **Pages 252–253:** On page 252, I see the title, "Chinatown," and the name of the author and illustrator. The picture looks like some kind of animal.
- **Pages 254–255:** I see a sign for a Chinese American grocery store. The sign has Chinese letters on it, too.
- **Pages 256–257:** I see an old woman and a boy crossing the street. There is lots of traffic.
- **Pages 258–259:** I see people holding their bodies in odd positions. It looks like they are exercising or dancing.
- **Pages 260–265:** I see people doing many different jobs—fixing shoes, working in a store, cooking, and working as a butcher.

Set purpose. Model setting a purpose for reading "Chinatown."

MODEL From what I have seen in my preview, I can see that many things in Chinatown are the same as where I live, but there are some very different things as well. I will read to see what is different about Chinatown.

AFTER
Reading "Chinatown"
pages 252–270

Reread and Summarize

Have children reread and summarize "Chinatown" in sections, as described below.

> Pages 252–255
> **Let's reread pages 252–255 to recall where the story takes place.**
> Summary: The story takes place in Chinatown, where the narrator lives with his parents and grandmother.
>
> Pages 256–259
> **Let's reread pages 256–259 to recall what the boy and his grandmother usually do each day.**
> Summary: The boy and his grandmother go for a walk through Chinatown and see the tai chi class in the park. Tai chi is an ancient form of exercise.
>
> Pages 260–265
> **Let's reread pages 260–265 to see whom they meet and where they go.**
> Summary: They meet Mr. Wong, the street cobbler and they see men making deliveries. Grandma and the boy go to the herbal shop, a seafood restaurant, and the outdoor market.
>
> Page 266
> **Let's reread page 266 to see what the boy does on Saturdays.**
> Summary: The boy goes to kung fu school on Saturdays. Kung fu is one of the martial arts.
>
> Pages 267–270
> **Let's reread pages 267–270 to see what his favorite holiday is.**
> Summary: His favorite holiday is Chinese New Year.

FLUENCY BUILDER Be sure children have copies of *Intervention Practice Book* page 99, which you used for the previous Fluency Builder activity. Call attention to the sentences on the bottom half of the page. The slashes break the sentences into phrases to allow you to work on natural phrasing. Tell children that their goal is to read each phrase or sentence smoothly. Model appropriate pacing, expression, and phrasing as you read each sentence and have children read it after you. Then have children practice by reading the sentences aloud three times to a partner.

INTERVENTION PRACTICE BOOK
page 99

Chinatown/Happy New Year! **251**

BEFORE

Making Connections
pages 274–275

Directed Reading of "Happy New Year!" pp. 198–204

Read aloud the title of the story. Tell children to read page 198 to find out what Jimmy and Grandmother are doing to get ready for New Year's Eve. Ask: **What are Jimmy and Grandmother doing to get ready for New Year's Eve?** (*Possible response: putting away anything sharp.*) **DETAILS**

SOUNDS OF SUNSHINE
pp. 198–204

Page 199

Have children read page 199 to find out what Jimmy's wish is. Ask: **What is Jimmy's wish?** (*Possible response: that his mother and father will be there for Chinese New Year*) **SUMMARIZE/RESTATE**

Ask: **Why is Jimmy staying with Grandma?** (*Possible response: His parents are away.*) **DRAW CONCLUSIONS**

Ask: **How does Jimmy feel?** (*Possible response: He misses his parents.*) **MAKE INFERENCES**

Pages 200–201

Have children read pages 200–201 to find out what **Jimmy and Grandma** buy. Ask: **Why does Grandma buy the fruit?** (*Possible responses: It is tastier and the price is better.*) **DRAW CONCLUSIONS**

Ask: **How is Jimmy feeling at the bakery?** (*Possible response: hungry*) **MAKE INFERENCES**

Ask a volunteer to read aloud the second paragraph on page 201 while children listen to create a mental image. Model using the Create Mental Images strategy:

> **MODEL** When I listened to this section, I heard it say they carried a "furious-looking lion mask." I know that *furious* means "very angry," so I imagine that the mask looks like an angry lion. **CREATE MENTAL IMAGES**

Discuss whether children agree with your thinking.

Pages 202–203

Have children read pages 202–203 to find out what happens at the New Year's celebration. Ask: **Who came to the celebration dinner?** (*Possible response: family members*) **DETAILS**

Ask: **Why did they have different fruits?** (*Possible response: Different fruits have different meanings.*) **INTERPRET STORY EVENTS**

Ask: **Why did Grandma give Jimmy melon?** (*Possible response: so that he would develop and grow*) **MAKE INFERENCES**

Why were there two empty chairs at the table? (*Possible response: for Jimmy's parents*) **MAKE INFERENCES**

Do you think Jimmy's parents will be at the celebration? (*Possible responses: No, they are on a trip. Yes, they pressed the buzzer and are at the door.*) **PREDICT OUTCOMES**

Lesson 25 • Intervention Teacher's Guide

Page 204

INTERVENTION PRACTICE BOOK page 101

Have children read page 204 to confirm their predictions about Jimmy's parents. Ask: **Who was at the door?** (*Possible response: Jimmy's parents*) **CONFIRM PREDICTIONS**

Ask: **Why does Jimmy say that New Year's is his favorite celebration?** (*Possible response: because his parents came home*) **MAKE INFERENCES**

Summarize the Selection. Ask children to think about what Jimmy learned about Chinese New Year. Then have them complete *Intervention Practice Book* page 101.

Answers to *Think About It* Questions

1. Jimmy and his grandmother clean the apartment. They put away sharp things and put out oranges. They hang up scrolls. They go shopping for new clothes, fruit, and cake. **SUMMARIZE**
2. It is Jimmy's favorite because his parents came home for the celebration. **INTERPRET STORY EVENTS**
3. Accept reasonable responses. **TASK**

AFTER
Skill Review *pages 275I*
USE SKILL CARD 25B

(Focus Skill) Details

RETEACH the skill. Have children look at **side B of Skill Card 25: Details.** Read the skill reminder with them, and have a volunteer read the paragraph aloud.

Read aloud the next set of directions. Explain that children will work with a partner to create their own webs. Remind them to write only the important details.

After children have completed their Details webs, have them display and explain their work. Point out that in the selection "Happy New Year" knowing the details can help you remember the story.

Review Phonics Skill from Chinatown

RETEACH **Prefixes: mis-, under-.** Have the children write the following base words on word cards. Have them sort the cards into piles to make new words by adding either the prefix mis- or the prefix under-. Then have them read each list of words.

judge (misjudge) **foot** (underfoot) **ground** (underground) **fit** (misfit)
line (underline) **print** (misprint) **water** (underwater) **read** (misread)

FLUENCY BUILDER Be sure that children have copies of *Intervention Practice Book* page 99. Explain that today children will practice the sentences on the bottom half of the page by reading them aloud on tape. Assign new partners. Have children take turns reading the sentences aloud to each other and then reading them on tape.

INTERVENTION PRACTICE BOOK page 99

Chinatown/Happy New Year! **253**

BEFORE Drafting a Summary
page 277C

Daily Writing: Summary

Build on Prior Knowledge. Tell children that they are going to talk and write about "Goldilocks and the Three Bears." Display the following information.

> Bears go for a walk while porridge cools.
> Goldilocks finds bears' house.
> Goldilocks tries chairs and breaks one.
> Goldilocks tries porridge and eats it.
> Goldilocks tries beds and falls asleep.
> Bears come home.
> Goldilocks runs away.

Construct the Text. "Share the pen" with children. Guide them in using the text above to write a summary of "Goldilocks and the Three Bears."

Revisit the Text. Go back and read the summary together. Ask: **Have we included only the most important details of the story?**

- Guide children to reread their work and edit for unnecessary details.
- Ask: **Have we included the most important events?** Make appropriate changes.
- Have children read the completed summary aloud and then copy it onto their papers.

On Your Own
Have children write a summary of "Happy New Year." Suggest that they include only the most important events.

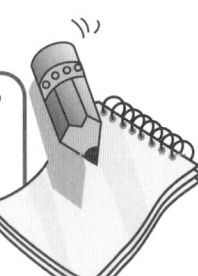

AFTER

Spelling
page 271H

Connect Spelling and Phonics

RETEACH **Long Vowel: /ō/ ow, oa.** Write the word *load* on the board. Tell children that in the words you say, /ō/ is spelled *oa* as in *load*. Dictate the words and have volunteers write them on the board.

| 1. float* | 2. coat | 3. loaf* | 4. roads* |
| 5. unloading | 6. soaked | 7. boat | 8. throat |

* Word appears in "Happy New Year."

Tell children that in the following sentence, /ō/ is spelled *ow*. Dictate the sentence: *Show me the plants that grow in the snow.*

Build and Read Longer Words

Write the word *snowman* on the board. Remind children that they can often figure out longer words by looking for smaller words in them. Cover the word *man*, and have children read the first part: *snow*. Follow a similar procedure to read the second part: *man*. Model how to blend the two smaller words to say the word *snowman*. Follow a similar procedure to have children read these words: *rowboat*, *snowball*, *railroad*. Encourage children to build other long words with the sound /ō/ spelled *ow* and *oa*. Suggest that they use a dictionary to look up words they are not sure about.

INTERVENTION ASSESSMENT BOOK

FLUENCY BUILDER Have children choose a passage from "Happy New Year" to read aloud to a partner. You may have children choose passages that they found particularly interesting, or have them choose one of the following options:

- Read pages 198–199. (From *It was almost . . .* through *. . . staying with Grandma.* Total: 119 words)

- Read pages 202–203. (From *At last . . .* through *. . . opened the door.* Total: 125 words)

Children should read the selected passage aloud to their partner three times. Have children rate each of their own readings on a scale from 1 to 4.

BEFORE Weekly Assessments

Review Vocabulary

To revisit Vocabulary Words prior to the weekly assessment, use these sentence frames. Have volunteers take turns reading aloud the sentence stem and the possible words to go in the blanks. Children identify the correct choice and explain why that choice makes sense in the sentence.

1. When you go to **celebrations**, you probably feel
    a. excited.
    b. glum.
2. A **grocery store** is a place where you can buy
    a. gas and oil.
    b. bread and carrots.
3. When you are **furious** with someone, you might
    a. laugh and sing.
    b. shout and turn red.
4. You can find **students**
    a. in every school.
    b. only on the bus.
5. If a movement is **graceful**, it
    a. looks good.
    b. sounds good.

Correct responses: 1a, 2b, 3b, 4a, 5a

You may want to display the Vocabulary Words and definitions on page 249 and have children copy them to use when they study for the vocabulary test.

INTERVENTION PRACTICE BOOK
page 102

(Focus Skill) Review Details

To review details before the weekly assessment, distribute *Intervention Practice Book* page 102. Have volunteers read aloud the first direction line and the paragraph. Guide children by helping them find the first detail.

Review Test Prep

Ask children to turn to page 277 of the *Pupil Edition*. Call attention to the tips for answering the test questions. Tell children that paying attention to these tips can help them answer not only the test questions but also other test questions like these.

BANNER DAYS
page 277

INTERVENTION ASSESSMENT BOOK

Have children follow along as you read each test question and the tip that goes with it. Discuss why it is important to pay attention to the important details of the story. (*Possible response: You may remember them.*) Discuss why it is important to reread the story. (*Possible response: You can go back and check to see that your answer is correct.*)

256 Lesson 25 • Intervention Teacher's Guide

AFTER **Self-Selected Reading**

Weekly Assessments

Have children select their own books to read independently. They might choose books from the classroom library shelf, or you may wish to offer a group of appropriate books from which children can choose.

- *Happy Chinese New Year!* by Jane Manners. (See page 277O of the *Teacher's Edition* for an Independent Reading Plan.)
- *Potluck* by Anne Shelby. Orchard Books, 1994.
- *My Many Colored Days* by Dr. Seuss. Knopf, 1996.

You may also wish to choose additional books that are the same genre or by the same author, or that have the same kind of text structure as the selection.

After children have chosen their books, give each child a copy of My Reading Log, which can be found on page R35 in the back of the *Teacher's Edition*. Have children fill in the information at the top of the form. Then have them use the log to keep track of their reading and to record their responses to the literature.

Conduct Student-Teacher Conferences. Arrange time for each child to confer with you individually about his or her self-selected reading. Have children bring their Reading Log to share with you at the conference. Children might also like to share a favorite passage to read aloud to you. Ask questions designed to stimulate discussion about the book. For example, you might want to ask what the problem and the solution are in a fiction text or how they figured out a new vocabulary word in a nonfiction text.

FLUENCY PERFORMANCE Have children read aloud to you the passage from "Happy New Year" that they selected and practiced with their partner. Keep track of the number of words the child reads correctly. Ask the child to rate his or her own performance on the 1–4 scale. If children are not happy with their oral reading, give them an opportunity to continue practicing and to read the passage to you again.

See *Oral Reading Fluency Assessment* for monitoring progress.

LESSON 26

BEFORE Building Background and Vocabulary

Use with

"Abuela"

Review Phonics: Vowel Variants /o͝o/ *oo*; /o͞o/ *oo*

Identify the sound. Have children repeat the following sentence three times: *The kangaroo at the zoo stood on the wood at noon.* Ask them which words in the sentence have the /o͝o/ sound that children hear in *hood.* (*stood, wood*) Then ask which words have the /o͞o/ sound that they hear in *food.* (*kangaroo, zoo, noon*)

Associate letters to sounds. On the board, write: *The kangaroo at the zoo stood on the wood at noon.* Circle the words *stood* and *wood.* Ask children to tell how the words are alike. (*Both have the /o͝o/ sound and the letters oo.*) Underline the letters *oo* in *stood* and *wood.* Tell children that the letters *oo* can stand for the /o͝o/ sound they hear in *stood* and *wood.* Remind children that sometimes the same letter or letters can stand for different sounds. Then follow a similar procedure to introduce the letters *oo* and the /o͞o/ sound in the words *kangaroo, zoo,* and *noon.*

Word blending. Write the words *pool, hook, stool, broom,* and *brook* on the board. Model how to blend and read the word *pool.* Slide your hand under the letters as you slowly elongate the sounds /po͞oll/. Then read the word *pool* naturally. Follow a similar procedure for *hook, stool, broom,* and *brook.* Emphasize the importance of trying a different sound for *oo* if a word does not sound right at first.

INTERVENTION PRACTICE BOOK page 104

Apply the skill. *Vowel Substitution* Write the first word in each pair of words below on the board, and have children read aloud. Make the changes necessary to form each word in parentheses. Have children read each new word.

coal (cool)	**goal** (good)	**roaster** (rooster)	**feet** (foot)
pail (pool)	**shake** (shook)	**boat** (boot)	**had** (hood)

Introduce Vocabulary

PRETEACH **lesson vocabulary.** Tell children that they are going to learn five new words that they will see again when they read a story called "Abuela." Use the following process to teach the Vocabulary Words.

Use the following suggestions or similar ideas to give the meaning or context:

flock — Relate with simple drawings of a flock of birds and only one bird. Have children contrast the two drawings.

> Write the word.
> Say the word.
> Track the word and have children repeat it.
> Give the meaning or context.

glide — Relate by showing how a paper airplane glides smoothly.

258 Lesson 26 • Intervention Teacher's Guide

harbor	Relate by showing a picture or photograph. Discuss where ships go when they are not sailing.
soared	Point out the -ed ending. Relate by using a toy or paper airplane and demonstrating the act of soaring.
swooping	Point out the -ing ending. Relate by using a toy or paper airplane and demonstrating the act of swooping.

> **Vocabulary Words**
> **flock** group of birds
> **glide** fly smoothly without effort
> **harbor** place where ships dock
> **soared** flew high
> **swooping** flying downward fast

For vocabulary activities, see Vocabulary Games on pages 2–7. (Intervention Teacher's Guide)

AFTER
Building Background and Vocabulary

Apply Vocabulary Strategies

Use familiar patterns. Write the word *harbor* on chart paper and underline the letters *ar*. Tell children that they can sometimes figure out a word by looking for letter patterns that they know.

MODEL The letter combination *ar* is familiar to me because I have seen it in words like *art*. I have seen the letter combination *bor* in the word *boring*. When I blend the letter patterns that I know all together with the initial consonant *h*, I read *harbor*. Guide children in using a similar strategy to decode the words *swooping* (p. 286) and *flock* (p. 284).

RETEACH lesson vocabulary. Have children listen to each of the following rhymes. Tell them to hold up the word card that completes each rhyme. Reread the rhymes aloud with the correct answer. Then discuss how children made their choices.

1. The flower started drooping as the bee started __(swooping)__.
2. Grapes grow in the arbor, and ships dock in the __(harbor)__.
3. Up over the dock, the seagulls flew in a __(flock)__.
4. On the ground the lion roared, and in the sky the birdie __(soared)__.
5. Down the hill I will slide, and in the air I will __(glide)__.

FLUENCY BUILDER Using *Intervention Practice Book* page 103, read aloud each word in the first column and have children repeat it. Then have children work in pairs to read the words in the first column aloud to each other. Follow the same procedure with each of the remaining columns. After partners have practiced reading aloud the words in each separate column, have them read aloud the entire list.

INTERVENTION PRACTICE BOOK
page 103

(Save Intervention Practice Book page 103 to use on pages 261 and 263.

Abuela/If I Could Fly

BEFORE
Reading "Abuela"
pages 282–299

(Focus Skill) Make Inferences

PRETEACH the skill. Point out to children that readers use story clues and what they already know to decide if something is real or make-believe in a story. Discuss how readers make these decisions, or make inferences, to figure out what is happening in a story. Guide children to see that an author does not always tell readers everything that is happening, but readers can use their own personal experience to help them understand the story.

USE SKILL CARD 26A

Have children look at **side A of Skill Card 26: Make Inferences.** Read the definition of Make Inferences. Next, read the story and have children read it with you.

Now call attention to the chart and have volunteers take turns reading the information aloud. Ask:

- **What does the story tell you that the grandson does?** (Possible response: *He calls his grandma every night.*)

- **Why might you want to call someone every night?** (Possible response: *Because I love the person and want to talk to him or her.*)

Prepare to Read: "Abuela"

Preview. Tell children that they are going to read a selection titled "Abuela." Explain that this is a fantasy story. Tell children that "Abuela" tells about a make-believe trip a girl takes with her grandmother. Then preview the selection.

BANNER DAYS
pages 282–299

- **Pages 282–283:** I see the title, "Abuela," and the name of the author on pages 282–283. I see a picture of a white-haired lady and a little girl flying in the sky. I think that the selection will tell who these people are and why they are flying.

- **Pages 284–285:** On these pages, I see pictures and read about a girl and her grandmother, Abuela. I read English words and Spanish words. I think that some of the story will be in English and some of the story will be in Spanish.

- **Pages 286–287:** On these pages, I read that the girl wonders what would happen if she and her abuela could fly. I see a picture of the girl and Abuela flying. I think I will read more words and see more pictures about what the girl imagines would happen if they could fly.

Set Purpose. Model setting a purpose for reading "Abuela."

MODEL From what I have seen in my preview, I think I will read more about where the girl and Abuela go on their make-believe flight. I will read to find out what they see as they fly and if they enjoy flying.

Lesson 26 • Intervention Teacher's Guide

AFTER
Reading "Abuela"
pages 282–299

Reread and Summarize

Have children reread and summarize "Abuela" in sections, as described below.

Pages 284–285

Let's reread pages 284–285 to recall who the story is about and what they do together in real life.

Summary: The story is about a girl and her grandmother, Abuela. They go to the park together and feed the birds.

Pages 286–293

Let's reread pages 286–293 to recall what happens in the girl's imagination.

Summary: The girl imagines that she and Abuela can fly over the city and glide close to the sea. They take a ride on the airplane that brought Abuela to this country. They go to Pablo and Elisa's store.

Pages 294–296

Let's reread pages 294–296 to remember some of the things the girl and Abuela see in the sky. Let's try to remember the Spanish words and what they mean in English.

Summary: The girl and Abuela see *las nubes*, which means *the clouds;* one cloud looks like *un gato,* which means *a cat;* one cloud looks like *un oso,* which means *a bear.*

Pages 297–298

Let's reread pages 297–298 to recall what happens to the girl and Abuela at the end of the story.

Summary: They are back in the park. They walk by the lake and Abuela probably wants to go for a boat ride and have another adventure.

FLUENCY BUILDER Be sure children have copies of *Intervention Practice Book* page 103, which you used for yesterday's Fluency Builder activity. Call attention to the sentences on the bottom half of the page. The slashes break the sentences into phrases to allow you to work on natural phrasing. Tell children that their goal is to read each phrase or sentence smoothly. Model appropriate pace, expression and phrasing as you read each sentence and have children read it after you. Then have children practice by reading the sentences aloud three times to a partner.

INTERVENTION PRACTICE BOOK
page 103

BEFORE
Making Connections
pages 302–303

Directed Reading: "If I Could Fly," pp. 206–211

SOUNDS OF SUNSHINE
pp. 206–212

Ask a volunteer to read aloud the title on page 206. Ask children why they think people might want to fly. Then have children read page 206 to find out about Luke. Ask: **What does the story tell you about where Luke would go if he could fly? What do you know about people who want to visit big cities? What kind of a person do you think Luke is?** (*Possible responses: The story tells me that Luke would fly to a big city because he has never been to one; people who like big cities like excitement, crowds, noise; Luke might be a person who is curious about new places.*) **MAKE INFERENCES**

Page 207

Have children read page 207. Ask: **What does Luke mean when he says he "would sail over the buildings"?** (*Possible response: He would fly high up in the sky over the city.*) **UNDERSTAND FIGURATIVE LANGUAGE**

Reread page 207 aloud. Model using the Look at Word Bits and Parts strategy in order for children to understand how to read and figure out the meanings of long or unfamiliar words.

MODEL As I read, I don't always know every word. If I have trouble reading a long word, I look at bits and parts that I know. I can find *be* and *eve* inside the word *believe*, and I can blend the *li* in the middle so now I can read the word *believe*, too. **LOOK AT WORD BITS AND PARTS**

Page 208

Have children look at the illustration to predict where June would fly. Then have them read page 208 to confirm their predictions. Ask: **Where would June go if she could fly?** (*Possible response: She would fly to a country where people love to play.*) **MAKE PREDICTIONS**

Page 209

Have children read page 209 to find out what June would do in that country. Ask: **Would June teach people to fly?** (*Possible response: Yes.*) **INTERPRET STORY EVENTS**

Ask: **What would June and her new friends do?** (*Possible response: They would have a big party in the sky, eat cake, and dance on the clouds.*) **NOTE DETAILS**

Page 210

Have children read page 210 to find out where Sally would go if she could fly. Ask: **Where would Sally go if she could fly? Why?** (*Possible response: She would visit her grandma because her grandma moved far away, and Sally misses her.*) **UNDERSTAND CHARACTERS' MOTIVES**

Page 211

Have children read page 211 to find out what Sally would do with her grandma after they ate. Ask: **What would Sally do with her grandma?** (*Possible response: She would take a walk, go fishing, look for whales, watch the sun go down, and read with her.*) **SUMMARIZE**

Ask: **How is Sally's adventure like Luke's and June's? How is it different?** (*Possible response: The adventures are alike because the children would all fly. Sally's is different because it could happen in real life. The others do*

262 Lesson 26 • Intervention Teacher's Guide

INTERVENTION PRACTICE BOOK
page 105

something make-believe.) **COMPARE AND CONTRAST**

Ask: **Why would Sally's adventure be the best for her?** (*Accept reasonable responses.*) **UNDERSTAND CHARACTERS' FEELINGS**

Summarize the Selection. Ask children to think about why people have different opinions about what a good adventure would be.

Answers to *Think About It* Questions

1. Luke would fly over a big city; June would fly to a place where people love to play; Sally would fly to visit her grandma, who has moved far away. **SUMMARY**
2. Sally loves her grandma. I can tell because Sally misses her grandma, would go to visit her grandma, and would do a lot of fun things with her grandma. **INTERPRETATION**
3. Accept reasonable responses. **TASK**

AFTER
Skill Review
pages 305C–305D

USE SKILL CARD 26B

(Focus Skill) Make Inferences

RETEACH the skill. Have children look at **side B of Skill Card 26: Make Inferences**. Read the skill reminder with them, and have a volunteer read the story aloud.

Read aloud the set of directions. Explain that children will work with partners to create their own charts. Remind them to think about the clues in the story as well as what they know as they read the story.

After children have completed their Make Inferences charts, have them display and explain their work. Point out that many inferences could be made about the selection "If I Could Fly." Ask volunteers to make some inferences about the characters in "If I Could Fly."

Review Phonics Skill from Abuela

RETEACH r-controlled vowels: /âr/ air, are. Read aloud the following sentence: *The glare from the sun made me move my chair.* Have children listen for the /âr/ sound. Then read this list aloud and have children raise their hands when they hear the r-controlled /âr/ sound: *blare, bland, unfair, stair, stop, dare, don't, square.*

FLUENCY BUILDER Be sure that children have copies of *Intervention Practice Book* page 103. Explain that today children will practice the sentences on the bottom half of the page by reading them aloud on tape. Assign new partners. Have children take turns reading the sentences aloud to each other and then reading them on tape.

INTERVENTION PRACTICE BOOK
page 103

Abuela/If I Could Fly

BEFORE

Drafting a Personal Narrative Paragraph
page 305E

Writer's Craft: Personal Narrative Paragraph

Build on Prior Knowledge. Tell children that they are going to talk about and write personal narrative paragraphs. Explain that personal narrative paragraphs tell about things the writer did or things that happened to the writer. Tell children that the events in the personal narrative paragraph happen in an order that makes sense. Have children share ideas for a personal narrative paragraph. Guide them to use time-order words in their narratives when they describe the events that occurred.

> My family ate the pie.
> I looked in a cookbook.
> I chose a recipe.
> I made a pie.
> I put all the ingredients on the table.

Construct the Text. "Share the pen" with children. Tell them that the list names events that took place in a personal narrative. Help children organize the items on the list into a personal narrative paragraph. Guide them to focus on the logic behind the order of the events. For example:

> I looked in a cookbook. I chose a recipe. I put all the ingredients on the table. I made a pie. My family ate the pie.

Revisit the Text. Go back and read the personal narrative paragraph together. Ask: **What happened first?** (*I looked in a cookbook.*) **What happened next?** (*I chose a recipe.*)

- Guide children to use time-order words to show the order of events. Ask: **How can I use time-order words to show the order of events?** (*First, I looked in a cookbook. Next, I chose a recipe. Then I put all the ingredients on the table. After that, I made a pie. Finally, my family ate the pie.*) Make appropriate changes.

- Ask: **What would happen if I wrote the events in a different order?** (*The story would not make sense.*)

- Have children read the completed personal narrative paragraph aloud and then copy it on their papers.

On Your Own

Have children write a list of events that could take place in a personal narrative paragraph. Tell them to put their list in the order in which they happen.

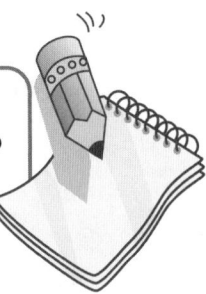

AFTER
Spelling Lesson
page 301H

Connect Spelling and Phonics

RETEACH Vowel Variants: /o͝o/oo; /o͞o/oo. Tell children to number their papers 1–8. Dictate the following words, and have children write them. After they write each word, write it on the board so children can proofread their work. They should draw a line through a misspelled word and write the correct spelling below it.

| 1. cook* | 2. boot | 3. soon | 4. book* |
| 5. hoof | 6. pool | 7. cool | 8. shook |

*Word appears in "If I Could Fly."

Dictate these sentences and have children write them: *I sit on the stool in my room. I look at my book. It tells me how to cook food.*

Build and Read Longer Words

Remind children that they have learned how to decode words with the /o͝o/ or the /o͞o/ sound. Explain that now they will use what they have learned to help them read some longer words.

Write the word *cookbook* on the board. Remind children that they can often figure out longer words by looking for smaller words in them. Cover the word *book*, and have children read the small word that is left. Follow a similar procedure to have them read the small word *book*. Model how to blend the two smaller words to read aloud the longer word *cookbook*. Do the same to have children blend word parts to read these longer words: *bedroom, broomstick,* and *noontime*.

INTERVENTION ASSESSMENT BOOK

FLUENCY BUILDER Have children choose a passage from "If I Could Fly" to read aloud to a partner. You may have children choose passages that they found particularly interesting, or have them choose one of the following options:

- Read pages 206–207. (From *Where would you . . . through . . . in the door!* Total: 95 words)
- Read pages 207–208. (From *Trucks on the street . . . . through . . . show them how.* Total: 113 words)

Children should read the selected passage aloud to their partners three times. Have children rate each of their own readings on a scale from 1 to 4.

Abuela/If I Could Fly

BEFORE Weekly Assessments

Review Vocabulary

To revisit vocabulary words prior to the weekly assessment, use these sentence frames. Have volunteers take turns reading aloud the sentence stems and choices. Then have children identify the correct choice and explain why that choice makes sense in the sentence.

1. If a bird is **swooping**, it
   a. flies downward fast.   b. does not move in the sky.
2. If you see a **flock** of birds, you see
   a. only one bird.   b. many birds.
3. When the birds **glide**, they
   a. fly smoothly.   b. have trouble flying.
4. If you **soared** up in the sky, you would
   a. not fly very high.   b. go high up in the sky.
5. When you go to the **harbor**, you see
   a. many trains.   b. many ships.

Correct responses: 1a, 2b, 3a, 4b, 5b.

You may want to display the Vocabulary Words and definitions on page 259 and have children copy them to use when they study for the vocabulary test.

Review Make Inferences

To review making inferences before the weekly assessment, distribute *Intervention Practice Book* page 106. Have volunteers read aloud the direction line and the story. Guide children to think about their own personal experience as they make their inferences.

Review Test Prep

Ask children to turn to page 305 of the *Pupil Edition*. Call attention to the Tips for answering the test questions. Tell children that paying attention to these tips can help them answer not only the test questions on this page but also other test questions like these.

BANNER DAYS page 305

Have children follow along as you read each test question and the tip that goes with it. Tell children to take their time as they think about each choice.

AFTER Weekly Assessments

Self-Selected Reading

Have children select their own books to read independently. They might choose books from the classroom library shelf, or you may wish to offer a group of appropriate books from which children can choose.

- *Working at the Airport* by Clair Daniel. See page 305Q of the *Teacher's Edition* for an Independent Reading Plan.
- *Let's Eat* by Ann Zamorano. Scholastic, 1997.
- *Busy Bea* by Nancy Poydar. Macmillan, 1992.

After children have chosen their books, give each child a copy of "My Reading Log," which can be found on page R35 in the back of the *Teacher's Edition*. Have children fill in the information at the top of the form. Then have them use the log to keep track of their reading and to record their responses to the literature.

Conduct Student-Teacher Conferences. Arrange time for each child to conference with you individually about his or her self-selected reading. Have children bring their Reading Logs to share with you at the conference. Children might also like to choose a favorite passage to read aloud to you. Ask questions about the book designed to stimulate discussion. For example, you might ask if children would like to fly and where they would like to go.

FLUENCY PERFORMANCE Have children read aloud to you the passage from "If I Could Fly" that they selected and practiced with their partners. Keep track of the number of words the child reads correctly. Ask the child to rate his or her own performance on the 1–4 scale. If children are not happy with their oral reading, give them an opportunity to continue practicing and then to read the passage to you again.

See *Oral Reading Fluency Assessment* for monitoring progress.

LESSON 27

BEFORE
Building Background and Vocabulary

Use with

"Beginner's World Atlas"

Review Phonics: Consonant: /j/g, dge

Identify the sound. Have children repeat the following sentence three times: *Gemma ate fudge in the giant gym.* Ask them which words in the sentence have the /j/ sound. (*Gemma, fudge, giant, gym*) Then have them raise their hands each time they hear a word with the /j/ sound as you say: *gum, gem, gave, gym, giant, got.*

Associate letters to sound. On the board, write: *Gemma ate fudge in the giant gym.* Have a volunteer underline the words that contain the letter *g.* Tell children that the letter *g* usually stands for the /j/ sound when it is followed by *e, i,* or *y.* Point to the word *fudge* and tell children that the letters *dge* usually stand for the /j/ sound.

Word blending. Model how to blend and read the word *gym.* Slide your hand under the letters as you slowly elongate the sounds /jiimm/. Then read *gym* naturally. Follow a similar procedure for *gem, giant, fudge* and *ledge.*

Apply the skill. *Letter Substitution* Write the first word in each pair below on the board, and have children read each aloud. Make the changes necessary to form the words in parentheses. Have a volunteer read aloud each new word.

game (gym)	**leg** (ledge)	**bug** (budge)	**gate** (germ)
peg (page)	**gas** (gem)	**hug** (hedge)	**gain** (giant)

INTERVENTION PRACTICE BOOK
page 108

Introduce Vocabulary

PRETEACH lesson vocabulary. Tell children that they are going to learn five new words that they will see again when they read a nonfiction selection called "Beginner's World Atlas." Teach every Vocabulary Word using the following process.

Use these suggestions or similar ideas to give the meaning or context.

> Write the word.
> Say the word.
> Track the word and have children repeat it.
> Give the meaning or context.

connects — Relate to movement by having a volunteer connect two children's hands. Say: **She or he connects the children.** Repeat the process by having volunteers connect other classroom objects.

distance — Relate to measurement by using a yardstick to measure the distance between two classroom desks.

features — Relate to physical features by having children touch the

268 Lesson 27 • Intervention Teacher's Guide

	features on their face; then point to the features on a map.
mapmaker	Point out the two small words *map* and *maker*. Have children role-play being mapmakers as they draw maps of the classroom or their neighborhood.
peel	Relate to peeling an orange.

For vocabulary activities, see Vocabulary Games on pages 2–7. *(Intervention Teachers Guide)*

> **Vocabulary Words**
> **connects** brings together
> **distance** how far it is from one place to another
> **features** traits or characteristics
> **mapmaker** a person who makes maps
> **peel** pull off

AFTER
Building Background and Vocabulary

Apply Vocabulary Strategies

Use synonyms. Write the word *connects* on chart paper and help children define it. Tell children that they can sometimes figure out the meaning of a word if they know its synonyms. Remind them that a synonym is a word that means nearly the same as another word.

MODEL If I want to understand what the word *connects* means, I can find synonyms, or other words that have the same meaning. *Connects* and *joins* are synonyms. I am familiar with the word *joins*. Now I know that the word *connects* means nearly the same as the word *joins*.

Use a similar strategy with *features* and *peel*.

RETEACH lesson vocabulary. Have each student make a set of word cards for the vocabulary words. Say the sentences below and tell children to hold up the word that tells about each sentence. Reread the sentences with the correct answer and discuss how children made their choices.

1. This word tells about the space between places. (*distance*)
2. This word tells about physical traits of a face or map. (*features*)
3. This word tells about taking the skin or cover off something. (*peel*)
4. This word tells about a person who draws something that shows places. (*mapmaker*)
5. This word tells about bringing two or more things together. (*connects*)

FLUENCY BUILDER Using *Intervention Practice Book* page 107, read each word aloud in the first column and have children repeat it. Then have children work in pairs to read the words in the first column aloud to each other. Follow the same procedure with each of the remaining columns. After partners have practiced reading aloud the words in each separate column, have them read aloud the entire list. (Save *Intervention Practice Book* page 107 to use on pages 271 and 273.)

INTERVENTION PRACTICE BOOK
page 107

Beginner's World Atlas/Map Games

BEFORE

Reading "Beginner's World Atlas"
pages 308–331

USE SKILL CARD 27A

(Focus Skill) Locate Information

PRETEACH the skill. Point out to children that readers can use the table of contents to locate information in books such as atlases. Discuss how a table of contents is organized. Guide children to see that using a table of contents saves readers time.

Have children look at **side A of Skill Card 27: Locate Information**. Read the definition of locate information. Next, read the table of contents and have children read it with you.

Now call attention to the chart and have volunteers take turns reading the information aloud. Ask:

- **What can you see on a map?** (*Possible response: Continents, oceans, physical features of places*)

- **What are rivers, lakes, and mountain ranges called when found on a map?** (*physical features*)

Prepare to Read: "Beginner's World Atlas"

Preview. Tell children that they are going to read a selection entitled "Beginner's World Atlas." Explain that this is a non-fiction selection. Tell children that "Beginner's World Atlas" tells facts about the places in the world. Then preview the selection.

BANNER DAYS
pages 308–331

- **Pages 308–309:** I see the title, "Beginner's World Atlas," on pages 308–309. I see a picture of children, animals, and the planet Earth. I think that the selection will tell facts about the planet Earth.

- **Pages 310–311:** On these pages, I learn about maps. I see pictures that show different views of a place, and read about the view a map shows. I think that I will learn more about maps in the selection.

- **Pages 312–313:** On these pages, I read about how to find places on a map. I see pictures that help me understand the features of a map. I think that I will be able to use maps to find out information about different places as I read the selection.

Set Purpose. Model setting a purpose for reading "Beginner's World Atlas."

MODEL From what I have seen in my preview, I think I will read more about maps and how to use them to learn information about the Earth and the people and animals that live there. I will read to find out what other information can be found in an atlas.

270 Lesson 27 • Intervention Teacher's Guide

AFTER

Reading "Beginner's World Atlas"
pages 308–331

Reread and Summarize

Have children reread and summarize "Beginner's World Atlas" in sections, as described below.

Pages 310–313

Let's reread pages 310–313 to recall facts about maps.

Summary: A map is a drawing of a place as it looks from above. A map can help you locate places. Maps have features called a compass, a scale, and a map key to help you find information about direction, distance, and other things found on a map.

Pages 314–319

Let's reread pages 314–319 to recall the difference between a map and a globe and some physical features of the world.

Summary: A globe is like a round map. Some physical features of the world are continents, islands, oceans, lakes, and rivers.

Pages 320–321

Let's reread pages 320–321 to recall some of the map symbols used on physical maps.

Summary: Symbols show mountains, deserts, coniferous forests, deciduous forests, rain forests, ice caps, tundras, wetlands, and grasslands.

Pages 322–328

Let's reread pages 322–328 to recall some facts about North America.

Summary: North America is shaped like a triangle. It has mountain ranges and grassy plains. The Great Lakes are the world's largest group of freshwater lakes. The climate in the far north is very cold, and temperatures get warmer as you move south. There is a big variety of animals. Mexico City is the biggest city in North America. The ancestors of most people in North America came from Europe. English and Spanish are the main languages.

FLUENCY BUILDER Use *Intervention Practice Book* page 107. Point out the sentences on the bottom half of the page. Remind students to pay attention to the slashes and to read each phrase or unit smoothly. Model appropriate pacing, expression, and phrasing as you read each sentence, and have students read it after you. Then have students practice by reading the sentences aloud three times to a partner.

INTERVENTION PRACTICE BOOK

page 107

BEFORE
Making Connections
page 332

Directed Reading: "Map Games," pp. 214–221

SOUNDS OF SUNSHINE
pp. 214–221

Pages 214–215

Ask a volunteer to read aloud the title on page 214. Ask children what a globe is like. Then have children read pages 214–215 to find out. Ask: **Who makes globes? How is a globe like a map?** (*Possible response: A mapmaker; a globe is like a round map*) **NOTE DETAILS**

Pages 216–217

Have children read pages 216–217. Ask: **What book will help you look up these facts? How will you locate information in this book?** (*Possible response: an atlas; I will use the table of contents.*) **LOCATE INFORMATION**

Ask: **What do you do first in a game that is played with a globe? What do you do next?** (*Possible response: First you spin your globe. Next you stop the globe with one finger.*) **SEQUENCE OF EVENTS**

Page 218

Have children read page 218. Model using the Decoding/Phonics strategy in order for children to understand how to figure out long or unfamiliar words.

> **MODEL** When I first see the word *continents*, I am not sure how to read it. I can begin by sounding it out and breaking it into syllables. I recognize the letters *ent* at the end of the word because I have seen them in other words like *tent* and *sent*. I have seen the *s* ending in other words like *cats* and *dogs*. I have seen the beginning letters *con* in words like *connect* and *contrast*. Now I know that the word I am trying to read is *continents*. **DECODING/PHONICS**

Page 219

Have children read page 219 to find out how to play What Is It Like There? Ask: **How do you play the new game?** (*Possible response: Ask things about the places your finger lands on. Each player writes down the answer. Then they look through the pages of books about the place to see who knew the most.*) **NOTE DETAILS**

Lesson 27 • Intervention Teacher's Guide

INTERVENTION PRACTICE BOOK page 109

Have children read page 220 to find out why people might want to play and make up new map games. Ask: **Besides being fun, why are map games important?** (*Possible response: They help people learn about the world.*) SPECULATE

Summarize the selection. Ask children to think about why people like to use maps and globes and atlases. Then have them complete *Intervention Practice Book* page 109.

Answers to *Think About It* Questions

1. Continents, oceans, rivers, lakes, and mountains are features of the earth that globes show. **NOTE DETAILS**
2. Possible response: What is it like there would be fun because you can learn about how people in other countries live. **PERSONAL OPINION**
3. Accept reasonable responses. TASK

AFTER
Skill Review
page 333I

USE SKILL CARD 27B

(Focus Skill) Locate Information

RETEACH the skill. Have children look at **side B of Skill Card 27: Locate Information**. Read the skill reminder with them, and have a volunteer read the table of contents aloud.

Read aloud the set of directions. Explain that children will work with partners to create their own charts. Remind them to look for clue words in the questions that match the information found on each page.

After children have completed their Locate Information charts, have them display and explain their work. Point out that a table of contents could be made for the selection "Map Games." Ask volunteers to suggest headings for a table of contents for "Map Games."

Review Phonics Skill from "Beginner's World Atlas"

RETEACH vowel variants /o͝o/oo, ou. Have children make word cards for the following words: *stood, could, book, goodnight, looking, would, shook, should.* Read the word together. Have children sort the words into two piles. One pile of words that makes the sound /o͝o/ spelled *oo* and another pile with words that make the sound /o͝o/ spelled *ou*. Then have children read the words in each pile with a partner.

FLUENCY BUILDER Be sure that children have copies of *Intervention Practice Book* page 107. Explain that today the children will practice the sentences on the bottom half of the page by reading them aloud on tape. Assign new partners. Have the children take turns reading the sentences aloud to each other and then reading them on tape.

INTERVENTION PRACTICE BOOK page 107

Beginner's World Atlas/Map Games

BEFORE
Drafting a Paragraph of Information
page 335C

Writer's Craft: Paragraph of Information

Build on Prior Knowledge. Tell children that they are going to talk about and write a paragraph of information, or an informational paragraph. Explain that informational paragraphs should be interesting and tell about one topic. Tell children that the ideas in an informational paragraph must be grouped in a way that makes sense. Explain that when writing an informational paragraph, it is often helpful to organize ideas by using time-order words. Have children discuss time-order words and how they think these words would be helpful in an informational paragraph. Display the list shown above.

> winter
> spring
> summer
> fall

Construct the Text. "Share the pen" with children. Tell them that the list names seasons of the year and that different places in the world experience the seasons at different times. Help children to organize the seasons on the list into an informational paragraph about the sequence of seasons around the world. Guide them to focus on the order of the seasons that happen where they live. For example:

> When it is winter where I live, it is summer in Australia. When it is spring where I live, it is fall in Australia. When it is summer where I live, it is winter in Australia. When it is fall where I live, it is spring in Australia.

Revisit the Text. Go back and read the informational paragraph together. Ask: **Why does the paragraph start by talking about the winter season?** *(Winter comes first in the year.)* **Why do we talk about spring next?** *(Spring comes after winter.)*

- Guide children to use time-order words to show the order of events. Ask: **How can I use time-order words to show the order of events?** *(When it is winter where I live, it is summer in Australia. Next, when it is spring where I live, it is fall in Australia. After that, when it is summer where I live, it is winter in Australia. Finally, when it is fall where I live, it is spring in Australia.)* Make appropriate changes.

- Ask: **What would happen if I used a different order?** *(The paragraph would not make sense.)*

- Have children read the completed informational paragraph aloud and then copy it on their papers.

On Your Own

Have children write a list of activities that they do throughout the seasons of the year. Tell them to put their list in an order which makes sense.

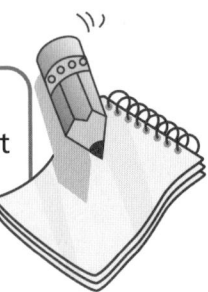

AFTER

Spelling Lesson
page 331H

Connect Spelling and Phonics

RETEACH consonant /j/g, dge. Tell children to number their papers 1–8. Dictate the following words, and have children write them. After children write each word, write it on the board so children can proofread their work. They should draw a line through a misspelled word and write the correct spelling below it.

| 1. orange* | 2. age* | 3. large* | 4. frigidly* |
| 5. Germany* | 6. village* | 7. range | 8. pages* |

*Word appears in "Map Games."

Dictate the following sentences and have children write them: *Mary sees a gem by the hedge. The gem is red.*

Build and Read Longer Words

Remind children that they have learned how to decode words with the /j/ sound. Explain that now they will use what they have learned to help them read some longer words.

Write the word *gigantic* on the board. Remind children that when they come across a word that has the VCV pattern, they should try saying the first syllable with a short vowel sound and then a long vowel sound to see which one sounds right. Then model saying the first syllable in *gigantic* with first a short and then a long vowel sound. Then ask children which part of the word says /jī/, which part says /gan/, and which part says /tik/. Follow the same procedure to have children read these longer words: *gymnastics* and *gentleness*.

INTERVENTION ASSESSMENT BOOK

FLUENCY BUILDER Have children choose a passage from *"Map Games"* to read aloud to a partner. You may have children choose passages that they found particularly interesting, or have them choose one of the following options:

- Read pages 214–215. (From *You can use . . .* through *. . . It is called Antarctica.* Total: 110 words)

- Read page 219. (From *On your spin . . .* through *. . . who knew more.* Total: 92 words)

Children should read the selected passage aloud to their partner three times. Have children rate each of their own readings on a scale from 1 to 4.

Beginner's World Atlas/Map Games

BEFORE Weekly Assessments

Review Vocabulary

To revisit Vocabulary Words prior to the weekly assessment, use these sentence frames. Have volunteers take turns reading aloud the sentence stems and choices. Students identify each correct choice and explain why that choice makes sense in the sentence.

1. When you **peel** an orange, you
   a. keep the skin on.   b. take the skin off.
2. If you know the **distance** between two places, you know
   a. how high the places are.   b. how far it is between them.
3. A **mapmaker** is a person who
   a. makes maps.   b. flies an airplane.
4. Some physical **features** on a continent are
   a. mountains and deserts.   b. words and paragraphs.
5. When you **connect** two things, you
   a. pull them apart.   b. bring them together.

Correct responses: 1b, 2b, 3a, 4a, 5b.

You may want to display the vocabulary words and definitions on page 269 and have children copy them to use when they study for the vocabulary test.

(Focus Skill) Review Locate Information

To review locate information before the weekly assessment, distribute *Intervention Practice Book* page 110. Have volunteers read aloud the directions and the table of contents. Guide children to look for clue words in the questions that match the headings in the table of contents.

Review Test Prep

Ask children to turn to page 335 of the *Pupil Edition*. Call attention to the Tips for answering the test questions. Tell children that paying attention to these tips can help them answer not only the test questions on this page but also other test questions like these.

BANNER DAYS page 335

Have children follow along as you read each test question and the tip that goes with it. Tell children to check over their answers after they have completed the test.

INTERVENTION PRACTICE BOOK page 110

INTERVENTION ASSESSMENT BOOK

276 Lesson 27 • Intervention Teacher's Guide

AFTER Weekly Assessments

Self-Selected Reading

Have children select their own books to read independently. They might choose books from the classroom library shelf, or you may wish to offer a group of appropriate books from which children can choose.

- *Getting to Grandpa's* by Clair Daniel. See page 335O of the *Teacher's Edition* for an Independent Reading Plan.
- *Parks Are to Share* by Lee Sullivan Hill. Carolrhoda, 1997.
- *Jonathan and His Mommy* by Irene Smalls. Brown Little, 1992.

After children have chosen their books, give each child a copy of My Reading Log, which can be found on page R35 in the back of the *Teacher's Edition*. Have children fill in the information at the top of the form. Then have them use the log to keep track of their reading and to record their responses to the literature.

Conduct student-teacher conferences. Arrange time for each child to confer with you individually about his or her self-selected reading. Have children bring their Reading Logs to share with you at the conference. Children might also like to choose a favorite passage to read aloud to you. Ask questions designed to stimulate discussion about the book. For example, you might ask children to share which places in the world they would like to visit, and what they know about those places.

FLUENCY PERFORMANCE Have children read aloud to you the passage from "Map Games" that they selected and practiced with their partner. Keep track of the number of words the child reads correctly. Ask the child to rate his or her own performance on the 1–4 scale. If children are not happy with their oral reading, give them an opportunity to continue practicing and to read the passage to you again.

See *Oral Reading Fluency Assessment* for monitoring progress.

Beginner's World Atlas/Map Games

LESSON 28

BEFORE Building Background and Vocabulary

Use with

"Dinosaurs Travel"

Review Phonics: Vowel Diphthongs /oi/*oi, oy*

Identify the sound. Have children repeat the following sentence three times: *Roy points to a coin in the soil by his toy.* Ask children to identify the words that have the /oi/ sound. (*Roy, points, coin, soil, toy*)

Associate letters to sound. On the board, write: *Roy points to a coin in the soil by his toy.* Circle the words *Roy* and *toy*. Ask children to tell how the words are alike. (*same vowel sound at the end; both end in* oy) Underline the letters *oy* in *Roy* and *toy*. Tell children that the letters *oy* can stand for the /oi/ sound they hear in *Roy* and *toy*. Then follow a similar procedure for the /oi/ sound in the words *points, coin,* and *soil*.

Word blending. Model how to blend and read the word *boil*. Write *boil* on the board. Slide your hand under the letters as you slowly elongate the sounds /boill/. Then read *boil* naturally. Follow a similar procedure for *coil, joy, moist,* and *Troy*.

Apply the skill. *Vowel Substitution* Write the following words on the board. Have children read each word aloud. Make the changes necessary to form the word in parentheses. Have children read the new word.

| **sail** (soil) | **by** (boy) | **tail** (toil) | **fail** (foil) |
| **jay** (joy) | **nose** (noise) | **tea** (toy) | **cone** (coin) |

Introduce Vocabulary

PRETEACH lesson vocabulary. Tell children that they will learn five new words that they will see again when they read a selection called "Dinosaurs Travel." Teach each Vocabulary Word using the following process.

Use these suggestions or similar ideas to give the meaning or context.

cassette	Demonstrate how to use an actual cassette tape.
companions	Have children role-play being companions.
luggage	Show a picture or have children role-play packing using actual suitcases or boxes.

> Write the word.
> Say the word.
> Track the word and have children repeat it.
> Give the meaning or context.

INTERVENTION PRACTICE BOOK
page 112

Lesson 28 • Intervention Teacher's Guide

relatives	Have children name members of their immediate and extended family.
sturdy	Contrast sturdy and weak classroom objects.

For vocabulary activities, see Vocabulary Games on pages 2–7.

AFTER
Building Background and Vocabulary

Apply Vocabulary Strategies

Use antonyms. Write the word *sturdy* on chart paper and help children define it. Tell children that they can sometimes figure out the meaning of a new word if they know its antonym. Remind children that an antonym is a word that means the opposite of another word.

> **MODEL** The word *sturdy* means *strong*, and *strong* means "not weak." Walls are sturdy. Hiking boots are sturdy. So I know that an antonym for *sturdy* is *weak*. Like *strong*, *sturdy* also means "not weak."

Guide children to use a similar process to figure out the meaning of *companions*.

RETEACH lesson vocabulary. Have children write each Vocabulary Word on a word card and then listen as you say each of the following groups of words. Tell them to hold up the word card that goes with each group. Reread the groups aloud with the correct answer. Then discuss how children made their choices.

1. suitcases	boxes	travel (*luggage*)
2. music	tape player	recording (*cassette*)
3. friends	people	come along (*companions*)
4. strong	lasting	made well (*sturdy*)
5. family	parents	cousins (*relatives*)

Vocabulary Words
cassette case with tape inside used to record music
companions people who came along with someone
luggage suitcases or boxes used by travelers
relatives people of the same family
sturdy strong and made to last

FLUENCY BUILDER Use *Intervention Practice Book* page 111. Read each word in the first column aloud and have children repeat it. Then have partners read the words in the first column aloud to each other. Tell children to follow the same procedure with each of the remaining columns. After partners have practiced reading aloud the words in each column, have them practice the entire list. (Save *Intervention Practice Book* page 111 to use on pages 281 and 283.)

INTERVENTION PRACTICE BOOK
page 111

Dinosaurs Travel/When You Visit Relatives

BEFORE
Reading
"Dinosaurs Travel"
pages 338–355

USE SKILL CARD 28A

(Focus Skill) Author's Purpose

PRETEACH the skill. Point out to children that the author's purpose is the reason why the author wrote the story. Explain that there are many purposes, or reasons, why authors write. Give examples of author's purposes, such as *to give information* and *to entertain*. Discuss why it helps authors to have a purpose before they begin to write.

Have children look at **side A of Skill Card 28: Author's Purpose**. Read the definition of author's purpose. Next read the paragraph and then have children reread it with you. Then have volunteers take turns reading the information in the chart aloud. Ask:

- **What would the author's purpose be if the story was about a space alien who washed a purple dog?** (*Possible response: to entertain.*)

- **How do the clues help you understand the author's purpose?** (*Possible response: They show what kind of story it is and help us know the author's reason for writing it.*)

Prepare to Read: "Dinosaurs Travel"

Preview. Tell children that they are going to read an informational story called "Dinosaurs Travel." Tell children that "Dinosaurs Travel" gives information about how to travel. Then preview the selection.

BANNER DAYS
pages 338–355

- **Pages 338–339:** I see the title, "Dinosaurs Travel," and the names of the authors, on pages 338–339. I read the subtitle, "A Guide for Families on the Go," and this tells me that I will find out information about how families can travel. I think that I will see more funny pictures of dinosaurs traveling.

- **Pages 340–341:** On these pages, I read about the places people might want to travel. I see pictures of dinosaurs traveling and doing things that many people like to do. Even though I know that dinosaurs can't really do these things, I think the pictures are funny. I enjoy them.

- **Pages 342–343:** On these pages, I read about how to get ready for a trip. I think I will probably learn more about how to plan and enjoy a trip.

Set Purpose. Model setting a purpose for reading "Dinosaurs Travel."

MODEL From what I have seen in my preview, I think I will read more about how to travel and what will happen on trips. I will also read to be entertained by the make-believe dinosaur characters who help me learn how to take a trip.

AFTER

Reading "Dinosaurs Travel" *pages 338–357*

Reread and Summarize

Have children reread and summarize "Dinosaurs Travel" in sections.

Pages 340–343

Let's reread pages 340–343 to recall why people travel and how to get ready for a trip.

Summary: People travel because they want to have adventures. Books and maps can help you get ready for your trip. You should take addresses of friends and relatives. You should pack small, light, and sturdy things.

Pages 344–347

Let's reread pages 344–347 to recall how to get from place to place.

Summary: You can walk, bike, or skateboard. Walking lets you stop and see the sights. Bikes and skateboards are faster than walking and you can go almost anywhere with them.

Pages 348–353

Let's reread pages 348–353 to remember some ways to get from place to place and why they are good ways to travel.

Summary: You can drive a car or you can ride a subway or bus in a city. You can drive a car on all kinds of roads. Subways are fast. Taking a train is a way to see new places. On an airplane, you fly high above the clouds.

Pages 354–355

Let's reread pages 354–355 to recall what happens when it is time to come home.

Summary: Remember to pack all your things. Souvenirs and pictures will remind you of your trip.

FLUENCY BUILDER Use *Intervention Practice Book* page 111. Point out the sentences on the bottom half of the page. Remind students to pay attention to the slashes and to read each phrase or unit smoothly. Model appropriate pace, expression, and phrasing as you read each sentence, and have children read it after you. Then have children practice by reading the sentences aloud three times to a partner.

INTERVENTION PRACTICE BOOK
page 111

Dinosaurs Travel/When You Visit Relatives

BEFORE
Making Connections
pages 360–361

Directed Reading: "When You Visit Relatives," pp. 222–228

SOUNDS OF SUNSHINE pp. 222–229

Page 222

Read aloud the title of the story. Ask children to name some relatives that they might like to visit. Then have children read page 222 to find out what to do before visiting relatives. Ask: **What should you do before you visit relatives?** (*Possible response: Call them.*) **SEQUENCE**

Ask: **Why should you call first?** (*Possible response: to give your relatives time to get ready for company*) **CAUSE AND EFFECT**

Page 223

Have children read the heading on page 223. Ask: **How do the headings in this story help you understand the author's purpose?** (*Possible response: The headings show me that the author wants to organize information about how to do something.*) **AUTHOR'S PURPOSE**

Have children read page 223. Model how to use the Use Context to Confirm Meaning strategy in order to understand the word *companion*.

> **MODEL** If I don't understand what a word means, I can use the other words in the sentence or paragraph to help me decide whether the meaning I am using is correct. After I read the word *companion* in the heading, I read the next sentence, which tells about inviting a friend to come along instead of traveling alone. That helps me to confirm that in the heading, *companion* probably means *friend*. **USE CONTEXT TO CONFIRM MEANING**

Page 224

Have children read page 224. Ask: **What should you do if you are biking?** (*Possible response: Bike in good weather; don't bike too far; avoid traffic; travel on safe roads; bring snacks.*) **SUMMARIZE**

Page 225

Have children read the heading on page 225. Ask children what luggage is. Then have them read page 225 to find out what to pack for a trip. Ask: **What should you pack for a trip?** (*Possible response: clothes, toys, and a raincoat*) **NOTE DETAILS**

Page 226

Have children read the heading on page 226. Then have them read page 226 to find out what rules to follow. Ask: **Which rule do you think is most important?** (*Responses will vary.*) **MAKE JUDGMENTS**

Page 227

Have children read the heading on page 227. Then have them read page 227 to learn how to help out. Ask: **What are some ways to help out?** (*Possible response: Make your bed; pick up your toys; make lunch; wash the dishes.*) **NOTE DETAILS**

Ask: **What other things might you do to help out?** (*Responses will vary.*) **EXTEND THE STORY**

Lesson 28 • Intervention Teacher's Guide

Page 228

INTERVENTION PRACTICE BOOK page 113

Have children read the heading on page 228. Then have them read the page to find out how to thank their relatives. Ask: **What are some ways to say thank you?** (Possible response: Tell your relatives that you had a good time; thank them for having you; invite them to visit you; send a thank-you note.) **NOTE DETAILS**

Summarize the selection. Ask children to think about why people want to travel to see their relatives and what they like to do once they get there. Then have them complete *Intervention Practice Book* page 113.

Page 229

Answers to *Think About It* Questions

1. First, you should call and tell your relatives about your travel plans. When you are there, you should follow the rules and help out. **SUMMARIZE**
2. A raincoat can keep you dry, and dry travelers are happy travelers. **NOTE DETAILS**
3. Accept reasonable responses. **SPECULATE**

AFTER

Skill Review page 363C

USE SKILL CARD 28B

(Focus Skill) Author's Purpose

RETEACH the skill. Have children look at **side B of Skill Card 28: Author's Purpose**. Read the skill reminder with them, and have a volunteer read the paragraph aloud.

Read aloud the set of directions. Explain that children will work with partners to create their own charts. Remind them to think about the reasons why the author might have written the paragraph.

After children have completed their charts, have them display and explain their work. Point out that the selection "Dinosaurs Travel" has an author's purpose and clues to that purpose. Ask volunteers to name the author's purpose and some clues to that purpose found in the selection.

Review Phonics Skill from "Dinosaurs Travel"

RETEACH vowel digraphs: /o͞o/ *ou, ou(gh)*. Read aloud the following sentence: **Lou and his group took a route through the mountains.** Have children identify words with the /o͞o/ sound. (*Lou, group, route, through*) Then read this list aloud and have children raise their hands when they hear the /o͞o/ sound: *you, cow, soup, cougar, fall, souvenir.*

FLUENCY BUILDER Use *Intervention Practice Book* page 111. Explain that today children will practice the sentences on the bottom half of the page by reading them aloud on tape. Assign new partners. Have children take turns reading the sentences aloud to each other and then reading them on tape.

INTERVENTION PRACTICE BOOK page 111

Dinosaurs Travel/When You Visit Relatives

BEFORE

Drafting a How-to Paragraph
page 363G

Writing Process: How-to Paragraph

Build on prior knowledge. Tell children that they are going to talk about and write how-to paragraphs. Explain that how-to paragraphs tell directions or instructions that must be followed to make or do something. Tell children that the directions or instructions in the how-to paragraph are listed in an order that makes sense. Have children share ideas for a how-to paragraph.

> 1. picnic basket
> 2. blanket
> 3. food
> 4. drinks
> 5. sunscreen
> 6. sandwich bags

Construct the text. "Share the pen" with children in a group writing effort. Guide them in using the list to formulate steps for planning a picnic. For example:

1. Make food.
2. Put food into sandwich bags.
3. Put sandwich bags into picnic basket.
4. Put drinks into picnic basket.
5. Put sunscreen into picnic basket.
6. Take blanket and picnic basket and go to the park.

Revisit the text. Go back and read the list of steps together. Ask: **What happens first?** (*Make food.*) **What happens next?** (*Put food into sandwich bags.*)

- Guide children to use time-order words to show the sequence of the steps. Ask: **How can I use time-order words to show how to plan a picnic?** (*Use words like* first, next, after that, then, *and* finally.) Make appropriate changes.

- Ask: **What would happen if I wrote the steps in a different order?** (*The instructions would not make sense.*)

- Have children read the how-to paragraph aloud and then copy it on their papers.

On Your Own

Have children write three or four steps for something they know how to do or make. Guide them to write their steps in an order that makes sense.

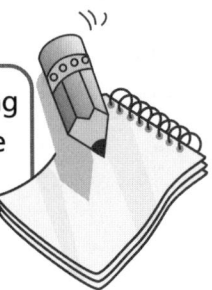

Lesson 28 • Intervention Teacher's Guide

AFTER

Spelling Lesson
pages 357H

Connect Spelling and Phonics

RETEACH vowel dipthongs. Tell children to number their papers 1–8. Write *boil* on the board, and tell children that in the words you will say, /oi/ will be spelled *oi* as in *boil*. Dictate the following words, and have children write them. After they write each word, write it on the board so children can proofread their work. They should draw a line through a misspelled word and write the correct spelling next to it.

1. soil	2. coin	3. point*	4. spoil*
5. join	6. foil	7. moist	8. oil

*Word appears in "When You Visit Relatives."

Tell children that in the following sentences the /oi/ sound is spelled *oy*. Dictate the sentences: *Roy is a boy. Joy is a girl. Roy and Joy play with toys.*

Build and Read Longer Words

Remind children that they have learned how to decode words with the /oi/ sound. Explain that now they will use what they have learned to help them read some longer words.

Write the word *enjoy* on the board. Remind children that they can often figure out longer words by looking for small words or word parts in them. Cover the word part *en*, and have children read the small word that is left. Follow a similar procedure to have them read the word part *en*. Model how to blend the two smaller parts to read aloud the longer word *enjoy*. Follow a similar procedure to have children read the words: *joyful*, *enjoyment* and *loyal*.

INTERVENTION ASSESSMENT BOOK

FLUENCY BUILDER Have children choose a passage from *"When You Visit Relatives"* to read aloud to a partner. You may have children choose passages that they found particularly interesting, or have them choose one of the following options:

- Read pages 222–223. (From *Call First . . .* through *. . . I'd love to Ernest!*) Total: 78 words.
- Read pages 224–225. (From *I forgot to bring . . .* through *. . . are happy travelers.*) Total: 93 words.

Children should read the selected passage aloud to their partners three times. Have the child rate each of his or her own readings on a scale from 1 to 4.

Dinosaurs Travel/When You Visit Relatives

BEFORE Weekly Assessments

Review Vocabulary

To revisit vocabulary words prior to the weekly assessment, use these sentence frames. Have volunteers take turns reading aloud the sentence beginnings and choices. Tell children to identify the correct choice and explain how they made their decision.

1. If something is **sturdy**, it is
   - **a.** weak.
   - **b.** strong and will last.
2. Travelers use **luggage** to
   - **a.** buy plane tickets.
   - **b.** hold their belongings.
3. You bring **companions** on a trip because
   - **a.** you want friends with you.
   - **b.** you need to pack.
4. If these people are your **relatives**, they are
   - **a.** not related to you.
   - **b.** members of your family.
5. When I play a **cassette**, I can hear
   - **a.** souvenirs.
   - **b.** music.

Correct responses: 1b, 2b, 3a, 4b, 5b

You may want to display the vocabulary words and definitions on page 279 and have children copy them to use when they study for the vocabulary test.

Focus Skill: Review Author's Purpose

To review Author's Purpose before the weekly assessment, distribute *Intervention Practice Book* page 114. Have volunteers read aloud the direction line and the story. Guide children to think about all the reasons authors write stories.

Review Test Prep

Ask children to turn to page 363 of the *Pupil Edition*. Call attention to the Tips for answering the test questions. Tell children that paying attention to these tips can help them answer not only the test questions on this page but also other test questions like these.

BANNER DAYS page 363

Have children follow along as you read each test question and the tip that goes with it. Tell children to get a good night's rest and eat a good breakfast before taking a test.

AFTER Weekly Assessments

Self-Selected Reading

Have children select their own books to read independently. They might choose books from the classroom library shelf, or you may wish to offer a group of appropriate books from which children can choose.

- *A Trip on Dinosaur Airlines* by Clair Daniel. See page 363S of the *Teacher's Edition* for an Independent Reading Plan.
- *The Berenstain Bears on the Road* by Stan and Jan Berenstain. Inchworm Press, 1996.
- *Dinosaurs* by Angela Royston. Simon and Schuster, 1991.

After children have chosen their books, give each child a copy of "My Reading Log," which can be found on page R35 in the back of the *Teacher's Edition*. Have children fill in the information at the top of the form. Then have them use the log to keep track of their reading and to record their responses to the literature.

Conduct student-teacher conferences. Arrange time for each child to confer with you individually about his or her self-selected reading. Have children bring their Reading Logs to share with you at the conference. Children might also like to choose a favorite passage to read aloud to you. Ask questions designed to stimulate discussion. For example, you might ask which method of travel children would like to experience and why.

FLUENCY PERFORMANCE Have children read aloud to you the passage from *"When You Visit Relatives"* that they selected and practiced with their partners. Keep track of the number of words the child reads correctly. Ask the child to rate his or her own performance on the 1–4 scale. If children are not happy with their oral reading, give them an opportunity to continue practicing and then to reread the passage to you.

See *Oral Reading Fluency Assessment* for monitoring progress.

Dinosaurs Travel/When You Visit Relatives

LESSON 29

BEFORE Building Background and Vocabulary

Use with

"Montigue on the High Seas"

Review Phonics: Vowel Variants /ô/ aw, au(gh)

Identify the sound. Have children repeat the following sentence three times: *Paul caught his puppy crawling on the lawn.* Ask children to identify the words that have the /ô/ sound. (*Paul, caught, crawling, lawn*)

Associate letters to sound. On the board, write: *Paul caught his puppy crawling on the lawn.* Circle the words *Paul* and *caught*. Ask children to tell how the words are alike. (*the /ô/ sound; the letters au*) Underline the letters *au* in *Paul* and *caught*. Tell children that the letters *au* can stand for the /ô/ sound they hear in *Paul* and *caught*. Then follow a similar procedure for the /ô/ sound for the letters *aw* in the words *crawling* and *lawn*.

Word blending. Model how to blend and read the word *taught*. Slide your hand under the letters as you slowly elongate the sounds. Then read *taught* naturally. Follow a similar procedure for *pause, claws,* and *fawn*.

Apply the skill. *Letter Substitution* Write the following words on the board, and have children read them aloud. Make the changes necessary to form the words in parentheses. Have children read each new word.

jay (jaw)   **lay** (law)   **pay** (paw)   **hail** (haul)
pail (Paul)   **stray** (straw)   **cat** (caught)   **fern** (fawn)

INTERVENTION PRACTICE BOOK page 116

Introduce Vocabulary

PRETEACH **lesson vocabulary.** Tell children that they are going to learn six new words that they will see again when they read a story called "Montigue on the High Seas." Teach every Vocabulary Word using the strategies in the box below..

Use the following suggestions or similar ideas to give the meaning or context:

cozy	Role-playing how a person feels in a cozy place.
drifted	Demonstrate with a toy or paper boat in the classroom sink.
fleet	Draw a simple picture of many boats. Have children contrast it with a simple picture of one boat.
launched	Point out the *-ed* ending. Relate meaning by demonstrating with a toy or paper boat in the classroom sink.
looming	Relate by role-playing something large and scary.

Write the word.
Say the word.
Track the word and have students repeat it.
Give the meaning or context.

288   Lesson 29 • Intervention Teacher's Guide

realized — Point out the -ed ending. Related words: *real*, *really*, *realize*.

For vocabulary activities, see Vocabulary Games on pages 2–7.

Vocabulary Words
cozy snug, comfortable
drifted pushed along by moving water
fleet group of ships or boats
launched caused to slide into the water
looming appearing large and scary
realized understood

AFTER — Building Background and Vocabulary

Apply Vocabulary Strategies

RETEACH lesson vocabulary. Write the word *cozy* on chart paper and help children define it. Tell children that they can sometimes figure out the meaning of a word if they know a synonym for it. A synonym is a word that means nearly the same as another word.

MODEL If I want to understand what the word *cozy* means, I can find synonyms, or other familiar words that have the same meaning. *Cozy* and *snug* are synonyms. I am familiar with the word *snug*. So now I know that the word *cozy* means nearly the same as the word *snug*.

Guide children in using a similar procedure to understand other words when you read.

Vocabulary Activity. Have children listen to each of the following descriptions of words. Tell them to hold up the word card that goes with each description. Reread the descriptions aloud with the correct answer. Then discuss how children made their choices.

1. This word tells about something horrible hanging over me. (*looming*)
2. This word tells about many ships at sea. (*fleet*)
3. This word is the opposite of *uncomfortable*. (*cozy*)
4. This word means *figured out*. (*realized*)
5. This word describes a boat that moved down a river. (*drifted*)
6. This word tells about a rocket that has set off into the sky. (*launched*)

FLUENCY BUILDER Read aloud each word in the first column on page 115. Have children repeat it. Then have children work in pairs to read the words in the first column aloud to each other. Follow the same procedure with each of the remaining columns. After partners have practiced reading aloud the words in each column separately, have them practice the entire list.

Save *Intervention Practice Book* page 115 to use on pages 291 and 293.

INTERVENTION PRACTICE BOOK
page 115

Montigue on the High Seas/Zelda Moves to the Desert

BEFORE
Reading "Montigue on the High Seas"
pages 366–379

USE SKILL CARD 29A

Homophones (Focus Skill)

PRETEACH **the skill.** Point out to children that homophones are words that sound alike but have different meanings. Explain that readers can recognize homophones by reading words aloud. Give examples of homophones, such as *so* and *sew*. Discuss why it is important for readers to know the exact meanings of words.

Have children look at **side A of Skill Card 29: Homophones.** Read the definition of *homophones*. Next, read the story and then have children reread it with you.

Now call attention to the chart and have volunteers take turns reading aloud the information in the boxes aloud. Ask:

- Why are *see* and *sea* homophones? (*They sound alike, but have different meanings.*)

- How does the story help you find the meanings of the homophones? (*Possible response: There are clue words in the sentences.*)

Prepare to Read: "Montigue on the High Seas"

Preview. Tell children that they are going to read a selection entitled "Montigue on the High Seas." Explain that this story has characters, a setting, and a plot. Tell children that "Montigue on the High Seas" is set on the high seas. Then preview the selection.

BANNER DAYS
pages 366–379

- **Pages 366–367:** I see the title, "Montigue on the High Seas," and the name of the author on pages 366–367. I see a picture of a mole sailing on the sea in what looks like a bottle. I think this mole might be Montigue.

- **Pages 368–369:** On these pages, I see a picture of the mole sleeping in his cozy hole. I read about how he has to find a new place to live. The last sentence on page 369 is not finished. This tells me that something surprising is going to happen.

- **Pages 370–371:** On these pages, I read that Montigue has been swept out to sea. I read that he is thrown into the air by a giant humpback whale. I think Montigue will have more adventures on the sea.

Set Purpose. Model setting a purpose for reading "Montigue on the High Seas."

MODEL From what I have seen in my preview, I think I will read more about what happens to Montigue on the high seas. I will read to be entertained by the adventures of a mole. I will also read to see what other characters are in the book and what happens when Montigue meets them.

290 Lesson 29 • Intervention Teacher's Guide

AFTER

Reading "Montigue on the High Seas"
pages 366–379

Reread and Summarize

Have children reread and summarize "Montigue on the High Seas" in sections, as described below.

Pages 366–371

Let's reread pages 366–371 to recall who Montigue is, why he had to leave his cozy hole, and where he went.

Summary: Montigue is a mole, and he had to leave his cozy hole because it was flooded by the rain. He crawled into a funny-looking house propped on a rock. Then he was swept out to sea and thrown into the air by a whale.

Pages 372–374

Let's reread pages 372–374 to recall how Montigue ended up on a ship.

Summary: He was in a bottle that was swallowed by a fish. The fish was caught in a huge net and yanked onto a ship. Montigue fell out of the fish's mouth.

Pages 375–376

Let's reread pages 375–376 to recall why the mice wanted to leave the ship and what they did.

Summary: The mice had to leave because Barnacles the Cat was trying to clear them off the ship. They collected things from a box of kitchen supplies and made a fleet of ships so that they could escape.

Pages 377–378

Let's reread pages 377–378 to recall what happened to Montigue at the end of the story.

Summary: He escaped with the mice and became their captain. He guided the ships through the waves until they found land. The mice carried him on their shoulders and asked him to live with them. He still had his bottle and his sail if he ever wanted to go off on the high seas again.

FLUENCY BUILDER Using *Intervention Practice Book* page 115, call attention to the sentences on the bottom half of the page. The slashes break the sentences into phrases to allow you to work on natural phrasing. Tell children that their goal is to read each phrase or sentence smoothly. Model appropriate pacing, expression, and phrasing as you read each sentence and have children read it after you. Then have children practice by reading the sentences aloud three times to a partner.

INTERVENTION PRACTICE BOOK
page 115

BEFORE
Making Connections
pages 380–381

Page 230

Directed Reading: "Zelda Moves to the Desert," pp. 230–236

SOUNDS OF SUNSHINE pp. 230–236

Help children read the title of the story aloud. Then have them describe what they see in the illustration. Point to the bat and tell children that this is Zelda, the main character. Ask children what kind of weather they see outside the cave. (*rain*) Then have children read page 230 to learn more about Zelda. Ask: **What does Zelda do at night?** (*She goes out flying to find bugs to eat.*) **NOTE DETAILS**

Ask: **What is another meaning for the word *bat*?** (*Possible response: a piece of sports equipment used to hit a ball in the game of baseball*) **HOMOPHONES**

Page 231

Have children read page 231. Model how to use the Create Mental Images strategy in order to understand that Zelda's cave will soon be flooded.

MODEL If I don't understand what is happening in the story, I can try to picture it in my mind. I know that the rain is falling very hard and the creek is getting bigger. All the rain falling into the creek is making the creek rise higher. Soon the creek will be as high as Zelda's cave. The creek water will then flow into her cave. If I picture this in my mind, I can understand that Zelda's cave will soon be flooded. **CREATE MENTAL IMAGES**

Pages 232–233

Have children read pages 232–233 to find out what Zelda does next. Ask: **What do the mice tell Zelda?** (*They tell her to find a new home.*) **NOTE DETAILS**

Ask: **What will Zelda do next?** (*Possible response: She will leave the forest to find a new home.*) **MAKE PREDICTIONS**

Page 234

Have children read page 234 to find out what Zelda has learned. Ask: **How did having her cave flooded teach Zelda that the sea is not a good home for her?** (*Possible response: Homes that are too wet are not good homes for her; the sea is too wet.*) **CAUSE AND EFFECT**

Page 235

Have children read page 235 to find out where Zelda makes her new home. Ask: **Why is the desert a good home for Zelda?** (*It is dry and has a cave that is cozy.*) **INTERPRET STORY EVENTS**

INTERVENTION PRACTICE BOOK page 117

Summarize the Selection Ask children to think about Zelda's problem and how she has solved it. Invite them to share their impressions about Zelda and the kind of character she is.

Then have children complete *Intervention Practice Book* page 117.

Page 236

Answers to *Think About It* Questions

1. Zelda leaves her cave because it is not cozy or safe. She moves to the desert because it is safe, dry, and cozy. **SUMMARY**
2. Possible response: Zelda would not like a home by a lake because she doesn't like the damp woods or the wet sea. **INTERPRETATION**
3. Accept reasonable responses. **TASK**

AFTER

Skill Review
pages 38 II

USE SKILL CARD 29B

(Focus Skill) Review Homophones

RETEACH the skill. Have children look at **side B of Skill Card 29: Homophones**. Read the skill reminder with them, and have a volunteer read the story aloud.

Read aloud the set of directions. Explain that children will work with partners to create their own charts. Encourage them to say the story aloud quietly to themselves in order to hear which words sound alike.

After children have completed their homophone charts, have them display and explain their work. Point out that the selection "Montigue on the High Seas" has some homophones in it. Ask volunteers to name the homophones, give their meanings, and tell how the story helps them figure out these meanings.

Review Phonics Skill

RETEACH **Vowel Variants: /ô/ *aw, au(gh)*** Read aloud the following sentence: *Saul taught Paul to draw a hawk and a fawn.* Have children raise their hands when they hear the /ô/ sound. Write the words *taught* and *draw* on the board and discuss the two spellings for the sound /ô/.

FLUENCY BUILDER Be sure children have copies of *Intervention Practice Book* page 115. Explain that they will practice the sentences at the bottom of the page by recording them on tape. Have children choose new partners. Tell the partners to take turns reading the sentences aloud to each other and then recording them. Have children listen to the tape and tell how they think their reading has improved. Then have them record the sentences one more time.

INTERVENTION PRACTICE BOOK
page 115

Montigue on the High Seas/Zelda Moves to the Desert

BEFORE
Drafting Directions
Page 381A

Writing Process: Directions

Build on prior knowledge. Tell children that they are going to talk about and write directions. Explain that directions are a set of steps or information that people follow in order to make or do something or go somewhere. Tell children that directions need to include exact words so that readers do not get confused. Guide children to see the difference between exact and general words, such as *111 Oak Street* versus *the street*.

> ➪ Turn right.
> Follow the river.
> Go 3 miles.
> ⬅ Turn left.

Construct the Text. On the board, copy the notes shown above. Tell children that these notes show directions for how to get to the desert. Then "Share the pen" with children. Guide them in using the notes to formulate four steps in a set of directions. For example:

1. Take a right turn.
2. Follow the river.
3. Walk three miles.
4. Take a left turn.

Revisit the Text. Go back and read the list of steps together. Ask: **How do the numbers help you know what to do?** (*They tell you which step to do first, next, and so on.*)

- Guide children to use exact words to help clarify the directions. Ask: **How can I make the directions clearer to readers? What other words can I add to help people know where to go?** (Possible responses: *Take a right turn on Smith Street. Take a left turn at the sand dunes.*) Make appropriate changes.

- Ask: **What might happen if you skipped a step?** (*The reader might not be able to find the desert.*)

On Your Own
Have children write directions telling others how to get from the front door of the school to their classroom.

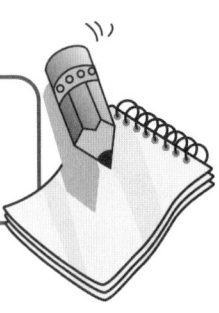

Lesson 29 • Intervention Teacher's Guide

AFTER

Spelling Lesson
Pages 379I

Connect Spelling and Phonics

RETEACH **Vowel Variants /ô/ *aw, au (gh)*.** Tell children to number their papers 1–8. Write *saw* on the board, and tell children that in the words you will say, /ô/ will be spelled *aw* as in *saw*. Dictate the following words, and have children write them. After each word display the correct spelling so children can proofread their work. They should draw a line through a misspelled word and write the correct spelling below it.

1. jaws*   2. dawn*   3. yawned*   4. saw*
5. awful* 6. crawled* 7. paws*   8. fawn*

* Word appears in "Zelda Moves to the Desert."

Tell children that in the following sentence, /ô/ is spelled *au*. Dictate the sentence and have children write it: *Paul hauls rockets to the launch pad.*

Build and Read Longer Words

Remind children that they have learned how to decode words with the /ô/ sound. Explain that now they will use what they have learned to help them read some longer words.

Write the word *because* on the board. Remind children that they can often figure out longer words by looking for small words or word parts in them. Cover the word *be*, and have children read *cause*. Follow a similar procedure to have them read the word *be*. Model how to blend the two smaller words to read aloud the longer word *because*. Have children blend word parts in this way to read these longer words: *granddaughter*, *strawberry*, and *seesaw*.

INTERVENTION ASSESSMENT BOOK

FLUENCY BUILDER Have children choose a passage from "Zelda Moves to the Desert" to read aloud to a partner. You may have children choose passages that they found particularly interesting, or have them choose one of the following options:

- Read pages 230–231. (From *Each night*, . . . through . . . *onto the ledge*.) Total: 119 words.
- Read pages 234–235. (From *Next Zelda flew*, . . . through . . . *her cozy new home*.") Total: 123 words.

Children should read the selected passage aloud to their partners three times. Have the reader rate each reading on a scale from 1 to 4.

BEFORE Weekly Assessments

Review Vocabulary

To revisit Vocabulary Words prior to the weekly assessment, use these sentence frames. Have volunteers take turns reading aloud the sentence stems and choices. Students identify the correct choice and explain why that choice makes sense in the sentence.

1. The boat **drifted**, so it
   a. did not move down the river.   b. moved down the river.
2. If something is **loom**ing over you, it is probably
   a. very nice.   b. not very pleasant.
3. The house was **cozy**, and we were all
   a. very comfortable.   b. miserable.
4. If you see a **fleet** of ships, you see
   a. many ships.   b. only one small ship.
5. If the boat was **launched**, it is no longer
   a. in the water.   b. on the land.
6. When she **realized** what happened, she
   a. understood it.   b. did not know what happened.

Correct responses: 1b, 2b, 3a, 4a, 5b, 6a.

You may want to display the Vocabulary Words and definitions on page 289 and have children copy them to use when they study for the vocabulary test.

⭐(Focus Skill) Review Homophones

To review homophones before the weekly assessment, distribute *Intervention Practice Book* page 118. Have volunteers read aloud the direction line and the story. Guide children to find the homophones and discuss their meanings.

Review Test Prep

Ask children to turn to page 383 of the *Pupil Edition*. Call attention to the tips for answering the test questions. Tell children that paying attention to these tips can help them answer not only the test questions but also other test questions like these.

BANNER DAYS page 383

Have children follow along as you read each test question and the tip that goes with it. Tell children to read each choice twice before making a decision.

INTERVENTION PRACTICE BOOK page 118

INTERVENTION ASSESSMENT BOOK

AFTER Weekly Assessments

Self-Selected Reading

Have children select their own books to read independently. They might choose books from the classroom library shelf, or you may wish to offer a group of appropriate books from which children can choose.

- *Hurricane!* by Elizabeth Field. (See page 383O of the *Teacher's Edition* for an Independent Reading Plan.)
- *The Adventures of Sparrowboy* by Brian Pinkney. Simon & Schuster, 1997.
- *Across the Big Blue Sea* by Jakki Wood. National Geographic Society, 1998.

After children have chosen their books, give each child a copy of My Reading Log, which can be found on page R35 in the back of the *Teacher's Edition*. Have children fill in the information at the top of the form. Then have them use the log to keep track of their reading and to record their responses to the literature.

Conduct student–teacher conferences. Arrange time for each child to confer with you individually about his or her self-selected reading. Have children bring their Reading Logs to share with you at the conference. Children might also like to choose a favorite passage to read aloud to you. Ask questions designed to stimulate discussion about the book. For example, you might ask if children have ever moved to a new home and how it felt, or how they think it might feel.

FLUENCY PERFORMANCE Have children read aloud to you the passage from "Zelda Moves to the Desert" that they selected and practiced with their partner. Keep track of the number of words each child reads correctly. Ask the child to rate his or her own performance on the 1–4 scale. If children are not happy with their oral reading, give them an opportunity to continue practicing and then to read the passage to you again.

See *Oral Reading Fluency Assessment* for monitoring progress.

LESSON 30

BEFORE Building Background and Vocabulary

Use with

"Ruth Law Thrills a Nation"

Review Phonics: Consonant /s/c

Identify the sound. Have children repeat the following sentence three times: *The city mice are in the center of an icy place.* Ask children to identify the words that have the /s/ sound. (*city, mice, center, icy, place*)

Associate letters to sound. On the board, write *The city mice are in the center of an icy place.* Circle the words *city*, *mice*, *center*, *icy*, and *place*. Ask children to tell how the words are alike. (*All have the /s/ sound and the letter* c.) Underline the letters *ci* in *city*. Remind children that sometimes the same letter or letters can stand for different sounds. Then tell children that when the letter *c* is followed by an *i*, it often stands for the /s/ sound that children hear in *city*. Then follow a similar procedure for the /s/ sound where *c* is followed by *e* in *mice*, *center*, and *place*; and in *icy*, where *c* is followed by *y*.

Word blending. Model how to blend and read the word *face*. Slide your hand under the letters as you slowly elongate the sounds /ffāāss/. Then read *face* naturally. Follow a similar procedure for *space*, *spicy*, and *cinder*.

Apply the skill. *Consonant Substitution* Write the following words on the board, and have children read them aloud. Make the changes necessary to form the words in parentheses. Have children read each new word.

bell (cell)   **lent** (cent)   **rake** (race)   **ride** (rice)
spine (spice)   **Mike** (mice)   **spider** (cider)   **trade** (trace)

INTERVENTION PRACTICE BOOK page 120

Introduce Vocabulary

PRETEACH lesson vocabulary. Tell children that they are going to learn six new words that they will see again when they read a story called "Ruth Law Thrills a Nation." Teach each Vocabulary Word using the strategies in the box below.

Use the following suggestions or similar ideas to give the meaning or context.

feat	Point out the homophone *feet* and discuss the different meanings of *feat* and *feet*.
heroine	Discuss heroines that children are familiar with and the accomplishments of each.
hospitality	Relate to the way you are treated when close family and friends meet.

> Write the word.
> Say the word.
> Track the word and have students repeat it.
> Give the meaning or context.

Lesson 30 • Intervention Teacher's Guide

refused	Point out the *-ed* ending. Role-play refusing to do or accept something.
spectators	Related words: *spectator, spectacle, speculate*
stood	Demonstrate by showing how someone "stands his or her ground."

For vocabulary activities, see Vocabulary Games on pages 2–7.

> **Vocabulary Words**
> **feat** an amazing deed
> **heroine** a woman who has done something very brave or helpful
> **hospitality** friendly treatment of guest or strangers
> **refused** would not do
> **spectators** people who watch
> **stood** was unchallenged

AFTER
Building Background and Vocabulary

Apply Vocabulary Strategies

RETEACH lesson vocabulary. Write the word *heroine* on chart paper and underline the letters *h-e-r-o*. Tell children that they can sometimes figure out the meaning of a word by looking for letter patterns that they know.

MODEL The letters *h-e-r-o* are familiar to me because they spell the word *hero*. I know that a hero is someone brave or who has done something important, like in sports. Maybe a heroine has something to do with being a hero.

Vocabulary Activity Have children listen to each of the following groups of words. Tell them to hold up the word card that goes with each group. Reread the groups aloud with the correct answer. Then discuss how children made their choices.

1.	unchallenged	certain	sure (*stood*)
2.	friendly treatment	guests	welcoming (*hospitality*)
3.	amazing	difficult	deed (*feat*)
4.	woman	brave	helpful (*heroine*)
5.	people	watch	cheering (*spectators*)
6.	no	don't want	will not accept (*refused*)

FLUENCY BUILDER Using *Intervention Practice Book* page 119, read aloud each word in the first column and have children repeat it. Then have children work in pairs to read the words in the first column aloud to each other. Follow the same procedure with each of the remaining columns. After partners have practiced reading aloud the words in each column separately, have them practice the entire list.

INTERVENTION PRACTICE BOOK
page 119

Save *Intervention Practice Book* page 119 to use on pages 301 and 303.

BEFORE
Reading "Ruth Law Thrills a Nation"
pages 386–403

USE SKILL CARD 30A

(Focus Skill) Predict Outcomes

PRETEACH **the skill.** Point out to children that readers use what they know from real life and clues from the story to make guesses about what might happen in the story. Explain that people make predictions about things every day. Give examples of predicting an outcome, such as looking at the sky to see what the weather will be. Discuss why it is important to be able to predict outcomes in real life and why predicting outcomes can help readers better understand and enjoy a story.

Have children look at **side A of Skill Card 30: Predict Outcomes**. Read the definition of *predict outcomes*. Next read the story and then have children reread it with you.

Now call attention to the chart and have volunteers take turns reading the information in the boxes aloud. Ask:

- **What do you know about people who work hard?** (*Possible response: They usually get what they want.*)
- **What else can you use to predict outcomes besides story clues?** (*Possible response: what you know or have experienced.*)

Prepare to Read: "Ruth Law Thrills a Nation"

Preview. Tell children that they are going to read a selection entitled "Ruth Law Thrills a Nation." Explain that this is a nonfiction biography that tells about something that really happened. Tell children that it is about a woman who flew a plane many years ago. Then preview the selection.

BANNER DAYS
pages 386–403

- **Pages 386–387:** I see the title, "Ruth Law Thrills a Nation," and the name of the author on pages 386–387. I see a picture of a woman flying an old-fashioned airplane. I think this woman might be Ruth Law.
- **Pages 388–389:** On these pages, I read about something that happened many years ago. I see pictures of Chicago and a picture of Ruth Law in her tent on top of a building. I think that Ruth must be a brave and unusual woman.
- **Pages 390–391:** On these pages, I read about how Ruth prepared for her trip. I see her working on her airplane. I think that Ruth must love to fly.

Set purpose. Model setting a purpose for reading "Ruth Law Thrills a Nation."

MODEL From what I have seen in my preview, I think I will read more about Ruth's flight from Chicago to New York City. I will read to find out if she can do what no one had ever done before.

300 Lesson 30 • Intervention Teacher's Guide

AFTER

Reading "Ruth Law Thrills a Nation"
pages 386–403

Reread and Summarize

Have children reread and summarize "Ruth Law Thrills a Nation" in sections, as described below.

Pages 388–391

Let's reread pages 388–391 to recall who Ruth Law was, what she was trying to do, and how she went about doing it.

Summary: Ruth Law was a pilot who lived many years ago. She was trying to fly from Chicago to New York City in one day. She slept in a tent on a roof to get used to the cold. She also dressed warmly and carefully prepared her plane for the journey.

Pages 392–394

Let's reread pages 392–394 to recall what happened in the early part of Ruth's trip.

Summary: The engine was hard to start because of the freezing weather. After an hour, the plane raced awkwardly across the ground before it lifted up into the sky. Ruth struggled to keep her plane steady in the fierce wind.

Pages 395–397

Let's reread pages 395–397 to recall what happened when Ruth neared Hornell, New York.

Summary: The plane's engine quit because the fuel tank was empty. Ruth was able to land the plane safely after flying 590 miles.

Pages 398–402

Let's reread pages 398–402 to recall what happened on the rest of Ruth's journey.

Summary: Ruth set out for New York City. When she was two hours away, she decided to land because it was too dark to see her instruments. The next morning, she made it to New York City.

FLUENCY BUILDER Be sure children have copies of *Intervention Practice Book* page 119, which you used for yesterday's Fluency Builder activity. Call attention to the sentences on the bottom half of the page. The slashes break the sentences into phrases to allow you to work on natural phrasing. Tell children that their goal is to read each phrase or sentence smoothly. Model appropriate pacing, expression, and phrasing as you read each sentence. Then have children practice by reading the sentences aloud three times to a partner.

INTERVENTION PRACTICE BOOK page 119

BEFORE
Making Connections
pages 406–407

Directed Reading: "An Amazing Feat," pp. 238–245

SOUNDS OF SUNSHINE
pp. 238–245

Pages 238–239

Help children read the title of the story aloud. Ask children what amazing feats they or people they know have accomplished. Explain that this selection is about the amazing feats of a woman named Amelia Earhart. Then have children read pages 238–239 to find out about Amelia Earhart. Ask: **Who was Amelia Earhart?** (*Possible response: an American heroine, a pilot.*) **NOTE DETAILS**

Ask: **Do you think Amelia will accomplish something amazing with her airplane? Why?** (*Possible response: Yes; The title of the story is "An Amazing Feat," and Amelia is a heroine*) **PREDICT OUTCOMES**

Page 240

Have children read page 240. Ask: **What did Amelia do after the war?** (*She took flying lessons and got her own plane.*) **SEQUENCE**

Page 241

Have children read page 241. Model how to use the Read Ahead strategy in order to understand the meaning of the word *spectators*.

> **MODEL** If I come to a word or sentence in the story that I don't understand, I can read ahead. I don't know what *spectators* means. If I read ahead, I read that they "came to cheer when she took off and landed." Now I can understand that spectators are people who watched and cheered for Amelia. **READ AHEAD**

Page 242

Read aloud the first sentence of page 242. Ask children what they think Amelia's dream was. Then have them read page 242 to find out. Ask: **What was Amelia's dream?** (*to fly all the way around the world*) **NOTE DETAILS**

Ask: **Why did Amelia want to take Fred Noonan on her trip?** (*Possible response: to help her on such a long trip*) **UNDERSTAND CHARACTERS' MOTIVES**

Page 243

Have children read page 243. Ask: **What did Amelia and Fred do before they left?** (*They filled the tanks with gasoline and checked the engine.*) **SEQUENCE**

Ask: **What happened to the plane?** (*It ran out of fuel and disappeared.*) **NOTE DETAILS**

Page 244

Read aloud page 244. Then ask children what they think Amelia Earhart meant when she said, "The dreams of long ago had come true." (*Accept reasonable responses.*) **INTERPRET STORY EVENTS**

INTERVENTION PRACTICE BOOK
page 121

Page 245

Summarize the Selection. Ask children what they learned about the beginning, middle, and the end of Amelia Earhart's life. Help them summarize the selection in three or four sentences. Then have children complete page 121 in their *Intervention Practice Book*.

Answers to *Think About It* Questions

1. She was a pilot who was courageous and who set many flying records. **SUMMARY**
2. The partner could look at the maps, help fly, or be good company. **INTERPRETATION**
3. Accept reasonable responses. **TASK**

AFTER

Skill Review
page 407I

USE SKILL CARD 30B

Focus Skill: Predict Outcomes

RETEACH the skill. Have children look at **side B of Skill Card 30: Predict Outcomes**. Read the skill reminder with them, and have a volunteer read the story aloud.

Read aloud the set of directions. Explain that children will work with a partner to create their own charts. Encourage them to ask or write down questions they have about what will happen next in the story as they read.

After children have completed their Predict Outcomes charts, have them display and explain their work. Point out that they can predict outcomes for the selection "Ruth Law Thrills a Nation." Ask volunteers to predict some outcomes for "Ruth Law Thrills a Nation."

Review Phonics Skill from "Ruth Law Thrills a Nation"

RETEACH Prefixes: *over-, un-*. Read aloud the following sentence: *Matt was unable to put his suitcase in the overhead bin.* Have children listen for the prefixes *over-* and *un-*. Then read this list aloud and have children raise their hands when they hear the prefixes *over-* and *un-*: unhappy, uncertain, overcoat, overpass.

FLUENCY BUILDER Be sure that children have copies of *Intervention Practice Book* page 119. Explain that today children will practice the sentences on the bottom half of the page by reading them aloud on tape. Assign new partners. Have children take turns reading the sentences aloud to each other and then reading them on tape.

INTERVENTION PRACTICE BOOK
page 119

Ruth Law Thrills a Nation/An Amazing Feat

BEFORE
Drafting Timed Writing
Pages 407A

Daily Writing: Timed Writing

Build on prior knowledge. Tell children that they are going to talk and do timed writing. Explain that sometimes people need to complete their work in a certain amount of time. Even though they are writing fast, they still need to pay attention to punctuation, spelling, and grammar. Guide children to see that timed writing works best if they choose a topic about which they know a great deal and if they keep their writing simple and clear. Display the list shown here.

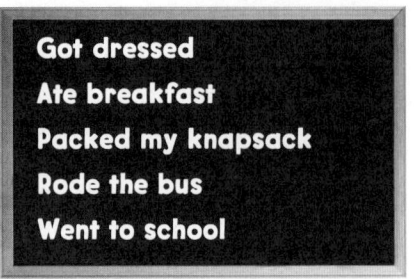

> Got dressed
> Ate breakfast
> Packed my knapsack
> Rode the bus
> Went to school

Construct the text. "Share the pen" with children. Tell them that the list shows information about someone's day. Guide them in using the list to do timed writing. Help them to use the activities on the list to write a paragraph in a set amount of time. For example:

> *Today I got dressed. Then I ate breakfast. Then I packed my knapsack. Then I rode the bus. Then I went to school.*

Revisit the text. Go back and read the timed-writing paragraph together. Ask: **Would it be easy for you to write a timed-writing paragraph about your day? Why?** (*Yes; I know a great deal about my day.*)

- Guide children to make the paragraph read more smoothly by combining sentences. Ask: **How can I combine sentences to make the paragraph read more smoothly?** (*Possible response: Today I got dressed and ate breakfast. Then I packed my knapsack. After that I rode the bus to school.*) Make appropriate changes.

- Ask: **What else could you add to the paragraph?** (*Possible response: things that happened at school*)

- Have children read the timed-writing paragraph aloud and then copy it on their papers.

On Your Own

Have children list three topics that they know a great deal about and could use for a timed-writing paragraph.

304 Lesson 30 • Intervention Teacher's Guide

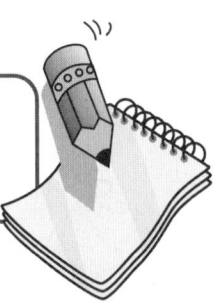

AFTER

Spelling Lesson
Page 403I

Connect Spelling and Phonics

RETEACH consonant /s/c. Tell children to number their papers 1–8. Tell them that in the words you say, the /s/ sound is spelled c, followed by e, i, or y. Dictate the following words and have children write them. After each word, display the correct spelling so children can proofread their work. They should draw a line through a misspelled word and write the correct spelling below it.

1. rice
2. chance
3. trace*
4. place*
5. circle
6. decided*
7. center*
8. city*

* Word appears in "An Amazing Feat."

Dictate the following sentence and have children write it: *The nice mice eat rice in the city.*

Build and Read Longer Words

Remind children that they have learned how to decode words with the /s/ sound spelled c. Explain that now they will use what they have learned to help them read some longer words.

Write the word *celery* on the board. Remind children that they can often figure out a longer word by looking for word parts they know in it. Ask children which part of the word says *cel*, which part says *er*, and which part says *y*. Then ask what word *cel*, *er*, and *y* all together make. (*celery*) Have children blend word parts to read these longer words: *palace*, *civil*, and *celebrate*.

INTERVENTION ASSESSMENT BOOK ✓

FLUENCY BUILDER Have children choose a passage from "An Amazing Feat" to read aloud to a partner. You may have children choose passages that they found particularly interesting, or have them choose one of the following options:

- Read pages 238–239. (From *Amelia Earhart is, . . .* through . . . *to fly herself.* Total: 115 words)

- Read pages 240–241. (From *Amelia had some . . .* through . . . *for their hospitality.* Total: 118 words)

Children should read the selected passage aloud to their partners three times. Have the child rate each reading on a scale from 1 to 4.

Ruth Law Thrills a Nation/An Amazing Feat **305**

BEFORE Weekly Assessments

Review Vocabulary

To revisit Vocabulary Words prior to the weekly assessment, use these sentence frames. Have volunteers take turns reading aloud the sentence stems and choices. Students identify the correct choice and explain why that choice makes sense in the sentence.

1. While her record **stood**, it was
   a. unchallenged.
   b. not very good.

2. She was a **heroine**, because she was
   a. brave and helpful.
   b. not very nice.

3. If they **refused** to do it, they would
   a. do it immediately.
   b. not do it.

4. The **spectators**
   a. flew the plane.
   b. watched the plane.

5. If the guest was given **hospitality**, he was
   a. treated well.
   b. treated poorly.

6. Her flight was a **feat**, because it was
   a. not hard to do.
   b. difficult and amazing.

Correct responses: 1a, 2a, 3b, 4b, 5a, 6b.

You may want to display the Vocabulary Words and definitions on page 299 and have children copy them to use when they study for the vocabulary test.

INTERVENTION PRACTICE BOOK
page 122

Review Predict Outcomes

To review predicting outcomes before the weekly assessment, distribute *Intervention Practice Book page* 122. Have volunteers read aloud the direction line and the story. Guide children to think about what might or might not happen in the story as they read it.

Review Test Prep

Ask children to turn to page 409 of the *Pupil Edition*. Call attention to the tips for answering the test questions. Tell children that paying attention to these tips can help them answer not only the test questions but also other test questions like these.

BANNER DAYS
page 409

INTERVENTION ASSESSMENT BOOK

Have children follow along as you read each test question and the tip that goes with it. Tell children not to rush as they think about their answers.

Lesson 30 • Intervention Teacher's Guide

AFTER Weekly Assessments

Self-Selected Reading

Have children select their own books to read independently. They might choose books from the classroom library shelf, or you may wish to offer a group of appropriate books from which children can choose.

- *The Journey of the Monarch* by Isabella Cummings. (See page 409M of the *Teacher's Edition* for an Independent Reading Plan.)
- *Gila Monsters Meet You at the Airport* by Marjorie Weinman Sharmat. Simon & Schuster, 1983.
- *The Trek* by Ann Jonas. Greenwillow, 1988.

After children have chosen their books, give each child a copy of My Reading Log, which can be found on page R35 in the back of the *Teacher's Edition*. Have children fill in the information at the top of the form. Then have them use the log to keep track of their reading and to record their responses to the literature.

Conduct student-teacher conferences. Arrange time for each child to confer with you individually about his or her self-selected reading. Have children bring their Reading Logs to share with you at the conference. Children might also like to choose a favorite passage to read aloud to you. Ask questions designed to stimulate discussion about the book. For example, you might ask if children would want to try to break a record, and why they would want to.

FLUENCY PERFORMANCE Have children read aloud to you the passage from "An Amazing Feat" that they selected and practiced with their partner. Keep track of the number of words each child reads correctly. Ask the child to rate his or her own performance on the 1–4 scale. If children are not happy with their oral reading, give them an opportunity to continue practicing and then to read the passage to you again.

See *Oral Reading Fluency Assessment* for monitoring progress.